Contents

Tables and Diagrams

Tables

Diagrams

Introduction

This book is based on *The Oxford Dictionary of English Grammar* (Chalker and Weiner, 1994), but aimed at the general reader who is primarily interested in the grammar of present-day English and the commoner terms used in describing it. I have, however, retained (*a*) some entries on word formation, the grammar of words, and (*b*) terms relating to the sounds of English, because we all speak more than we write and yet phonetics is strangely neglected.

At the same time I have taken the opportunity of adding several new entries, and in particular a number of completely new tables. These tables bring together, with examples, the main terms relating to particular grammatical features. They are intended to serve as summaries or reminders, but fuller details will be found either at the adjoining entry or at the relevant alphabetical entry. For example, many of the terms included in the table for Adjectives are explained at the **adjective** entry, but separate entries will also be found at **attributive**, **predicative**, and so on.

Thus, this volume combines a dictionary format, which makes it easy to check on individual terms, with a grammar book's advantage of grouping related concepts together. In addition, some important aspects of language often neglected in grammar books are explained—for example, **information structure** (the relationship between word order and meaning).

Terms consisting of two (or more) words are usually listed only once, at the place judged to be the more obvious, but with cross-referencing where this is felt to be necessary. Thus **adjective clause**, **adjective complementation**, and **adjective order** all follow the entry for **adjective**, but at **adjective clause** the reader is referred to the table RELATIVE CLAUSES (another name for this type of clause). Similarly **split infinitive** is listed under S, as the whole term is familiar to many people as a unit, but the reader looking for this at infinitive will find a cross-reference.

On the other hand, a specialist term such as *mandative subjunctive* is given only at the **subjunctive** entry. Other two-word terms, even well-known ones, may also appear only under their second word if this enables related terms to be dealt with together. For example, *first person*, *second person*, etc. are entered only at **person**. Readers are therefore advised to try again if they do not find an entry where they expect it! But I hope that *The Little Oxford Dictionary of English Grammar* will prove user-friendly. I hope also that readers will come to see, if they do not do so already, that grammar is not a set of arbitrary rules but a meaning-based system.

S. C.

Conventions

1 Where an entry mentions another entry which the reader may find helpful to consult, this second entry is signalled in SMALL CAPITAL LETTERS. Thus the entry for **abbreviated language** includes references to ELLIPSIS, BLOCK LANGUAGE, and CONTRACTIONS.

2 Elsewhere the reader's attention may be drawn to the fact that a particular word or phrase is a specialist term by the use of *italics*. For example, at **absolute** there is a reference to *gradable* adjectives.

3 In some of the entries on word formation, words and phrases quoted as examples are given abbreviated dates indicating their earliest known recorded appearance in English. In these the number is that of the century and the preceding E, M, L means 'early', 'mid', and 'late': 'E19' means 1800–29, 'M19' means 1830–69, and 'L19' means 1870–99.

4 The following symbols are used

*   grammatically deviant.

    e.g. *an asleep child; *the silence was utter

?   grammatically doubtful

    e.g.? When buying statuary, its impact on the garden will be strong

( ) the words inside the brackets are grammatically optional

    e.g. I want (you) to go

    i. the words either side are grammatically alternatives

       e.g. You may/can go

    ii. the words either side belong to different clause elements

       e.g. The cat /sat/on the mat (= SVA)

/ / phonetic symbols are enclosed

    e.g./kæt/cat

[ː]   length mark (for vowels), e.g. /dɑːk/ dark

[ˌ]   syllabic consonant, e.g. /bʌtn̩/ button

[ˈ]   primary stress
[ˌ]   secondary stress } e.g. ˌanti-ˈaircraft (secondary, primary)

[▲]   ellipsis, e.g. ▲Coming? (= Are you coming?)

A   Adverbial
C   Complement
O   Object   } as an element of clause structure
S   Subject
V   Verb

NP   noun phrase
VP   verb phrase

A

abbreviated language

Abbreviated language is not a precise term, because individuals vary in how severely they abridge and how exactly they do it, when, for example, writing diaries or making lecture notes.

Most written and spoken language omits some words that are 'recoverable' from the context, and the rules governing such omissions are codified as ELLIPSIS.

Specialized 'rules' apply to particular types of language. Notices, newspaper headlines, and titles of books, plays, and films often use BLOCK LANGUAGE. Labels and printed instructions may contain 'sentences' with clause structure, but often with subject or object omitted, e.g.

> Contains natural herb extracts
>
> Avoid getting into the eyes

Broadcasters also use abbreviated language, e.g.

> And now back to the studio

Abbreviated forms representing two words run together, such as *I'm* or *don't* are called CONTRACTIONS.

See p. 157 OMISSION.

abbreviation

An abbreviation is a shortened form of a word or phrase.
Abbreviations are of various kinds:

(*a*) A word (sometimes called a CLIPPING) retaining at least one syllable of the original word, e.g.

> *ad* (advertisement), *demo* (demonstration), *flu* (influenza), *pub* (public house), *phone* (telephone), *sitcom* (situation comedy)

Some clippings are informal, e.g. *mike* (microphone), *wellies* (wellington boots). Others are completely acceptable in formal contexts, e.g. *bus* (omnibus), *maths* (US *math*) (mathematics), or their origins may even be virtually forgotten, e.g. *mob* (from Latin *mobile-vulgus*).

(*b*) A string of letters, pronounced as such, formed from the initial letters of the (main) words of a phrase. Also called INITIALISM, e.g.

> *BBC* (British Broadcasting Corporation); *UN* (United Nations); *OTT* (over the top); *PCW* (personal computer word processor); p.t.o. (please turn over).

Sometimes the letters represent syllables of a word, e.g.

> *ID* (identity or identification card)
> *TB* (tuberculosis)

Initialism is sometimes classified as a type of ACRONYM.

(*c*) A written convention which is unpronounceable as a word. This includes abbreviations of personal titles, e.g. *Col.*, *Dr*, *Mrs*, *Sgt.*, etc.; also such common abbreviations as *St* (street or saint), *Fr.* (French), *Gk* (Greek), *etc.* (etcetera), *kg* (kilogram), *rpt* (repeat), *ms.* (manuscript).

Written Latin abbreviations are sometimes read out in their English equivalents, or pronounced as letter strings, e.g.

> *e.g.* (*exempli gratia*)   for example, /ˌiːˈdʒiː/
> *i.e.* (*id est*)   that is, /ˌaɪˈiː/
> *a.m.* and *p.m.*
> (*ante* and *post meridiem*)   /ˈeɪˌem/, /ˈpiːˌem/

absolute

1 The absolute form or 'degree' of a *gradable* adjective or adverb is the uninflected (or POSITIVE or *base*) form, e.g. *kind*, *soon*, in contrast to comparative (*kinder*, *sooner*) and to superlative (*kindest*, *soonest*) forms.

2 Adjectives and adverbs that are non-gradable, that is they have no comparative or superlative forms, are sometimes called absolute adjectives or adverbs, e.g. *unique*, *chemical*, *nuclear*; *uniquely*, *chemically*.

absolute clause

An absolute clause is a non-finite or verbless clause that contains its own subject. In the first sentence the two absolute clauses contain non-finite verbs (*crushed, clutching*). In the second sentence, the absolute clause is verbless:

> The fight to board the train—*the women crushed against the doors, the children desperately clutching their mothers*—repeated itself at this provincial station.
>
> *The platform empty once more*, I settled down for the night.

Except for a few set phrases (*all being well, weather permitting, present company excepted*) absolute clauses tend to be formal and written. If the subject is a pronoun it must be in subject, not object, case, e.g. *I refusing to go, Nicholas went alone* (not **Me refusing to go*).

See p. 42 CLAUSES.

abstract noun

An abstract noun refers to an idea, quality, or state, in contrast to a CONCRETE NOUN.

The traditional division of common nouns into abstract and concrete nouns is meaning-based. It cuts across the more strictly grammatical classification into UNCOUNT and COUNT NOUNS, and as a way of trying to deal with syntactic differences is unsatisfactory.

The abstract label does fit many uncount nouns (e.g. *Everybody needs advice/fun/luck*; not **an advice/*funs/*two lucks*). But abstract nouns also include count nouns (e.g. *We had an idea/another quarrel/better solutions*; not ** We had idea/*quarrel/*better solution*). Other abstract nouns have both count and uncount uses (e.g. *several important discoveries, an important discovery, a voyage of discovery*).

See p. 151 NOUNS.

accent

1   A way of speaking—of an individual, a region, a country, etc., as in 'he has a north country/Irish/Scottish/American/French/German accent'.

Accents in Britain may be regional (e.g. a Scottish accent) or social (related to educational and cultural background). So everyone speaks with an accent. The accent characteristic of many middle-class speakers, BBC news readers, and so on is sometimes called 'standard', which is a rather broader term than RECEIVED PRONUNCIATION (RP).

Accent refers only to pronunciation and is distinct from a regional DIALECT, which usually has some differences of grammar and vocabulary.

2 In the phonetic analysis of spoken English, the terms *accent* and *stress* are loosely used interchangeably.

Some phoneticians, however, distinguish the terms, and use accent to mean emphasis involving a PITCH change. (Stress then means emphasis, but without a change of pitch.)

3 An accent in the sense of a punctuation mark is sometimes used to indicate (*a*) that a letter or letter sequence is pronounced as a separate syllable (e.g. *an agèd man*, in contrast to the corresponding one-syllable verb, *He's aged a lot recently*), or (*b*) that a word has a 'foreign' pronunciation (e.g. *café, entrée.*)

accusative

Accusative is a traditional term taken from Latin grammar for what is now called the OBJECT or the objective case.

acronym

1 Strictly, a word formed from (*a*) the initial letters of other words, or (*b*) a mixture of initials and syllables, e.g.

- (*a*) NATO (North Atlantic Treaty Organization)
    NIMBY (not in my back yard)
    TINA (there is no alternative)
- (*b*) radar (radio detection and ranging)
    yuppie (young urban professional + diminutive ending)

Acronyms are sometimes included under the general term ABBREVIATION and sometimes contrasted.

2 More loosely, the term acronym is extended to cover an ABBREVIATION pronounced as a letter string (e.g. *BBC, USA*), for which the more precise term is INITIALISM.

action verb

A verb (also called an *event verb*) that describes a happening that occurs in a limited time and has a beginning and an end, e.g. *arrive*, *make*, *listen*, *walk*. Contrasted with STATE verb.

The terms *action* or *event* to describe verbs are popular terms for DYNAMIC. (Similarly *state verb* is a popular label for *stative verb*).

active

Verb tenses are either active or PASSIVE, and the distinction is discussed as VOICE. When the verb is in the active voice the subject of the sentence is often the 'actor', the 'doer' of the verb, as in

> The sun *rises* in the east
> The early bird *caught* the worm

However, this is a grammatical, not a meaning-based, distinction. The following are all active sentences with active verbs

> Books do furnish a room
> Curiosity killed the cat
> Faith will move mountains
> I can't hear you

Intransitive verbs (e.g. *rise*) can occur only in the active.

adjectival

Any word or phrase functioning as an adjective can be described as an *adjectival*. So the term includes single-word adjectives, but it is a much wider term, embracing for example

> nouns in attributive position (e.g. *guide* price, the *greenhouse* effect, *compassion* fatigue)

> prepositional phrases (e.g. the man *in the white suit*)

> and other parts of speech (e.g. an *I'm-all-right-Jack* attitude, Don't be so *holier-than-thou*).

Some grammarians loosely use the term adjective to describe all these, but it is sometimes useful to distinguish between true single-word adjectives and other words functioning adjectivally in a particular context.

ADJECTIVES AT A GLANCE

....

POSITION

attributive:	an old man
predicative:	He is old. He looks old
postpositive:	something old, the president elect
attributive-only:	I felt an utter fool (*That fool is utter)
predicative-only:	She's asleep (*an asleep person)

MEANING AND FORM

qualitative v. classifying

  qualitative adjectives (usually gradable):

positive (absolute) *degree*:	good, kind, beautiful
comparative:	better, kinder, more beautiful
superlative:	best, kindest, most beautiful

  classifying adjectives (usually ungradable):

      annual (*more annual, *most annual)

      domestic, golden, wooden . . .

inherent v. non-inherent meaning

inherent:	that old man, he is old
	a poor person, she is poor
	pure water, it's pure
non-inherent (in attributive position):
	an old friend, you poor darling
intensifying	— pure fantasy, downright nonsense, utter madness
restrictive (limiting)	— the former champion, the main chance,
	a certain person

....

ADJECTIVES AND OTHER PARTS OF SPEECH

  used with a noun-like function:

    the poor, the unattainable, in short

  identical in form to *some*

adverbs:	monthly payments (adj.) It's paid monthly (adv.)
nouns:	a chemical reaction (adj.) dangerous chemicals (noun)
verbs:	the singing detective (participial adj.) he is singing (verb)
	unclaimed items (pseudo-participle)

....

ADJECTIVE COMPLEMENTATION

optional:	I'm glad.
	We're all glad about your success. I'd be glad of your
	opinion. I'm glad to hear that you've passed. I'm glad (that)
	you agree.
obligatory:	She's fond of children (*She's fond)

....

adjective

Adjectives are one of the major parts of speech. They are traditionally defined as 'describing words', words 'that tell us something about a noun', e.g. *difficult, grey, nice, pretty, usual.* This is only roughly true, and in modern grammar adjectives are usually defined in more grammatical terms.

(*a*) **Position**

A typical 'central' adjective can

   (i) be used before a noun (attributive position), e.g. *an old man*
   (ii) follow *be* or some other 'linking' verb without a following noun (predicative position), e.g. *He looks old*
   (iii) be graded, which means it can be:
       modified by an adverb such as *very* (e.g. *He's very old*)
       have comparative and superlative forms (*an older person, most extraordinary*).

Not all adjectives meet all these conditions. For example, some can only be used in position (i) or (ii), not both (e.g. *an utter fool*, but not **that fool is utter*; *she is asleep*, but not **that asleep child*). Other adjectives are ungradable (*extremely unique, **more unique than . . .*).

Adjectives, except the 'before-noun-only' kind, can sometimes come after their noun (in *postpositive* position), e.g.

   people *impatient* with the slow progress of the talks

This position is obligatory for a few adjectives (e.g. the president *elect*, the body *politic*, the harbour *proper*) and for any adjective used with an indefinite pronoun (e.g. nothing *special*, someone *silly*).

(*b*) **Meaning**

Adjectives are sometimes divided on grounds of meaning into two kinds:

   qualitative (usually gradable) ascribing a quality to a noun, e.g. *extraordinary, lovely, small classifying* (usually ungradable) assigning a category to a noun, e.g. *domestic, golden, wooden*

Most adjectives usually have inherent meaning—that is, the meaning of the adjective belongs directly to its noun (e.g. *He's an old man. That man is old*).

When adjectives do not refer directly, they are non-inherent, e.g.

an *old* friend *of mine* (It is the friendship that is old)
a *hard* worker (He works hard)

Some attributive adjectives have various kinds of non-inherent meaning, e.g.

intensifying meaning: a *downright* falsehood, *utter* madness, *sheer* genius, a *complete* stranger, *total* rubbish

restrictive (limiting) meaning: a *certain* person, an *only* child, the *main* reason

(c) Adjectives and other parts of speech

Some adjectives are used with *the*, to function rather like a noun. Used of people, the meaning is plural, 'people of that sort' in general, e.g. *the great and the good, the poor, the disabled*. But notice *the Almighty*. A few participles also can, exceptionally, have singular meaning, e.g. *the accused, the deceased*.

Other adjectives, prefaced by *the*, refer to abstract qualities, e.g.

the bizarre, the unattainable, the worst, the occult

and some have a noun-like use in set phrases:

in *public*, in *short*, for *better* or worse . . .

Some words are both adjectives and adverbs, e.g.

an *early* start (adj.); We must leave *early* (adv.).
a *better* result (adj.); I did *better* than I'd expected (adv.).

Some are both adjectives and nouns, e.g.

a *chemical* reaction (adj.), dangerous *chemicals* (n.)

Some are both adjectives and parts of verbs, e.g.

the *singing* detective (PARTICIPIAL ADJECTIVE),
The birds are *singing* (present participle of verb)

Participial adjectives (verbal in form, adjectival in use) also include *pseudo-participles* (words that have no corresponding verb), e.g. *wooded* slopes, an *unexpected* pleasure, a *breathtaking* view.

adjective clause

Commonly another name for RELATIVE clause, a clause that in some
way describes the noun (or noun phrase) it follows. See p. 205
RELATIVE CLAUSES.

adjective complementation

Adjectives often have other words after them to complete their
meaning; this is called *adjective complementation*.

See p. 6 ADJECTIVES.

An adjective complement may be

(i) a prepositional phrase

They were innocent *of the crime*
She is brilliant *at chess*

or (ii) various kinds of clause

I am sorry (*that*) *you don't like it*
You were mad *to tell them*
It's a very easy place *to find*
I've been busy *answering letters*

Such complementation may be obligatory, e.g. *She is fond of her
mother* (*She is fond) or optional, e.g. *I am so glad* (*that you got the
job*).

adjective order

The order in which two or more adjectives come in attributive
position.

When two or more adjectives premodify a noun, there is usually a
'natural' or a 'better' order for them. *Your wonderful new cream
woollen jumper* is likely; **your woollen cream new wonderful jumper*
is deviant. It has proved difficult to formulate comprehensive,
satisfactory rules to describe the ordering, and there are often
alternative possibilities, but in general the order is related to the
semantic properties of the adjectives; inherent characteristics (e.g.
woollen) are closest to the noun and subjective judgements (e.g.
wonderful) are furthest from it.

A typical order is:

> determiners (if any) *your*
> 'central' adjectives (*wonderful/expensive/useful*)
> colour adjectives (*cream*)
> inherent characteristics: origin (*Welsh*)
>   material (*woollen*)
> attributive noun describing purpose (*golfing* jacket)

adjective phrase

An adjective (or adjectival) phrase is a phrase consisting of an adjective as the HEAD plus, optionally, words before and/or after, e.g. It was *very difficult/too difficult to understand/simple enough.*

See p. 176 PHRASES.

adjunct

1 The older meaning of adjunct was something that formed an optional, inessential element in a structure. But in current usage the term is usually restricted to a word or words functioning like an adverb, whether a single-word adverb, an adverb phrase, or an adverb clause; sometimes the same as ADVERBIAL.

2 In some modern grammar, where adverbs are classified in considerable detail on the basis of how they function syntactically, adjunct is a specialized label for the most important kind of adverb, an adverb when it functions as an element of clause structure. By this definition, *clearly* is an adjunct in the first sentence below, but not in the second:

> He spoke clearly and to the point
> Clearly, I could be wrong

See p. 11 ADVERBS.

adverb

(*a*) Position

Adverbs are one of the major parts of speech. They get their name because they often modify or qualify the verb (or the whole predicate) of a sentence, e.g. She dances the tango *beautifully.*

ADVERBS AT A GLANCE

....

ADJUNCT

A 'central' adverb modifying the verb (or entire predicate). Adjuncts include
adverbs of

manner	Please speak *slowly*
place	We drove *there* yesterday
time	We drove there *yesterday*

....

SUBJUNCT

An adverb with a subordinate role. This includes many traditional 'degree'
adverbs:

intensifying adverb:	*very* surprising, *too* late, *completely* mad
focusing adverb:	*only* a rose, *just* in time, you *especially*

Subjuncts also include:

'viewpoint' adverbs:	*Technically*, we broke the rules (= from a technical point of view/technically speaking)
courtesy subjuncts:	*Please* do agree
	Kindly leave the room

....

DISJUNCT

An adverb with a more detached relationship to the clause or sentence. A
disjunct may be:

style disjunct:	*Frankly*, I am extremely worried. (= I am speaking frankly)
content (or attitudinal) **disjunct**:	The visit, *sadly*, was not a success. (= that's my opinion of the facts)

....

CONJUNCT

(Or *connector* or *linking adverb*) connecting one sentence or clause with
another:

> *First*, I have to admit . . .
> *Next*, it is important to remember that . . .
> We took a taxi. We weren't in time, *however*.
> *Nevertheless*, I'm glad we went.

....

Notes: These four terms can be applied to adverbials generally, not only to
single-word adverbs.
Both disjuncts and conjuncts are sometimes called sentence adverbs.

....

Typically such adverbs occur in final (end) position—that is, after
the verb, and the object if there is one, e.g.

> We are leaving town *tomorrow*

But other positions are possible, including initial:

> *Tomorrow*, we are leaving town

and mid (medial), i.e. between the subject and the lexical verb:

> They have *recently* left town

Adverbs that modify other parts of speech usually occur next to the word being modified, which could be:

> an adjective (e.g. *really* awful, *too* difficult)
> another adverb (e.g. *very* quietly)
> a noun or pronoun (e.g. *only* a rose, *just* you)

(*b*) **Meaning and function**

Adverbs form a notoriously mixed word class. Traditionally they are divided into various meaning-related categories, such as

> manner (which includes many typical *-ly* adverbs, e.g. *hurriedly, sensibly*)
> place (e.g. *there*)
> time (e.g. *soon, often, tomorrow*)
> degree (e.g. *only, too, very*)

In modern grammar adverbs are sometimes analysed in much greater detail. One analysis begins with an initial classification into four kinds, based primarily on four different syntactic functions. See p. 11 ADVERBS.

In this analysis the traditional categories of manner, place, time, and others are classed as *adjuncts*, the most central of the four types, because these adverbs are most closely integrated in clause structure. Many of the old degree adverbs, that modify individual words, are—in this analysis—*subjuncts* (adverbs of subordinate status); while various types of adverb that are more marginal to clause structure are distinguished as *disjuncts* (standing apart from clause structure and perhaps commenting on it) *or conjuncts* (linking one clause or sentence to another).

Within these four categories, many further classifications can be made. Even in popular grammar time adverbs (and adverbials) may be subdivided on grounds of both position and meaning into frequency (e.g. *often*) and duration (e.g. *for a month*), while degree adverbs may be divided into intensifying adverbs (e.g. *too* difficult) and focusing adverbs (I'm *only* here for the beer).

ADVERB CLAUSES AT A GLANCE

Comment: It's quite difficult, *you know*, to decide

Comparative [or Comparison]:
    I worked as hard *as I could*
    I worked harder *than I'd ever done in my life*

Comparison: (1) See Comparative
              (2) See Manner

Concession:
    Although you don't like it, perhaps you should accept
    While I don't actually know, I have a good idea
    We fear the worst, *though hoping for the best*

Condition: *If winter comes*, can spring be far behind?
          I wouldn't do that, *if I were you*
          He wouldn't have paid, *unless they had made him*
          Do let us know, *if possible*

Contrast: I adore jazz, *whereas my sister prefers classical music*

Manner [or Comparison]: You look *as though you'd seen a ghost*
                   He speaks *just like his father did*

Place: Put your money *where your heart is*
       Where there's a will, there's a way

Proportion: *As* you sow, *so* shall you reap
           The more I think about it, *the less* I like it
           The fewer, the better

Purpose: He's getting new glasses, *so that he won't keep falling over the cat*
         To open, cut along the dotted line

Reason [or Cause]: They climbed it *because it was there*
              Since you're so clever, why don't you try?

Result: He's so shortsighted, *(that) he keeps falling over the cat*

Time: Don't fire *until you see the whites of their eyes*
      As I was going to St Ives, I met a man with seven wives
      Things are different *since she left*
      I'm ready *when you are*
      After driving all day, we felt tired

Notes: Comment clauses and Comparative clauses (as shown here) are excluded
    from some classifications—as also are non-finite and verbless clauses.
The label Comparison is given to two different types of adverb clause—the types
    that are shown here as Comparative and Manner.
Contrast is sometimes included in Concession.

Some adverbs are gradable like adjectives, e.g.

> soon, sooner, soonest; well, better, best
> beautifully, more beautifully
> intelligently, less intelligently

Loosely, in popular grammar, the term *adverb* is often used to cover ADVERB PHRASES and adverbials in general. More strictly, where the latter terms are used, *adverb* may be restricted to single words functioning adverbially.

adverb clause

Any clause functioning as the adverbial element in clause structure is an adverb clause. Adverb (or adverbial) clauses are often classified on semantic grounds into such categories as clauses of time, reason, condition, etc., e.g.

> I'll come *when I'm ready* (compare I'll come *soon*)
> They succeeded *because they persevered*
> Don't do it *unless you're sure*

In traditional usage, only finite structures are clauses, but some modern grammar includes non-finite and verbless clauses, e.g.

> *Although injured*, he struggled on
> *While travelling*, he contracted jaundice
> Make it Thursday, *if possible*

See p. 13 ADVERB CLAUSES.

adverbial

1 In some modern grammar Adverbial (indicated by A) is one of the five elements of clause or sentence structure, along with Subject (S), Verb (V), Object (O), and Complement (C). See p. 42 CLAUSES.

In this sense, the adverbial may be a word, phrase or clause:

> You / 've done / that / *(very) well (indeed)*: SVOA
> Hang / your coat / *on a hanger*: VOA
> They / arrived / *the Sunday before last*: SVA
> *When you've quite finished*, / we / can begin: ASV
> *Though disappointed*, / she / said / nothing: ASVO

2 An adverbial can also mean any word, phrase, or clause used like an adverb (including a single-word adverb alone), whether functioning as an element in clause structure (as above) or at some other level.

Compare:

> She dresses simply
> That was a simply dreadful thing to say

In the first sentence *simply* modifies the verb and the sentence has the overall pattern of SVA. In the second, *simply* is part of a noun phrase (*a simply dreadful thing to say*), which functions as a complement, making the sentence SVC.

Adverbial is a useful term to cover words and phrases functioning adverbially but that belong to other parts of speech, e.g. They arrived *last night*.

adverb phrase

A phrase containing an adverb as head and so functioning like a single adverb:

> He speaks *very quickly indeed*
> We were able to use the pool *as often as we wished*

See p. 176 PHRASES.

affirmative

An affirmative sentence or verb states that a fact is so; or answers 'yes' to a question. In some grammars the term POSITIVE is used with the same meaning. The opposite is NEGATIVE.

affix

An affix is an addition to a word or root etc. in order to form a new word.

Affixes added at the beginning are PREFIXES (e.g. *un*natural, *over-*weight); those added at the end are SUFFIXES (e.g. natural*ness*, weight*less*/*ness*.) An affix may be derivational, producing a new word: *garden* + *er* gives *gardener*; or inflectional, giving another form of the same word—*garden* + *s* gives plural *gardens*.

affricate

A consonant sound combining the characteristics of a PLOSIVE and a FRICATIVE. There is a complete closure in the vocal tract, but the plosive release is slow enough for there to be accompanying friction.

There are two affricates in standard English: [tʃ], the voiceless sound heard at the beginning and end of *church*, in the middle of *feature*, and at the end of *catch*; and [dʒ], the voiced sound at the beginning of *gin* and *jam*, in the middle of *soldier*, and the beginning and end of *judge*. See p. 264 THE CONSONANTS OF ENGLISH.

agent

The 'doer', in semantic terms, of the action of the verb.

The term is particularly applied to the 'doer' of a passive verb, because here the grammatical subject is not the doer, as the subject of an active verb often is. The agent is often indicated with a *by*-phrase;

> The two were kidnapped by *masked terrorists*
> The child was saved by *the dog*

An agent is typically animate, and contrasts with INSTRUMENT and MEANS.

agent noun

An agent noun indicates 'someone who does something', e.g. *doer*, *farmer*, and *lover*.

Most agent nouns are formed by adding the *agentive* suffix *-er* or *-or* to a verb, e.g. *actor*, *manufacturer*, *teacher*, *worker*. But some agent nouns are inanimate (e.g. *computer*, *shocker*); and a few have no independent base (e.g. *author*, *butcher*).

agreement

Agreement (also called *concord*) is a necessary grammatical relationship between two (or more) words in a clause or sentence, because of person, number, or gender.

In English, the most generally recognized agreement is the relationship between a subject and its verb. As verbs have few inflections, this mainly affects the third person of the present simple of ordinary (lexical) verbs, where the singular *-s* ending contrasts with the plural and with other persons (e.g. *He/she works*, but *I/we/you/they work*). The verbs *be* and *have*, and progressive and perfect tenses formed with them (I *am* working, She *has* worked) also must agree with their subjects.

Prescriptivists favour strict grammatical agreement. However, *notional concord*—where agreement follows the meaning, is a common feature of English, and acceptable to many grammarians:

> Everybody knows this, don't they?
> Neither of them approve (*more strictly* approves)
> The committee have decided (. . . has . . .)
> £10 is all I have (*not* *£10 are all . . .*)

A minor type of verb agreement, called *proximity agreement*, *proximity concord*, or *attraction*) means agreement of the verb with a closely preceding noun instead of the actual noun head. Such agreement may be marginally acceptable when it supports notional concord, but is generally considered ungrammatical:

> ? No one except my parents care what happens to me
> ?? A parcel of books have arrived for you

Number and gender agreement affects pronouns and possessives, e.g.

> *He* has lost *his* umbrella
> *She* blames *herself*
> There were *many* problems and *much* heartsearching

allomorph

Any variant of a MORPHEME, any form in which a meaningful morpheme is actually realized.

For example, the regular English plural is pronounced in three different ways, according to the preceding sounds. Thus we can say

that the English plural morpheme has three regular allomorphs—
an /s/ sound as in *cats*, a /z/ sound as in *dogs*, and an /ɪz/ sound as in
horses. We can also talk of a *zero allomorph* in *sheep* (plural), and
various irregular allomorphs in *mice*, *geese* and so on.

allophone

Any of the variants in which an (idealized) PHONEME is actually
pronounced.

A single phoneme of a language may be pronounced in slightly
different ways by different speakers. But the main variants—the
allophones—are conditioned by the surrounding sounds. Thus in
standard English the LATERAL phoneme /l/ has a *clear* sound when
it precedes a vowel (as in *listen* or *fall in*); a somewhat DEVOICED
sound when following a voiceless plosive (as in *please*), and a *dark*
sound when it occurs word-finally after a vowel (as in *fall down*) or
when it is syllabic (as in *muddle*).

alveolar

A consonant sound made by the front of the tongue against the
alveolar ridge, the hard ridge formed by the roots of the upper
teeth.

The main alveolars in English are /t/ and /d/ (often dental consonants in other languages), which are alveolar plosives; /n/, an
alveolar nasal; and /s/ and /z/, which are alveolar fricatives.

The actual articulation of these alveolar phonemes is affected by
adjacent sounds, so that their actual pronunciation is not always in
fact alveolar.

See p. 264 THE CONSONANTS OF ENGLISH.

ambiguity

If a word or phrase is ambiguous, it can be understood in more
than one way.

(*a*) *Lexical ambiguity* can occur when a word has more than one
meaning, e.g. *I don't seem to have a chair* (was the lecturer
complaining that she had nothing to sit on or that there was
nobody to introduce her?).

(b) *Grammatical ambiguity* has a variety of causes including—

- ellipsis (or possible ellipsis):

    He was wearing new red socks and boots (were the boots new and red too?)
    I had better taste in films than girls (than in girls? or than girls did?)

- prepositional phrases (which may either form part of a noun phrase or have an adverbial function):

    These claims have been dismissed as mere bravado by the police (bravado by the police? or dismissed by the police?)

- to-infinitive clauses (which also have several functions):

    Railmen defy union order *to stop coal shipments* (they are refusing to stop the shipments? or they are stopping them in defiance of union orders?)

In complex sentences, a whole finite clause may be open to more than one interpretation. (Intonation may disambiguate if the sentences are spoken.) E.g.

    He said he wouldn't lend me the money and I couldn't go (did he say that I couldn't go, or was I unable to go as a consequence of not being lent the money?)

    I'll tell you when they arrive (am I going to inform you of their arrival, or am I going to tell you something when they arrive?)

(c) Many English words can be interpreted as different parts of speech, so sometimes lexical and grammatical ambiguity results. Headlines and other types of abbreviated language provide many examples of such ambiguity:

    Free Worktops Last 7 Days (hardly worth having if you interpret *last* as a verb)

anacoluthon (plural **anacoluthons, anacolutha**)

Anacoluthon is a break in syntax. Either a sentence breaks off though incomplete, or it starts one way and finishes another. This is generally an error in written English, but it occurs frequently in spoken language and often passes unnoticed by the listener, e.g.

    One of my sisters—her husband's a doctor, and he says if you take aspirin your cold will go in a week, but if you do nothing it will take seven days
    It's a course which I don't know whether it will be any good
    I thought that you were going—well, I hoped that you were going to help
    Why don't you—it's only a suggestion—but you could walk

analogy

Imitation of the inflections and constructions of existing words in the formation of new words.

Word formation normally follows regular patterns by analogy. Recent years, for example, have seen numerous new verbs with the prefixes *de-* (e.g. *deselect*) and *dis-* (e.g. *disinvest*) and nouns beginning *Euro-* (e.g. *Eurocrat, Eurofare, Eurospeak*). Other new nouns have been formed with such established suffixes as *-ism* (*endism, handicapism*). New verbs almost always inflect regularly (*faxing, faxes, faxed*) by analogy.

See p. 145 NEW WORDS.

analysis

Analysis is distinguishing the grammatical elements of a sentence, phrase, or word.

There are many ways in which this can be done. Simple sentences or clauses may be analysed into subject and predicate, or into such elements as subject, verb, object, complement, and adverbial. (Compare Immediate CONSTITUENT analysis.)

Complex and compound sentences are often analysed into types of clauses, e.g. coordinate and subordinate; adverbial, nominal, and so on. A word may be analysed into its base and suffixes (e.g. *dis-interest-ed-ness*).

anaphora

1 When we use a word or phrase as a substitute for a previous word or phrase, in order to refer back to some thing, person, or happening that has been mentioned previously, the process is *anaphora* and the substitute word or phrase is an *anaphor* (more generally called a PRO-FORM).

In *My cousin said he was coming*, *he* refers back to *my cousin* (which is its ANTECEDENT).

Pronouns and other pro-forms are frequently used anaphorically to avoid repetition. But sometimes a noun is repeated, and then the identity of reference is usually shown by a marker of definiteness (*the, that . . .*) in the later (anaphoric) reference:

Old Mother Hubbard
went to the cupboard
to get her poor dog a bone;
But when *she* got *there*,
the cupboard was bare,
and so *the* poor dog had none.

She and *there* refer back to *Old Mother Hubbard* and *the cupboard*
(line 2). *The cupboard* (line 5) and *the poor dog* (line 6) refer back
to lines 2 and 3.

2 Loosely the term anaphora is extended to cover the use of
pro-forms to refer forward, which is more accurately called CATA-
PHORA.

animate

Animate means 'living'. The term is particularly used in the
classification of nouns. Animate nouns (e.g. *girl*, *tiger*, etc.) refer to
persons and animals in contrast to *inanimate* nouns (e.g. *girlhood*,
zoo) referring to things, states, ideas.

In English this distinction is almost entirely a matter of meaning, not
grammar, although there is rough correspondence in some personal
and relative pronouns: *he*, *she*, *who* usually have animate reference;
it, *which* are mainly used in connection with inanimate referents.

antecedent

1 A word or words to which a following word or phrase refers
back.

Typically antecedents are noun phrases to which personal and
relative pronouns refer. For example, in

My brother telephoned to say he'd be late

My brother is the antecedent of *he*.

Less obviously *do*, *so*, *do so*, *there*, *then*, and a few other pro-forms
can refer anaphorically to antecedents which may be verbal,
adverbial, or clausal, e.g.

I *cried* more than I'd ever *done* before in my life
You could *buy a yearly season ticket*, but I don't advise *doing so*
'*Air fares are going up again*.' 'Who told you *that*?'

2 Loosely, despite the meaning of the word, the term antecedent is sometimes extended for phrases that come later than their pro-forms, e.g. *Mary* in

If you see *her*, will you give *Mary* a message for me?

anticipatory *it*

The word *it* is *anticipatory* if used as a grammatical subject, or more rarely object, when the 'real' subject or object is postponed until later in the sentence:

It is better *to have loved and lost* than never to have loved at all
I take *it that you agree with me*?

There is considerable confusion in the usage of the several terms available to describe various functions of the word *it*. For some grammarians, anticipatory *it* (used with the subject or object placed later) and *preparatory it* are identical, but they distinguish this usage from DUMMY (or EMPTY or PROP *it*). Others use all or some of these terms differently, or use one of them as an umbrella term.

antonym

Pairs of words opposite in meaning to each other are antonyms, e.g. *good/bad*, *thick/thin*, *few/many*. More accurately we should talk of words that are opposite to others in some of their meanings. For example the antonym of *old* is sometimes *young*, and sometimes *new*.

Some linguists distinguish various kinds of opposite meaning and reserve the term *antonym* for gradable opposites (e.g. *good/bad*), excluding both non-gradable COMPLEMENTARY terms (e.g. *life/death*), and relational CONVERSES (e.g. *buy/sell*; *husband/wife*).

apostrophe

The sign ⟨'⟩ has two main uses:

1 To indicate the omission of a letter or letters, as in *don't*, *thro'*, the *'90s*. The apostrophe is not normally used in established abbreviations such as *(in)flu(enza)* or *info(rmation)*. *O'clock* is an obvious exception (the *o'* originally being *of*).

2 To indicate the genitive (possessive) case of nouns. The current rules for possessive apostrophes are:

- Add *'s* to a singular word (e.g. *the boy's statement, an hour's time, Doris's husband, her boss's address*)
- Also add *'s* to plural words that do not end in *s* (e.g. *the men's action, the people's will*)
- With plural words ending in *s*, only add an apostrophe at the end (e.g. *ladies' shoes; the Lawsons' house*).

Names from ancient times ending with *s* do not necessarily follow these rules (e.g. *Socrates' death*).

It is an error to use the apostrophe with possessive pronouns (e.g. *hers, its, ours, theirs, yours*). *It's* means 'it is' or 'it has'. For 'belonging to it', the correct form is *its* (e.g. *The cat hasn't eaten its food*).

Note: the use of the apostrophe to mark ordinary plurals (e.g. **potato's, *ice-cream's*) is a mistake. It is, however, generally acceptable with the less usual plurals of letters and dates, e.g.

> Dot your *i's* and cross your *t's*
> That is what people did in the *1960's/1960s*

apposition

Two (or more) words or phrases—particularly noun phrases—that are used together and refer to the same person or thing are in apposition (to each other):

> *Our longest reigning monarch, Queen Victoria*, reigned from 1837 to 1901
> The second edition of *OUP's biggest dictionary, the Oxford English Dictionary*, was published in 1989

In *full apposition* (as above) both parts are identical in their reference and either part could be omitted without affecting the grammar or essential meaning.

In *partial apposition*, these conditions only partly apply:

> A monarch, for example a twentieth-century monarch, may have limited powers (a relationship of example, not identity)
> A very important person is coming—the Queen (where we could not say **is coming—the Queen*)

Grammarians disagree about whether such structures as the following show apposition or not:

> the number thirteen, my sister Mary, the author Graham Greene, the expression 'greenhouse effect'

and structures joined by *of* where the two parts share identity, as in *the city of Oxford, that fool of a man*.

appositive clause

An appositive clause is a particular type of postmodifying clause, e.g.

They had the idea *that everything would be all right* in *the end*

Such clauses are grammatically different from relative clauses. The *that* is a conjunction, not a pronoun, so these clauses have their own subject (and object), and *which* is never possible. The preceding noun is an abstract noun such as *belief, fact, idea*. Contrast a relative clause: The idea *(that/which) Tom put forward* was ingenious.

archaism

A word or grammatical structure characteristic of an earlier period of the language but no longer in ordinary use is *archaic*. Some archaisms survive in special registers, such as legal or religous language, or they are familiar from literature, proverbs, and so on. Archaisms include

(*a*) individual words, e.g. *albeit, methinks, perchance, thou, thine, thee, whence, whereat, ye*

(*b*) verbal inflections, e.g. *goeth, knowest*

(*c*) some grammatical structures, e.g.

Our Father, *which art* in heaven (= who are . . .)
He who hesitates is lost (= Anyone who . . .)
All that glisters is not gold (= Not everything that . . . is)
We *must away* (= must go/leave/be off)
Would that I could help (= I wish . . .)
So be it
If it *please* your lordship

article

A name for *the* (DEFINITE ARTICLE) and *a/an* (INDEFINITE ARTICLE).

The articles are sometimes classified as a distinct part of speech. Earlier grammarians considered them to be a special kind of adjective. But in fact articles are much more like DETERMINERS than adjectives in their usage, and modern grammarians usually classify them as a subclass of determiner. See also ZERO ARTICLE.

See p. 66 DETERMINERS, p. 190 PRONOUNS AND DETERMINERS.

articulation

This is a term in phonetics for the physical production of speech sounds.

Consonant sounds are classified in terms of both their PLACE and their MANNER of articulation. For example, English /p/, /b/, and /m/ are bilabial sounds (made with both lips). In manner, /p/ and /b/ are plosives—that is they are made by a complete closure followed by a release (an 'explosion') of air, though /p/ is voiceless and /b/ is voiced. By contrast, /m/, though bilabial in place, is articulated in a nasal manner, as even when the lips are closed air escapes through the nose. See p. 264 Diag. 1. The articulation of vowel sounds is described mainly in terms of tongue position. See VOWEL.

aspect

Aspect relates to the meaning and form of verbs.

English is often considered to have two aspects—PROGRESSIVE (as in *I am/was writing to Robert*), which stresses action in progress (or incomplete action) and PERFECT or *perfective* (as in *I have written to Robert*), which stresses completed action, although the distinction of incomplete versus complete meaning is an oversimplification.

Traditionally both aspects are treated as part of the tense system in English, and we commonly speak of tenses such as the present progressive (e.g. *We are waiting*) or even the past perfect progressive (e.g. *We had been waiting*), which combines two aspects. There is a distinction to be made, however, between tense and aspect. Tense is more concerned with past versus present time and is based on form (e.g. *write/writes, wrote*); aspect is concerned with duration, and in English is a matter of syntax, using parts of *be* to form the progressive, and *have* to form the perfective.

aspiration

Popularly the sound of *h* is an aspirate. This usage is illustrated by the old joke:

A: I've got a 'orrible 'eadache.

B: What you need is a couple of aspirates.

In phonetic terms, aspiration means articulating a sound with an audible release of air. The term is relevant to the description of the English voiceless plosives /p/, /t/, and /k/. These sounds are aspirated in their final release stage when they come at the beginning of a stressed syllable (e.g. *pun, two, careful*). In contrast, the same phonemes have little or no aspiration when initial in unstressed syllables (*per'*mission), when preceded by s (*s*tory) or in final position—i.e. followed by silence (Bad lu*ck* !).

assertive

Words that are typically used in positive statements are *assertive*, in contrast to NON-ASSERTIVE words (which are typical of questions and negative statements).

Certain determiners, pronouns, and adverbs, by reason of their meaning, tend to be confined to positive statements, and are replaced by corresponding non-assertive forms in negative and interrogative sentences. Assertive forms include the *some* series of words (*some, someone, somewhere*, etc.) plus a few other words (e.g. *already, plenty, several*)—in contrast to *non-assertive* words (particularly the *any*-series, plus e.g. *at all, much, yet*). Compare, for example:

I've *already* planted *some* spring bulbs

with

I haven't planted *any* bulbs *yet*

Have you planted *any yet*?

The line between assertive and non-assertive is not rigid. Although non-assertive forms are often impossible in positive statements (**I've already planted any*), assertive forms may be possible in questions and negative clauses, where they suggest a markedly positive meaning (e.g. *Have you planted some bulbs already?*). Non-assertive forms occasionally occur in positive statements (e.g. *Any small bulbs would be suitable*).

• **assertive territory** means the part of a sentence where assertive forms may be expected, i.e. the whole predication in positive statements.

Similarly the predication of negative statements and questions is *non-assertive territory*. Non-assertive territory also includes clauses expressing other kinds of tentativeness, such as condition (e.g. *If anyone calls*, say I'm designing St Paul's).

assimilation

Speech sounds are often affected by adjacent sounds, and they *assimilate* some of the other sounds' characteristics.

This is a common feature of speech, though one that many native speakers are unaware of.

In *anticipatory assimilation* (*or regressive assimilation*), a sound is influenced by the following sound. For example, in some people's pronunciation of *width* the voiced /d/ has been assimilated to a voiceless /t/ by the following voiceless /θ/.

In current speech, assimilation frequently occurs across word boundaries, as when *that case* becomes /ðæk keɪs/ or *this shop* becomes /ðɪʃ ʃɒp/ or *ten more* becomes /tem mɔ:/.

A reverse type of assimilation (*progressive assimilation*) is found when a sound is influenced by a previous one. This is an established and regular feature of the *-s* ending of verbs and nouns, where the ending is a voiceless /s/ after voiceless sounds (*taps, heats, dock's, griefs*), but a voiced /z/ sound after another voiced sound (*tabs, heeds, dog's, grieves*). (The /ɪz/ ending follows both voiceless and voiced sibilants—*pieces, pleases*). Similarly the past tense *-ed* ending is devoiced to a /t/ sound after a voiceless consonant (*roped, lacked, bussed*, versus *robed, lagged, buzzed*).

attachment rule

The 'rule' that the notional subject of a subjectless non-finite clause is the same person or thing as the subject of the clause it is subordinate to. Failure to observe this rule often results in a HANGING PARTICIPLE.

attraction

The same as *proximity* AGREEMENT.

attributive

An adjective or noun preceding a noun, and so usually 'attributing' some characteristic to it, is attributive, or 'in attributive position', e.g. *new* in *the new library* or *power* in *power struggle*. The term contrasts with PREDICATIVE.

Some adjectives can only be attributive (e.g. *former, inner, mere, lone, main, indoor*). Similarly, nouns used attributively cannot normally be transferred to predicative position (**the effect is greenhouse*, **this book is library*).

Attributive adjectives are sometimes classified according to meaning into such subclasses as *intensifying* and *restrictive*.

See p. 6 ADJECTIVES.

auxiliary

(*a*) A verb used in forming tenses, moods, and voices of other verbs is an auxiliary (verb).

The chief verbs used like this are *be, do*, and *have* and the MODAL VERBS (sometimes called *modal auxiliaries*).

An auxiliary cannot function as the only verb in a complete sentence. Apparent exceptions to this principle are in fact examples of ellipsis or substitution.

Auxiliaries thus contrast functionally with MAIN VERBS.

(*b*) On formal grounds, the auxiliaries contrast with LEXICAL VERBS (full verbs) in the way that they form questions by inversion of subject and verb (e.g. *Are you ready? Can you help?*), and negatives by simply adding *n't* (*They aren't, We mustn't, She doesn't*).

Both definitions of auxiliary verb, (*a*) and (*b*), describe the modal verbs. The verbs, *be, do*, and *have*, however, do not quite fit, since they can also function as main verbs. They are therefore sometimes classified separately as PRIMARY VERBS.

See p. 250 VERBS.

a-word

a-*words* begin with the syllable a- and form a class of words, some more like adjectives, and some more like adverbs, that mainly function predicatively. E.g.

The children were abroad/afraid/alone/ashamed/awake

but not

*An afraid/alone/ashamed/awake child was crying

Some of the more adjective-like words can be used attributively if modified (e.g. *a very ashamed person*); the more adverb-like words can follow verbs of motion (e.g. *They've gone abroad*).

B

back-formation

The formation of a new word by the removal of (real or apparent) affixes etc. from an existing word; or such a word itself.

A back-formation is revealed by the fact that the date of its first use is later than that of its apparent derivative. The majority of back-formations in English are verbs, e.g.

burgle (L19)   from *burglar* (M16)
housekeep (M19)   from *housekeeping* (M16)
shoplift (E19)   from *shoplifting* (L17)

See p. 145 NEW WORDS.

backshift

When using a reporting verb in the past tense (*He said, They thought, I remarked*) it is common to 'backshift' the tenses of the words spoken or thought into past tenses too. Thus

'I am sorry I haven't asked them yet. I will.'

may (with backshift) become

Mark said he was sorry he hadn't asked them yet, but he would.

Similarly a past tense (e.g. *I asked them*) may become a past perfect (*He said he had asked them*). Backshift (which is related to the *sequence of tense rule*) is not, however, automatic. Importantly, if the time frame of the person writing or speaking now is the same as that of the original speaker whose words are being reported, tenses do not need to change:

He said $\left\{\begin{array}{l}\text{he wouldn't}\\\text{he won't}\end{array}\right\}$ be around in the year 2050

This explains why past tenses are often not subject to backshift: She told us that both her parents (had) died when she was ten (and not **when she had been ten*).

bare infinitive

The infinitive of a verb without a preceding *to* particle.

Bare infinitives are identical in form with the BASE form of the verb. They are used after:

- the main modal verbs; e.g. *I must go, I shall return!* and can occur with semi-modals: e.g. *You needn't bother*
- the verb *do* in questions and negatives; e.g. *Does he know? They didn't say*
- verbs of perception; e.g. *We saw/heard them go, I felt it bite me*
- *make* and *let*; e.g. *Make/Let them wait*

and in:

- a few fixed expressions; e.g. *make do, make believe, (live and) let live, let go*
- various other patterns; e.g. *I'd rather try than do nothing*

A bare infinitive is only rarely interchangeable with a *to*-INFINITIVE, and some of the verbs listed above need a *to*-infinitive when used in the passive, e.g. *We were made to wait.* The verb *help* is unusual, in that both the bare infinitive and the *to*-infinitive are often possible, e.g. *Please help (me) (to) do the washing-up.*

See p. 250 VERBS.

base

1 The basic or uninflected form of a verb. Also called *base form*. *Go*, *like*, *sing* are all bases or base forms, in contrast to *went*, *likes*, *sang*, which are not.

The base form of a verb functions

  (*a*) non-finitely, as the infinitive (e.g. You must *go*)

  (*b*) finitely:

- as the imperative (*Listen*!, *Be* quiet, *Have* a biscuit)
- as the present indicative tense for all persons other than the third person singular, e.g. *I always listen* as opposed to *He always listens* (the verb *be* is an exception to this)
- as the so-called present subjunctive (e.g. They insisted that he *listen*).

2 An element in word formation.

(*a*) The terminology of word formation is confused. Many words consist of an irreducible 'core' word (a free morpheme) to which one or more affixes (bound morphemes) are attached, e.g. *sing* + *s* = *sings*, *great* + *er* = *greater*, *great* + *ly* = *greatly*, *infect* + *-ious* = *infectious*, *in* + *discreet* = *indiscreet*. Such basic core words as elements in larger words may be called *base morphemes*, but are more often called ROOTS (or STEMS).

(*b*) Another type of word when stripped of an affix is no longer a complete word, but a 'bound morpheme'. E.g. *gratuitous* apparently has the suffix *-ous* (compare *pompous, monstrous, outrageous*) just as *gratuity* has a noun suffix *-y* but there is no word **gratuit*. Such a form may be termed a *base* (or a base morpheme) in some systems. (But the terms STEM and root are also used.)

(*c*) A different problem arises with a word such as *unanswerable*. It clearly consists of the prefix *un-*, the word *answer*, and the suffix *-able*. But we do not have a word **unanswer*; we can only attach *un-* to *answerable*. Some linguists therefore specifically reserve the term *base* for a word such as *answerable* in the context of *unanswerable*. In this usage, a base is not as basic as the 'core' element (here *answer*). But other linguists use STEM as the label here, possibly also including forms such as *gratuit-*.

before-past

A popular name for the past perfect tense, which often refers to a time before another past time, e.g. *I realized that I had lost the key.*

bilabial

Bilabial is a place-of-articulation label for consonants. It means a sound made with both lips closed or nearly closed. The English bilabials are the consonants /p/, /b/, and /m/ as in *pan, ban,* and *man*. See p. 264 THE CONSONANTS OF ENGLISH.

Actually, the semi-vowel /w/ is also bilabial, but all vowels involve both lips, so the label is usually restricted to consonants.

binary

A term applied to a pair of features in a language which are mutually exclusive, or the opposition between them.

(*a*) The phonetic contrasts between nasal and non-nasal or voiced and voiceless articulations are said to be *binary oppositions* or *binary features*.

(*b*) Binary contrasts are a notable feature of vocabulary, which contains many pairs of words of opposite meaning (ANTONYMS).

binary noun

A noun that both by form and function is plural only and which denotes something, particularly a tool or a garment, with two joined parts (e.g. *scissors*, *trousers*). See p. 151 NOUNS.

blend

A word, phrase, or other structure formed by merging or blending parts of two other words etc. The term can refer to word formation and to syntax.

(*a*) Examples of *lexical blends* (also called *blend words*, *word blends*) are:

> *bit* (= binary + digit) (M20)
> *brunch* (= breakfast + lunch) (L19)
> *camcorder* (= camera + recorder) (L20)
> *smog* (= smoke + fog) (E20)
> *televangelist* (= television + evangelist) (L20)
> *motel* (= motor + hotel) (E20)

Note that while most blends are formed by joining a pair of words at the point where they have one or more letters or sounds in common (e.g. mo*tor* + *ho*tel), a few are not formed in this way (e.g. *brunch*, *camcorder*).

See p. 145 NEW WORDS, p. 157 OMISSION.

(*b*) Syntactic blends include such structures as:

> I would have liked to have done it (*I would have liked to do it* + *I would like to have done it*)

Neither claim impressed us, nor seemed genuine (*Neither claim impressed us or seemed genuine* + *The claims neither impressed us nor seemed genuine*)

block language

A type of ABBREVIATED structure differing from normal clause or sentence structure, but often conveying a 'complete' message.

Block language is found especially in notices and newspaper headlines. It sometimes consists of single noun phrases (e.g. *No exit, County's snappy reply to a negative image*). Other block language has a sort of abbreviated clause structure, with articles, auxiliary verbs, and other minor words omitted (e.g. *Tanks met by rain of stones, Jailed racing driver's bail request rejected*). Some block language could be included in some wider category such as *irregular sentence* or *non-sentence*.

borrowing

Taking over a word from a foreign language; or a word so borrowed (also called a LOANWORD). The term is somewhat misleading because 'borrowed' words usually become a permanent part of the borrowing language.

English has borrowed from many other languages. Some loanwords are totally assimilated (e.g. *butter, fail, umbrella*). Others retain foreign traces in pronunciation, spelling, or inflection (e.g. *phenomenon, genre, faux pas*). Other words remain semantically tied to a foreign context (e.g. *matador, rajah, tundra, intifada*).

Surprisingly few words have been borrowed into English from the neighbouring Celtic languages. Examples here are *coracle, flannel* (Welsh); *clan, slogan, whisky* (Gaelic); *galore, shamrock* (Irish).

Borrowing from Latin has been constant from earliest times, and has always included quite central vocabulary items, such as *cheese, pillow,* and *tile*. Many Latin borrowings have come through French. Similarly some Greek loanwords have come through Latin, and others direct.

Scandinavian loanwords in late Old English times even included form words, such as *they, them, their*.

French has contributed more than any other language to the English vocabulary, starting with early post-Conquest loanwords (e.g. *castle*, *prison*, *war*). Other important European sources have been Dutch, Low German, Italian, and Spanish.

Loanwords from outside Europe tended, in the earlier period of exploration, to come through languages such as Dutch and Portuguese. Later, borrowings came direct from many other languages, e.g. *sheikh* (Arabic), *boomerang*, *kangaroo* (Australian aboriginal), *lychee* (Chinese), *taboo* (Tongan), *mocassin*, *skunk* (Algonquian), *judo*, *tycoon* (Japanese), *caddy*, *rattan* (Malay), *thug* (Hindi), *bungalow* (Gujarati).

See p. 145 NEW WORDS.

bound form

A morpheme that normally can only occur joined to another form, e.g. *-ly* (as in *normally*) or *-ed* (as in *joined*). Also called *bound morpheme*.

brackets

A pair of rounded marks ( ) that are used to separate off a word, a number, etc. that interrupts the main structure of the sentence. Dashes or hyphens are sometimes used for the same purpose. Other brackets [ ] or ⟨ ⟩ are used for specialist purposes.

- **bracketing** is sometimes used to show the internal structure of a clause or sentence. At a simple level the technique is useful. We might for example contrast

[He]	[looked up]	[the word]	[in his dictionary]
subject	verb	object	adverbial

with

[He]	[looked]	[up the chimney]
subject	verb	adverbial

More complicated sentences may involve brackets within brackets, which make the analysis difficult to read. For these TREE DIAGRAMS are often preferred.

branching

A linguistic term for the connections between main and sub-ordinate clauses, often shown in a TREE DIAGRAM.

Right-branching subordinate clauses tend to be easier to understand than left-branching ones. Compare

I danced with a man
        who danced with a girl
                who danced with the Prince of Wales

and (left-branching)

I danced with a man
      a girl
      the Prince of Wales danced with
          danced with

C

cardinal number

A number denoting quantity (*one*, *two*, *three*, etc.) in contrast to an ORDINAL number (*first*, *second*, *third*).

cardinal vowels

A standard set of eighteen vowels, devised by the phonetician Daniel Jones (1881–1967) as a basis for describing the vowels of any language.

There are eight primary vowels: four front vowels, defined according to the height of the front of the tongue, and four back vowels, where the height of the back of the tongue is relevant. These tongue heights are *close* (or *high*), *half-close*, *half-open*, and *open* (or *low*). The eight secondary cardinal vowels have the same tongue positions, but the LIP-POSITION (rounding or spreading) is different. Two further vowels depend on the centre of the tongue being raised.

The cardinal vowel system is conventionally presented in a stylized diagram of the mouth, on which the actual vowels of a particular language can be superimposed. Thus the /iː/ sound in English *need* is a high (or close) front vowel, but not quite so high as the idealized cardinal vowel 1; while English /ɑː/ in *hard* is a low back vowel, near in sound to cardinal 5, the lowest or most 'open' back vowel.

case

The form of a noun (or noun phrase), shown by inflection; and its meaningful function in relation to other words in the clause or sentence.

(*a*) **Form** In English (unlike Latin, which has six cases) the only case distinction in nouns is between the COMMON case, i.e. the

CASE

....

FORM

nouns:
    common case: boy, boys, child, children, Tom Smith, the Smiths
    genitive (or possessive) case: boy's, boys', child's, children's, Tom
        Smith's, the Smiths'
pronouns:
    common case: one, someone, anybody . . .
    genitive case: one's, someone's, anybody's . . .
Six pronouns have:
    subject(ive) case: I, he, she, we, they, who
    object(ive) case: me, him, her, us, them, whom

....

FUNCTION

Subject: *Old Mother Hubbard* went to the cupboard . . .
Indirect object (or **dative**): to fetch *her poor dog* . . .
Direct object (or **objective**): . . . *a bone*
Genitive: Tom, he was a *piper's* son
Agent(ive): Cock Robin was killed *by the sparrow*
Instrument: Who killed Cock Robin? I, said the sparrow, *with my bow
    and arrow* . . .
Means: The sparrow killed the robin *by shooting him*

....

ordinary base form for the singular—*boy* (with plural *boys*) and the
GENITIVE (*boy's, boys'*). And even genitive is slightly dubious, because we can add the inflection to a phrase (e.g. *the King of Spain's
daughter, the man next door's car*).

Among English pronouns, a few have a genitive case (e.g. *one's*),
and six distinguish SUBJECT and OBJECT—*I/me, he/him, she/her, we/us,
they/them, who/whom*.

(*b*) **Meaning** As a category of meaning, 'case' is usually shown
in English by word order or by the use of prepositions. So the
traditional case names taken over from Latin are generally, except
for *genitive*, considered inappropriate. Instead, terms such as *subject* and *direct* and *indirect object* are preferred to the nominative,
accusative, and dative of Latin grammar. See also VOCATIVE.

Other case roles commonly recognized in English are AGENT, usually
indicated by a *by*-phrase following a passive tense (e.g. *He was
chased by a bull*), and INSTRUMENT, often indicated by a *with*-phrase
(*He defended himself with his stick*).

cataphora

The use of a pronoun or other PRO-FORM as a substitute that points forward to a later word, phrase, or clause. Usually contrasted with ANAPHORA, but sometimes loosely included. Examples:

> What I want to say is *this*. Please drive carefully.
> If you see *him*, will you ask Bob to telephone me?
> Here is *the news*. A hurricane has devastated . . .

catenative

Catenative means 'linking' and describes any lexical verb capable of linking with a following verb, e.g.

> *want* (to go); *enjoy* (going); *go* (shopping); *get* (hurt)

Popularly, catenatives include similar verbs with an intervening object, e.g.

> *want* (them to go); *watch* (them go/going); *have* (the house painted)

Chance juxtapositions are not catenative. Contrast:

> We stopped + to talk to the old man (= in order to talk)

with

> We stopped talking to the old man (catenative)

causative

In classic semantic theory, the verb *kill* (meaning 'cause a person or animal to die') is a causative verb, whereas *die* is not. Other causatives include verbs such as *place* or *put* i.e. cause something to be in such-and-such a place (*Put the book on the shelf*).

Popularly, *get* and *have* are the prime causative verbs, when used in the pattern get (or have) something done, e.g. *Get your hair cut* or *We've had the house painted*.

cause

Cause is one of the meaning categories used in the classification of adverb clauses — see p. 13 ADVERB CLAUSES — and also prepositions (e.g. *because of*). An alternative term here is REASON.

central

1 At, or forming, the centre.

- **central determiner**: a determiner (e.g. *a*, *an*, *the*, *my*, *that*) which must follow a predeterminer (e.g. *both*) but precede a postdeterminer (such as a number). See p. 66 DETERMINERS.

- **central vowel**: a vowel made with the centre of the tongue raised towards the middle of the roof of the mouth, i.e. /ʌ/, /ɜ:/, /ə/, and ʊ. See VOWEL.

2 Having the main features of a particular word class.

- **central adjective**: a typical adjective that can be used in both attributive and predicative position (e.g. *a pretty girl*; *she is pretty*).

- **central coordinator**: *and*, *but*, and *or*.

- **central modal**: a true modal verb (e.g. *can*, *must*), in contrast to a semi-modal (e.g. *dare*, *used to*). See p. 137 MODAL VERBS.

- **central passive**: a 'true' PASSIVE verb, a verb having a regular active counterpart, in contrast to a *semi-passive* or *pseudo-passive* verb.

- **central preposition**: a 'true' preposition (e.g. *at*, *in*, *on*) in contrast to a MARGINAL preposition (e.g. *considering*).

chain and choice

Chain and *choice* represent the two contrasting ways in which elements of language relate to each other in a larger unit. In a chain relationship, items are linked serially in a *syntagm*, e.g. *b* + *a* + *t* forms *bat*, *c* + *a* + *t* = *cat* and so on. In a choice relationship we can choose *b* or *c* or *f* or *h* before *-at* (but only one at a time) to produce a word. Similarly at a higher level, if we wish to add one word to complete the sentence: *The cat . . . on the mat*, the chain relationship requires a verb, but the choice is a wide range of alternatives, a *paradigm*, (*is*, *jumped*, *lay*, *lies*, *sat*, *slept*, etc.).

classifying

Indicating membership of a class.

In describing the meaning of the ARTICLES many grammars contrast SPECIFIC and GENERIC (in addition to the better known distinction between *definite* and *indefinite*). But not all non-specific usage has generic reference. Thus, while *the* + a singular count noun can refer to a class as a whole (e.g. *The black rhino is in danger of extinction*), the indefinite article cannot have this meaning (**A black rhino is in danger of extinction*). Some grammars therefore prefer the label *classifying* for the use of *a/an* or ZERO ARTICLE with various non-specific meanings:

> *A black rhino* can be very dangerous
> We cannot afford *a new car*
> More people should train as *engineers*

- **classifying adjective**: classifying adjectives (e.g. a *medieval* castle, a *wooden* spoon) contrast with *qualitative* adjectives, and are usually ungradable. See p. 6 ADJECTIVES.

- **classifying genitive**: classifying genitives indicate type, not possession (e.g. *a women's college*, *a moment's thought*).

- Nouns can classify in attributive position (e.g. a *birthday* party, *country* houses, a *peace* process).

clause

A grammatical unit operating at a lower level than a sentence but higher than a phrase.

(*a*) In traditional grammar, a clause has its own subject and a finite verb, and is part of a larger sentence. Thus *I was ten when I got my scholarship* consists of a MAIN CLAUSE (*I was ten*) and a SUBORDINATE CLAUSE (*when I got my scholarship*).

(*b*) Some modern grammar also classifies as clauses various NON-FINITE and VERBLESS structures which can be analysed as containing some of the functional elements that are distinguished in finite clauses. For example, in

> Whenever possible, I walked to school

Whenever possible is a verbless clause containing a conjunction and a complement, with subject and verb (*it was*) elliptted. In this sort of analysis the following, though containing only one finite verb, has four clauses:

> *My father travelled by two buses each day / to get there on time / leaving home at 5.00 a.m. / and usually returning after 10.00 p.m.*

CLAUSES AT A GLANCE

....
CLAUSES IN RELATION TO SENTENCES

Coordinated clauses: I like it / and I'm going to buy it.
[two main clauses]

Main clause: I like it . . .
[not subordinate]

Subordinate clause: . . . because it reminds me of you.
[needs a main clause]

....
SUBORDINATE CLAUSES BY FORM

Finite (any clause containing a finite verb):
                    although it is expensive
                    if you agree
                    whenever I can
                    so that you won't worry

Non-finite:
  participle: Complete the sentence, *using your skill and judgement*
                    Spoken rapidly, the words were confusing
                    We'll be there, *weather permitting*. [= absolute]
                    Do you recognize that man *waving at us*? [= reduced
                    relative]

  to-infinitive: *To open*, cut along the dotted line
                    For him to do that was outrageous
Verbless: *If in doubt*, say nothing
                    The party over, everyone disappeared [= absolute]
....
SUBORDINATE CLAUSES BY FUNCTION

1 **Nominal (or noun) clause**: see p. 152 NOUN CLAUSES
2 **Relative (or adjectival) clause**: see p. 205 RELATIVE CLAUSES
3 **Adverbial (or adverb) clause**: see p. 13 ADVERB CLAUSES
....
THE FIVE ELEMENTS OF CLAUSE STRUCTURE:
SOME COMMON CLAUSE PATTERNS

SV   Time / will tell
SVO   Not many people / know / that
SVC   Small / is / beautiful
SVA   A funny thing / happened / on the way to the forum
SVOO   The world / doesn't owe / you / a living
SVOC   They / were painting / the town / red
SVOA   I / 'll forget / my own name / in a minute
....

An ABSOLUTE clause is a non-finite or verbless clause containing its own subject.

(*c*) Clauses are also defined functionally into three main types: *nominal* (functioning like a noun phrase), *relative* (functioning like an adjective), and *adverbial*. Further distinctions are sometimes made—with the *nominal relative* separated from noun clauses, and the *comparative clause* no longer treated as an adverbial clause.

(*d*) Some modern grammar takes the clause, rather than the SENTENCE, as the basis of structural analysis. The five possible elements of clause structure are Subject (S), Verb (V), Object, including indirect object (O), Complement (C), and Adverbial (A).

clear | See LATERAL.

cleft sentence

A sentence derived from another, by dividing the latter into two clauses, each with its own finite verb, so as to emphasize a particular part of the original sentence. The form is *It* + part of the verb *be* +. . .+ *who/that* . . . For example:

Bob always plays golf on Sundays

could be reworded as any of the following cleft sentences:

It is Bob / who always plays golf on Sundays (e.g. not his brother)
It is golf / (that) Bob always plays on Sundays (not tennis)
It is on Sundays / that Bob always plays golf (not Mondays)

In these sentences the chief focus comes at the end of the main clause (the first clause) and the subordinate clause contains information which is assumed to be 'known' and which is therefore less important.

In another type of cleft sentence, more carefully distinguished as *pseudo-cleft*, the focus of information comes at the very end. A pseudo-cleft has a nominal relative clause, beginning with *what*, as subject:

What Bob plays on Sundays / is golf

Unlike the cleft sentence proper, the pseudo-cleft can focus on the verb element:

What Bob does on Sundays / is (to) play golf.

click

A type of stop consonant made with sucked-in air. Clicks are not part of the ordinary English speech system, but they are heard—for example, in the sound made to express disapproval (conventionally written as *tut-tut*); in the sound made to encourage horses to move on and hurry up; and in the kissing sound.

clipping

The formation of a new word by shortening an existing one; or an example of this. (A type of ABBREVIATION.) E.g. (omni)bus, exam(ination), (in)flu(enza), (tele)phone.

See p. 145 NEW WORDS p. 157 OMISSION.

cognate

When a word or language is related in form to another word or language because both are derived from the same source it is cognate with it, and the two are cognates.

French, Italian, and Spanish are cognate languages (cognates), being all derived from Latin. Latin *mater*, German *mutter*, English *mother* are cognates (cognate words).

A *cognate object* is an object related in form and meaning to the verb it is used with, e.g. sing a *song* of sixpence.

coherence

Coherence is the relationships within a TEXT that link sentences by meaning. The term contrasts with COHESION.

Coherence often depends on shared knowledge, implication, or inference. A dialogue such as

A: You weren't at the meeting yesterday.
B: My daughter's ill.

shows coherence. A's statement can be understood as a question, and B's statement can be understood as an explanation. But if he had replied with a rather different statement, e.g. 'Marmalade is a kind of jam', the conversation would normally lack coherence.

cohesion

Cohesion is the grammatical or lexical relationships that bind different parts of a TEXT together, in contrast to COHERENCE, e.g.

> A: You weren't at the meeting yesterday.
> B: No, I'm sorry I wasn't there. How did it go?

Here *there* substitutes for *at the meeting*, and *it* refers to *the meeting*. When pronouns and other words (e.g. *it, there*) are used in this way they are sometimes called *cohesive devices*.

coinage

Word coinage—the coining of words—means the invention of new words.

See p. 145 NEW WORDS.

collective noun

A noun that refers to a group of individual people or animals, and which in the singular can take either a singular or plural verb: *army, audience, committee, family, herd, majority, parliament, team,* etc. (Also called *group noun*.)

The choice of singular or plural verb—and corresponding pronouns and determiners—depends on whether the group is considered as a single unit or a collection of individuals: e.g.

> The audience, *which was* a large one, *was* in *its* place by 7 p.m.
> The audience, *who were* all waving *their* arms above *their* heads, *were* clearly enjoying *themselves*

Even when followed by a plural verb, such a noun still takes a singular determiner (e.g. *This family are all accomplished musicians*).

Loosely the term is sometimes applied to any noun referring to a group—including nouns that can only (in the sense used) take a plural verb: *cattle, clergy, people, police*.

See p. 151 NOUNS.

collocation

Words that regularly and to some extent predictably go together *collocate* with, or are collocates of, each other.

Any word is to some extent restricted in its usage. But many are much more restricted and can occur only with a limited set of other words or be used only in a particular type of structure. For example, the prepositions used with some nouns, adjectives, and verbs are often fixed, e.g.

adherence to, under the auspices of;
by chance, on foot;
similar to, inconsistent with;
account for, consist of, long for, rely on

Thus the noun *adherence* and the adjective *similar* are said to collocate with *to*; and *adherence* and *to*, and *similar* and *to* are collocates. And so on.

Two kinds of collocation may be distinguished:

• **grammatical collocation**: here, a verb, adjective, etc. must be followed by a particular preposition (e.g. *account for, afraid of*) or a noun must be followed by a particular form of the verb (e.g. the *foresight to do* it, not *of doing* it).

• **lexical collocation**: here particular nouns, adjectives, verbs, or adverbs form highly predictable connections with each other (e.g. *cancel a* (luncheon) *engagement*, or *break off an engagement* (to be married), not normally *withdraw, *revoke, or *discontinue an engagement*; compare also such collocations as *take advantage of*.

Special cases of collocation (*come a cropper, kith and kin*), in which one of the elements is completely predictable from the other merge into *archaisms* or *idioms*.

colloquial

Colloquial language is informal, and *colloquialisms* are the kinds of words and expressions that are mainly found in casual speech.

In ordinary everyday language, especially between speakers who know each other well, a casual style of speech is both frequent and appropriate. *Are you doing anything tomorrow evening?* as a preliminary to an invitation is probably more suitable than *Have you an engagement for tomorrow evening?* Colloquial speech is not substandard, nor is it the same as SLANG.

comma   See PUNCTUATION.

command

A command in the ordinary sense often takes the grammatical form of an IMPERATIVE (e.g. *Speak up! Leave me alone! Stop teasing the cat*), so the terms are sometimes used interchangeably. However, what is meant and understood as a command or order can be expressed grammatically in other ways (e.g. *You will do as I say; Could you make less noise?*). Conversely, grammatical imperatives can have other functions, such as requests (e.g. *Please give generously*) or invitations (*Have some more coffee*). Some grammarians therefore use separate sets of words for sentence forms and sentence functions, and *command* may be confined to either form or function only, but unfortunately this is an area where terminology is not agreed.

See p. 212 SENTENCE TYPES.

comment

In an analysis of information structure, the comment is that part of a sentence that says something about the TOPIC.

comment clause

A parenthetical clause, only loosely connected with the rest of the sentence. Comment clauses are sometimes analysed as a kind of adverbial clause (see p. 13 ADVERB CLAUSES).

Comment clauses may be finite or non-finite. They include many cliché conversation fillers, e.g.

you know, you see, as I said
to be frank, generally speaking

common

General, in some way basic or unmarked.

- **common case**: the unmarked case of a noun (e.g. *boy*, *week*) which is used for subject, object, and after prepositions—in contrast to the marked GENITIVE case (*boy's*, *week's*).

- **common core**: the basic grammar and vocabulary of English which theoretically is shared by all varieties of the English language. A rather indefinable concept.

- **common gender**: the characteristic shared by many animate nouns of having no gender distinctions, e.g. *baby*, *person*, *horse*, *sheep*.

- **common noun**: a noun which is not the name of any particular person, place, or thing—for example *boy*, *city*, *paper*—as opposed to PROPER NOUN. See p. 151 NOUNS.

communicative

Conveying meaning.

- **communicative competence**: a speaker's ability to understand the implications of utterances, to appreciate what language is appropriate in different situations—in contrast to grammatical competence (which is an ability to manipulate the syntactical rules).

- **communicative function**: the purpose and meaning of an utterance, whatever its FORM. Thus an interrogative sentence (*Isn't it a lovely day*) may have the communicative function of an exclamation.

comparative

The comparative (*comparative form*, *comparative degree*) of an adjective or adverb is the form expressing the middle degree of COMPARISON between positive and superlative. The comparative inflection is *-er*, as in *better*, *happier*, *sooner*. Long adjectives and most adverbs do not inflect, but use the word *more*, e.g. *more beneficial*, *more cheaply*.

Only gradable adjectives and adverbs can be compared in this way—*firster*, *more weekly*.

comparative clause

Narrowly, the term *comparative clause* can be restricted to a clause following a main clause containing a comparative form, e.g.

It was colder *than we expected*

It was more/less expensive *than last year*

but usually clauses expressing equivalence, beginning with *as* are included, e.g.

It was as cold *as it was last year*

We were not so/as well looked after *as we had hoped*

See p. 13 ADVERB CLAUSES.

comparison

This is a very general term and can be used to cover any grammatical way of comparing one thing with another. It may include expressions with *enough* or *too*, e.g.

They did not arrive *early enough to help*

They arrived *too late to help*

The three degrees of comparison are POSITIVE, COMPARATIVE, and SUPERLATIVE (e.g. *good, better, best; kind, kinder, kindest*).

• **comparison clause**: a clause containing some kind of comparison. This label may include the COMPARATIVE CLAUSE (as defined above) and also clauses introduced by *as if, as though*, e.g.

He looked *as if/as though he'd seen a ghost*

However, *as if* and *as though* clauses are alternatively analysed as MANNER clauses, because they explain *how* he looked. See p. 13 ADVERB CLAUSES.

complement

1 Complement is one of the five elements of clause structure, along with Subject, Verb, Object, and Adverbial. See p. 42 CLAUSES.

Typically complements of this type 'complete' the verb *be* or another linking verb, and are either adjective phrases or noun phrases, e.g.

My brother-in-law is *very clever*

He's *a brain surgeon*

This type of complement is called a *subject(ive) complement*, because the complement refers back to the subject. There are also *object(ive) complements* referring back to the object, e.g.

I consider tranquillizers *dangerous*
They make some people *addicts*

2 More widely, *complement* can mean any element needed to 'complete' an adjective, preposition, or verb; an example of *complementation*.

Complements of adjectives include prepositional phrases, (e.g. fond *of chocolate*) and clauses (e.g. sorry *that you are ill*, sorry *to hear your news*).

Complements of prepositions (also called *objects* of prepositions) are usually noun phrases, e.g.

out of *order*, in *the bag*, over *the moon*

The 'complement of a verb', in this wider sense, is a very unspecific term, and can include almost anything that in some way 'completes' the verb, including objects and adverbials.

complementary

One of a pair of ungradable opposites, e.g. *alive/dead*, *boy/girl*. A special type of ANTONYM.

complex

Consisting of at least two unequal parts—often in contrast to either SIMPLE or COMPOUND.

● **complex conjunction**: a two- or three-word conjunction (e.g. *in that*, *providing that*, *as soon as*).

● **complex preposition**: a two- or three-word preposition (e.g. *out of*, *because of*, *prior to*, *on behalf of*).

● **complex sentence**: a sentence containing at least one subordinate clause, in addition to its main clause: *When you've quite finished*, *we can begin*. This contrasts with a COMPOUND sentence. See p. 212 SENTENCE TYPES.

● **complex word**: generally, a word consisting of at least two parts, usually a base and one or more affixes.

Thus *im-polite*, *rude-ness* contrast both with unanalysable words, long or short (*dog*, *hippopotamus*), and with COMPOUND words (e.g. *dogfood*).

complex transitive verb

Some transitive verbs just take an object (e.g. *Eat your greens*). But some can or must be followed by more complicated structures, and the term complex transitive verb is applied to the verb in such cases, e.g.

> Let's paint / the town / red
> They made / him / leader
>
> She put / the car / in the garage
> He threw / himself / into the role

compound

Consisting of two or more parts of equal value; in contrast to SIMPLE and COMPLEX.

• **compound sentence**: a sentence containing two or more coordinate clauses. See p. 212 SENTENCE TYPES.
• **compound word**: a word formed by combining two or more independent words (*compounding*), in contrast to a word formed by DERIVATION or INFLECTION, e.g.

> bookcase, handlebar, laptop, mind-set, windshield, fact-finding, home-made, south-facing, tax-free

See p. 145 NEW WORDS.

compound-complex sentence

A sentence containing at least two coordinated clauses (making it compound) plus at least one subordinate clause (making it complex).
See p. 212 SENTENCE TYPES.

concession

Conceding, admitting; one of the meaning categories used in the analysis of adverb clauses.

A *concessive clause* is usually introduced by a concessive conjunction, e.g. *although, though, whereas, while*, which indicates that the situation in the main clause is contrary to what might be expected, e.g.

Although he was angry
Although feeling angry } he did not raise his voice
Although angry

Concessive prepositions include *despite, in spite of, for all, notwithstanding*, e.g.

For all his protestations, nobody believed him.

There are also concessive conjuncts, e.g. *anyhow, anyway, however, nevertheless, still, though, yet, in any case, all the same*, and many more, e.g.

He was angry; he did not raise his voice, though.

concord

The same as AGREEMENT.

concrete noun

A noun denoting a physical object; a person, animal, or observable, touchable thing—in contrast to an ABSTRACT NOUN. Most concrete nouns are countable, but some are uncountable (e.g. *furniture, luggage*).

See p. 151 NOUNS.

condition

Conditional clauses are a type of ADVERB CLAUSE. (See p. 13). A distinction is often made between *open condition* and *hypothetical condition*.

An open condition (also called *real condition*) is neutral. The condition, and therefore the rest of the sentence, may or may not be true, e.g.

If it rains tomorrow, we won't go
If Bob's there already, he'll have heard the news

A hypothetical condition (also called *unreal/rejected/closed/ unfulfilled condition*) implies that the speaker does not think that the condition will be, is, or has been fulfilled, and therefore the whole thing is either in doubt or untrue, e.g.

> If he made a bit more effort, he might get somewhere
> If you hadn't told me, I'd never have guessed
> I could if I were younger

The commonest subordinators introducing clauses of condition are *if* and *unless*. Others are: *on condition (that)*, *providing (that)*, *provided (that)*.

Most conditional clauses posit a *direct condition*. An *indirect condition* occurs when there is a *logical gap* in the meaning between the two parts of a conditional sentence. For example, the stated outcome in the following does not depend on the fulfilment of the *if*-clause:

> You look tired, if you don't mind my saying so

Traditional grammarians often label *should/would* + infinitive (e.g. *I should/you would be late*) and *should/would* + perfect infinitive (e.g. *We should have been late/He would have forgotten*) as conditional tenses. But this analysis is somewhat out of favour today.

conjunct

An adverb or adverbial that has a joining (or connective) function, often that of joining a sentence to an earlier sentence. Popularly called CONNECTOR.

Conjuncts have a variety of meanings, including (*a*) listing, (*b*) reinforcement, (*c*) result, and (*d*) concession, e.g.

> (*a*) *First* of all, I'd like to thank all those people . . .
> (*b*) *Moreover* (or *Above all*), I owe a debt of gratitude to . . .
> (*c*) I would like, *therefore*, to . . .
> (*d*) I must *nevertheless* point out . . .

In some analyses of adverbials, conjuncts contrast with ADJUNCTS, DISJUNCTS, and sometimes SUBJUNCTS (see p. 11 ADVERBS). But different grammars make different distinctions, and conjuncts (roughly as here defined) may be called *discourse* or *linking adjuncts*, or, of course, they may just be grouped together with other adverbs.

conjunction

A word used to join clauses, words in the same clause, and sometimes sentences.

Conjunctions are one of the generally recognized word classes (parts of speech). (See p. 165 PARTS OF SPEECH.) Two main types are generally distinguished:

(*a*) *coordinating conjunction* (also called COORDINATOR) joining units of 'equal' status:

> free *and* easy, poor *but* honest, speak now *or* forever hold your peace

(*b*) *subordinating conjunction* (also called SUBORDINATOR) introducing a subordinate clause, e.g. *although, because, if, since, when*, etc.

connector

The same as CONJUNCT.

connotation

Connotation belongs to the terminology of semantics rather than grammar, but the difference between connotation and DENOTATION (objective 'dictionary meaning') is important in language use.

Connotation is the meaning that a word or phrase etc. has by virtue of cultural or personal associations. It may be highly subjective. For example, the connotations of *police* for some people may be 'reliable', 'helpful', 'protectors of law and order', 'the front line against crime', while for others they may be 'breathalysers', 'arrests', and so on.

consonant

1 (*a*) A speech sound in which the escape of air is at least partly obstructed; in contrast to a VOWEL.

(*b*) A sound that functions marginally within a syllable.

While most sounds popularly thought of as consonants meet the definitions of both (1*a*) and (1*b*), there are some discrepancies. For example, /j/ and /w/, are marginal in syllable structure, like consonants, but vowel-like in articulation, and so are usually classified in phonetic terms as SEMI-VOWELS. The nasals /m/ and /n/ are usually marginal (as in *man*) and are classified as consonants, but they can be syllabic (e.g. in *mm*, *frighten*).

2 Traditionally any letter except *a*, *e*, *i*, *o*, and *u*.

This roughly corresponds to the definition of a consonant in (1), although the letter *y* in particular clearly often represents a vowel sound (e.g. *city*, *my*).

There are twenty-two consonant phonemes in standard English, which are defined by place (where in the mouth they are made) and manner (how they are made). See p. 264 THE CONSONANTS OF ENGLISH.

consonant cluster

A series of consonant sounds, occurring at the beginning or end of a syllable and pronounced together without any intervening vowels.

English has some quite complicated consonant clusters. Initial clusters can have up to three consonants, if the cluster begins with *s* (e.g. *spread*, *splendid*, *street*). Also *squint* /skw . . . / and *skewer* /skj . . . /.

Two-consonant clusters are much more usual, but only some combinations can occur. Native speakers who usually have no problem with an initial plosive followed by /r/ or /l/ (as in *proud*, *bread*, *true*, *drew*, *cream*, *grew*, *plate*, *blue*, *clue*, *glad*) might have difficulty in pronouncing *tlew* or *dlad* (which are also initial plosive + *l*) because /tl/ and /dl/ are not members of the English system.

Final clusters can contain as many as four consonants, because of inflectional endings, e.g. *texts*, *twelfths*, and *glimpsed*. (Again, we are talking about consonant sounds, not letters.)

constituent

Constituent is a very general term, applied to any item which forms part of some larger unit.

Immediate constituent analysis, breaking a whole down into its parts, is sometimes applied to sentences. For example, in the sentence

The cost includes air travel by scheduled services

we might say the constituents are

[The cost] [includes air travel by scheduled air services]

and we might break the predicate down further into

[includes] [air travel] [by scheduled air services]

What we would not do is say that there are any constituents such as *travel by* or *scheduled air*. See also TREE DIAGRAM.

contact clause

A defining relative clause joined to its noun phrase without any connecting word.

(*a*) Normally this means a clause in which the missing relative pronoun would function as an object of the verb or of a deferred preposition, e.g.

the woman + *I love*
a crisis + *we could have done without*

Similar contact clauses are possible where the relative word expresses time, cause, or manner:

The moment (that/when) *I saw it*, I knew it was mine
The reason (that/why) *I asked* was that I needed to know
This is the way (that) *you should do it*

(*b*) More rarely, since subject relative pronouns are not normally omissible, a relative clause in which a subject is omitted:

There's someone at the door + *says you know him.*

See p. 205 RELATIVE CLAUSES.

content disjunct See DISJUNCT.

content word

A word with a statable meaning, also called *lexical* or *full* word; contrasted with a FORM word.

Content words include most open-class words—nouns, verbs, adjectives, adverbs, but the distinction between content and form words is blurred rather than rigid.

See p. 165 PARTS OF SPEECH.

continuous

The same as PROGRESSIVE.

contraction

A shortened form of a word that can be attached to another word; or the two words together. Also called *abbreviated form*, *contracted form*, or *short form*.

Thus both *'m* and *I'm* are described as contractions. Other contractions in English are:

> *'s*, (is/has, also *us* in *Let's*); *'re* (are); *'ve* (have); *'d* (had/would); *'ll* (shall/will); *n't* (not)

See p. 157 OMISSION.

contrast

1 In syntax *contrast(ive)* is a general term applied to clauses, conjunctions, conjuncts.

Contrastive clauses (also called *clauses of contrast*), are sometimes classified with concessive clauses (see p. 13 ADVERB CLAUSES), and are introduced by some of the same conjunctions such as *whereas*, *while*, and *whilst*, e.g.

> I adore jazz, whereas my sister prefers classical music

Contrastive conjuncts include *by contrast*, *alternatively*, *rather*, *more accurately*.

2 In phonetics, *contrastive stress* is stress on a word or syllable that would normally be unstressed, in order to convey a contrastive meaning:

> What 'ARE you doing? (i.e. you are doing something surprising)
> What are 'YOU doing? (i.e. never mind about the others)

converse

A special type of ANTONYM, where one meaning presupposes the other, e.g. *buy/sell*, *husband/wife*, *teacher/learner*.

conversion

A term in word formation for the process by which a word belonging to one word class gets used as part of another word class without the addition of an affix.

Words produced by conversion are mainly nouns, verbs, or adjectives. Conversion is a very old process in English, as the date-range of the instances given below shows:

> Nouns from verbs: a bounce (E16), a meet (M19), a retread (E20), a swim (M16; M18 in current use)

> Verbs from nouns: to fingerprint (E20), to highlight (M20), to holiday (M19), to mob (E18), to necklace (E18; L20 in current sense)

> Adjectives from nouns: average (L18), commonplace (E17), cream (M19), damp (L16, E18 in current sense), game (plucky; E18)

Minor types of conversion include conversions of closed class words (e.g. *the ins and outs*, *the whys and wherefores*); of affixes (e.g. *So you've got an ology*); and even of whole phrases (e.g. *his holier-than-thou protestations*). Notice a recent noun from adjective: a video *nasty*. An unusual recent conversion (to what is effectively a closed class) is the use of *plus* (already a preposition and a noun) as a colloquial conjunction, e.g.

> 10% bonus offer, plus you'll get a mystery present.

See p. 145 NEW WORDS.

coordination

Coordination occurs when two or more units of equal status (e.g. two clauses or two words) are joined or *coordinate(d)*. Coordination contrasts with SUBORDINATION, the joining of a grammatically less important unit to a more important one.

The units joined by coordination may be anything from clauses (as in compound sentences) to single words (*knife and fork*, *poor but honest*, *double or quits*).

The main coordinating conjunctions (or *coordinators*) are *and*, *but*, and *or*.

• **pseudo-coordination**: apparent coordination, but the units joined are not equal. This is an idiomatic feature found with some verbs, e.g. *try and come, went and complained.* It is condemned by purists as illogical, but it seems acceptable colloquially. Other pseudo-coordination is found with adjectives, e.g. *nice and warm*, and there is the very colloquial adverbial *good and proper.*

copula

The term 'the copula' or 'the copula verb' usually means the single verb *be*, particularly when it is linking a subject with a complement:

She is a pilot.   They are pleased

But any linking verb can be described as a copula verb:

It *seemed* good at the time
Will it *turn* cold?

corpus (plural **corpuses, corpora**)

A collection of spoken and/or written texts. The study of the English language has been transformed in recent years by the collection of large quantities of authentic texts into corpora on which grammatical and lexicographic analyses and descriptions of use can be based.

The British National Corpus, a government-sponsored collaborative project begun in 1991 and involving three publishers, the British Library, and the Universities of Oxford and Lancaster, contains 100 million words.

correlative

Correlatives are pairs of words or phrases that join two similar parts of a sentence together.

Coordinating correlatives include *both . . . and, either . . . or, neither . . . nor, not only . . . but also.* E.g.

You either like it or loathe it
It's not only dangerous but silly

Subordinating correlatives include *so/such . . . that, less/more . . . than, hardly . . . when, if . . . then.* E.g.

It was so late that we decided to get a taxi
We had hardly got home when the storm broke

count noun

A noun that can be used with numbers (also called a *countable* noun); in contrast to an UNCOUNT (or *uncountable* or *non-count*) noun.

Count nouns usually have different singular and plural forms (*book/books, child/children*), and when used in the singular must be preceded by a determiner: *a/my/this/one book*; not **I bought book*.

In the plural, count nouns can be combined with certain determiners, some of them exclusive to the plural: e.g. *few, many, several, these*.

See p. 151 NOUNS.

D

dangling participle

The same as HANGING PARTICIPLE, a participle that is not grammatically related to the noun phrase it is intended for by meaning.

dark I See LATERAL.

dative

The case expressing an indirect object or recipient (as in They gave *Susan* a present; Tell *me* the truth). The term is not really applicable to an uninflected language like English, and *indirect object* is preferred.

See p. 38 CASE.

declarative

In grammatical terms, a declarative (sentence) in English is a sentence in which the subject precedes the verb, e.g. *I love Lucy. All power tends to corrupt.*

Such sentences are typically used (as here) to make *statements*, and the two terms are often used interchangeably. Where a distinction is made, *declarative* is often used as a syntactic formal category (as in the definition above), leaving *statement* to be used as a functional, meaning-based category.

Sentences that are declarative in form may be used not only for making statements, but also to ask questions.

See p. 212 SENTENCE TYPES.

defective verb

This is a slightly old-fashioned term for a verb that lacks a complete set of forms, and particularly the MODAL VERBS.

An interesting defective verb is *beware*, which is used only as an imperative (e.g. *Beware of the dog*) or a *to*-infinitive (*I warned him to beware of the dog*).

defining

Identifying; restricting meaning in some way.

(*a*) **defining relative clause**: a clause that follows a noun phrase and uniquely identifies it by restricting its meaning. (Also called *restrictive relative clause*, *identifying relative clause*.) Contrasted with NON-DEFINING (or *non-restrictive*). Examples of defining clauses:

> News is what a chap [what sort of chap?] *who doesn't care much about anything* wants to read

> All the news [all of it?] *that's fit to print*

> There are only two posh papers on a Sunday—the one [which one?] *you're reading* and this one

See p. 205 RELATIVE CLAUSES.

(*b*) Other words that identify can also be called defining. For example, in *my blind friend*, the adjective may well be understood to give uniquely defining reference, identifying one particular friend. (By contrast, in *my blind mother*, the adjective is non-defining, merely adding some information about my mother.)

definite

(*a*) **definite article**: the determiner *the* (contrasted with INDEFINITE *a/an*). *The* is typically used with a noun phrase whose referent has either just been mentioned (or implied) or is assumed to be familiar or uniquely identifiable in some way, e.g.

> I had to call a taxi. *The* driver couldn't find *the* house
> *The* sun's out at last
> I heard it on *the* radio

(*b*) Other determiners, besides *the*, can make a noun phrase definite, including the demonstratives (*this*, *that*, etc.) and possessives (*my*, *your*, etc.). All of them are sometimes collectively labelled *definite* determiners or *definite* identifiers. Proper names are inherently definite (at least in context), and so are personal pronouns (*he*, *she*, etc.), in contrast to indefinite *somebody*, *something*, etc.

(*c*) Definiteness is also part of the meaning of some adverbs (e.g. *daily*) in contrast to adverbs of indefinite frequency such as *often*, *sometimes*.

degree

1 Gradable adjectives and adverbs can be compared on a threefold scale, called *degrees*. The three degrees are positive (*good*, *soon*), comparative (*better*, *sooner*) and superlative (*best*, *soonest*).

2 Degree, meaning greater or lesser intensity, is one category of adverb meaning. *Degree adverbs* (or *adverb(ial)s of degree*) express a meaning of greater or lesser intensity. Examples: *much*, *quite*, *so*, *too*, *very* . . .

Degree adverbs traditionally contrast with adverbs of manner, time, and place. Some modern grammarians prefer to use INTENSIFIER more or less as a synonym. Others make various subtle distinctions between *degree adverb*, *intensifier*, and *emphasizer*.

See p. 11 ADVERBS.

deictic

Pointing. Relating (an utterance) to its context in time and place.

The four demonstrative determiners and pronouns are the prime *deictics*. *This* and *these* point to what is here or now, while *that* and *those* point to there or then.

Other deictic words are *here/there*, *now/then*, *today/yesterday/tomorrow* and personal pronouns (*I/we/you* etc.). Tense too (present versus past) is a category of **deixis**.

delexical verb

A verb that has little meaning in itself, because the meaning has been transferred to the object.

Perhaps to give more end-focus or end-weight to a sentence English sometimes uses a verb + an object noun where a plain intransitive verb could be used. For example instead of saying *I looked*, you can say *I had a look*; instead of *I'll think about it* you can say *I'll give it some thought*.

Verbs particularly used in this way include *do, have, give, make,* and *take,* and when so used they retain little of their usual meaning, and the main meaning is carried by the object noun.

demonstrative

The demonstratives are the four pronouns and determiners *this, that, these, those.* They refer to things (or people) in relationship to the speaker or writer in space or time.

denotation

The *denotation* of a word or phrase is its primary (often literal) meaning. It is contrasted with CONNOTATION.

Denotation relates to the naming function of words, and so often to their primary dictionary meanings. Thus the denotation of *(the) police* is 'the civil force of a State, responsible for maintaining public order'.

dental

A place-label for a consonant made with the tongue coming in contact with the teeth.

The English dental consonants are the voiceless fricative /θ/ as in *thick* and *thin* and the voiced fricative /ð/ as in *this, them*.

In some languages the *t* and *d* sounds are dental, but in standard English RP these two sounds are normally alveolar. See p. 264 THE CONSONANTS OF ENGLISH.

deontic

This word is taken over from philosophy and relates to duty and obligation as moral concepts. It is used to describe those uses of modal verbs intended to influence behaviour, e.g.

    You must obey your parents
    You may go now
    You shouldn't mislead me

In a sense the deontic modals actually do something (e.g. they order, permit, advise, etc.), and can be regarded as a special type of PERFORMATIVE verb.

The deontic meaning of modals is usually contrasted with EPISTEMIC (or theoretical) meaning and sometimes also with DYNAMIC meaning.

See p. 137 MODAL VERBS.

derivation

Derivation is the process of forming (*deriving*) a new word by adding an affix to an existing word, in contrast to both COMPOUND-ING and inflection. Examples:

> *alleviation* (from *alleviate*)
> *interference* (from *interfere*)
> *sub-editor* (from *editor*)
> *unhelpful* (from *helpful*)

Some words are derived from other languages. Thus *denim* ultimately comes from French *serge-de-Nîmes* (serge made in the town of Nîmes) via 17th-century English *serge de Nim*.

Roughly speaking, derivation produces a new word (e.g. *driver* from *drive*), whereas an inflectional suffix produces another form of the same word (e.g. *driven, driving, drives*).

See p. 145 NEW WORDS.

descriptive

Many modern grammarians try to describe language objectively, as it is actually used, and try to avoid laying down idealized, unrealistic rules. They seek to produce descriptive 'rules', in contrast to the more PRESCRIPTIVE aims of usage books.

determiner

Determiners form a class of words that precede nouns, and for this reason they were sometimes called adjectives in traditional grammar. But they have to come before ordinary adjectives in noun phrase structure.

DETERMINERS AT A GLANCE

POSITION

predeterminers (1)	central determiners (2)	postdeterminers (3)
all, both, half, double, one-third, such, what	a, an, the	few, many, much, little
	this, that . . .	Cardinal numbers
	my, your, his . . .	Ordinal numbers
	every, each, no	

examples

(1)	(2)	(3)	adjective	noun
all	our	many	blue	friends
both	those	two		suitcases
half	the			time
double	your		annual	salary
such	a		good	opportunity
	every	second		day
	my	few	remaining	pleasures

SOME MEANING LABELS

article: a, an, the
cardinal (number): one, five, seven hundred, etc.
demonstrative: this, that, these, those
dual: both, either, neither
multiplier: twice, double, three times, etc.
ordinal (number): first, second, last, etc.
possessive: my, your, our, etc.
quantifier: all, half, some, any, no, (a) few, (a) little, many, much, several, every, each, etc.

Determiners are also subject to fairly strict rules of word order among themselves, so that *predeterminers*, *central determiners*, and *postdeterminers* can be distinguished.

Most determiners are also restricted by number-related meaning as to the category of noun they can occur with, e.g. *many/few* apples (count plural), but *much/little* food (uncount).

Determiners are also classified on grounds of meaning into such categories as DEMONSTRATIVES, QUANTIFIERS, etc.

Determiners form a mainly closed class, but variants are possible on some items—*a (good) few*, *a (very) little*, *(a great) many* — and numbers are open-ended (*seventh*, *three times . . .*)

See p. 66 DETERMINERS; also p. 190 PRONOUNS AND DETERMINERS.

devoiced

A speech sound is *devoiced* when it is spoken with less VOICE than is usual for that particular sound.

English voiced sounds are often partly devoiced under the influence of surrounding sounds (*assimilation*). This happens so completely with /b/, /d/, and /g/ following /s/ that they are 'neutralized' with /p/, /t/, and /k/, so that we have no words distinguished by sp . . . and sb . . . etc. (Try distinguishing *spray/sbray*, *stone/sdone* or *skit/sgit*!)

diaeresis

A mark (as in *naïve*) over a vowel to indicate that it is sounded separately.

dialect

A variety of language that is distinct from other varieties not merely in ACCENT, but also in grammar and vocabulary.

Dialects may be regional, or based on class differences, when they are usually called social or class dialects—or a mixture of the two. Although such dialects are usually recognizable from the speaker's accent, the term dialect embraces wider differences of grammar, e.g.

I likes it
I ain't done it
I didn't have no breakfast
It needs washed
We got off of the train
Look at them cows

and vocabulary, e.g. *while* meaning 'until' (*Wait while the lights are green*, a dangerous level-crossing notice if you only know *while* as 'all the time that'); *learn* meaning 'teach'.

The term *dialect* tends to imply deviation from some standard educated norm, but linguists regard the standard variety as just another dialect.

digraph

1 A group of two letters representing one sound, as *ph* (in *phone*) or *ey* in *key*.

2 Two letters that are physically joined together in a writing or printing system as in *æon*, *ædema*. Also called a *ligature*.

diminutive

A suffix denoting smallness, or the complete word containing such a suffix, is a diminutive.

The smallness may be literal or metaphorical. Some diminutives are objective (*manikin*, *piglet*), but many are used as a mark of informality (*bunny*, *comfy*, *sweetie*) or to show affection (*auntie*) or to belittle (*starlet*). Proper names often have diminutive forms— *Teddy (Edward)*, *Jimmie (James)*, *Lizzie*, *Bessie*, *Betsy*, *Betty* (*Elizabeth*).

diphthong

1 A vowel that glides from one quality to another within the same single syllable. (Sometimes called *gliding vowel*.)

The English diphthongs in modern standard 'RP' are:

three that glide towards an /ɪ/ sound from different starting points:

/eɪ/ as in *day, late, rain, weigh, they, great*
/aɪ/ as in *time, cry, high, height, die, dye, aisle, eider*
/ɔɪ/ as in *boy, voice*

two that glide towards /ʊ/:

/əʊ/ as in *so, road, toe, soul, know*
/aʊ/ as in *house, now*

three that glide towards /ə/:

/ɪə/ as in *deer, dear, here, weird, idea*
/eə/ as in *care, air, wear, their, there*
/ʊə/ as in *pure, during, tourist*

A diphthong gliding to a closer sound (i.e. one ending in /ɪ/ or /ʊ/ in English) is called a *closing diphthong*; a diphthong finishing at /ə/ is called a *centring diphthong*.

Formerly a fourth centring diphthong was used, /ɔə/, which distinguished words such as floor /flɔə/ and flaw /flɔː/, but /ɔə/ has largely coalesced with /ɔː/ among standard speakers.

A number of words formerly pronounced with /ʊə/, such as *moor* and *tour*, are often now said with the single vowel /ɔː/. This has led to the proliferation of homophones (*moor, more, maw; tour, tore, taw; poor, pour, pore, paw;* etc.).

See p. 265 THE SOUNDS OF ENGLISH.

2 Two vowel letters representing a diphthong sound—as in *rain* /reɪn/ or *toe* /təʊ/ may be called a diphthong. An *improper diphthong* is two vowel letters representing a single vowel sound as in *heat* /hiːt/, *soup* /suːp/.

directive

A sentence or clause giving a command or order. This is a meaning-based category. Directives typically take an IMPERATIVE form; but can also take declarative form, e.g. *You will apologize immediately*.

See p. 212 SENTENCE TYPES.

direct object

The noun phrase most clearly affected or 'acted upon' by the action of a transitive verb. A verb taking only one object is normally immediately followed by the direct object in a declarative statement. Thus the direct object is *some vegetables* in:

Rachel ate/bought/cooked/grew some vegetables

The direct object (DO) is often simply called the object, unless there is likelihood of confusion with the INDIRECT OBJECT.

direct question   See DIRECT SPEECH.

direct speech

Direct speech is the reporting of speech by repeating the actual words used, without making any grammatical changes. Quotation marks are used in writing.

'Is there anybody there?' said the listener is an example of direct speech, including a direct question. This contrasts with INDIRECT SPEECH, as in *The listener asked if there was anybody there.*

discontinuity

The splitting of a construction by the insertion of a word or words, or a particular instance of this. For example:

Have you *finished?* (verb phrase)
Look the word *up* (phrasal verb)
That's a *hard* act *to follow* (modification)
There's *a man* outside *who wants to see you* (noun phrase and its relative clause)
The time has come, the Walrus said, *to talk of many things* (noun phrase and modification)

Discontinuity is very common in sentences containing comparative clauses, e.g.

I spend *more money* on clothes *than I can really afford*

discourse

Although the sentence is the biggest unit of language that grammar is traditionally concerned with, there are many grammatical and semantic connections between sentences. The term *discourse* is applied to stretches of language longer than a sentence, particularly viewed as interaction between speakers or between writer and reader.

disjunct

An adverbial with a rather detached role in clause or sentence structure. Sometimes called SENTENCE ADVERBIAL.

Disjuncts either express the speaker's or writer's attitude to the content of the sentence (*content disjuncts*), e.g.

> *Tragically*, the rescue party arrived too late

or they claim that the statement is being made in a particular way (*style disjuncts*), e.g.

> *Honestly*, nobody could have done any better
> *To be frank*, the whole thing was hopeless

See p. 11 ADVERBS.

distributive

Relating to individual members of a class separately, not jointly.

Words like *each* and *every* are distributive words. Phrases like *once a week* and *three times per year* are distributive expressions.

Distributive plural concord is common in expressions such as *The children all had such eager faces* (where clearly each child had only one face), but a *distributive singular* is often possible—*They all had such an eager expression.*

disyllabic

Having two syllables, in contrast to MONOSYLLABIC and polysyllabic.

The term is commonly used to talk about comparative and superlative forms, where some disyllabic words take inflection (*cleverer, cleverest*) and others use *more/most* (*more/most eager*).

ditransitive

A verb having two objects is a ditransitive verb. (Also called *double transitive.*) Ditransitive verbs take an indirect object plus a direct object, e.g.

I gave *my mother flowers*

I gave *flowers to my mother*

Some grammarians include verbs that take an indirect object and a clause:

She told *me (that) she was delighted*

But others call these *complex transitive verbs*.

do-support

do-support is the use of *do, does, did* to form questions, negatives, tag-questions, etc. with simple present and past tenses. The device means that there is a structural regularity between these and other verb phrases. Thus *Do you understand?* has the same pattern of auxiliary + subject + verb as *Are you listening* or *Can you hear?* and *They knew* (= did know), *didn't they?* is comparable to *He could explain, couldn't he?*

double consonant

(*a*) Double consonant letters generally represent a single sound in English (e.g. *batter, puppy, shallow*, etc.). The main exception is *cc* before *i* or *e*, pronounced /ks/ as in *accident* or *succeed*.

(*b*) Double consonant sounds are heard when the two consonant phonemes occur across syllable or word boundaries, as in

unnatural, shell-like, part-time, hat trick, fish shop

Such double sounds are not pronounced completely separately. They are more like one sound lengthened. The main exception here—with both sounds fully articulated—is when one affricate follows another, as in *which child?*

Sometimes what in careful speech is a double consonant sound is elided into one, so that, for example, *Prime Minister* sounds more like *pry minister*. (Contrast *prime mover*.)

double genitive   See GENITIVE.

double negative

It is usually incorrect in standard English to negate a clause more than once (**I never said nothing*, **I haven't got none*) because the first negative could be omitted or the second replaced by a non-assertive form (*anything, any*). But the argument, from logic, that 'two negatives make a positive' is unjustified, as many English dialects and many other languages do have reinforcing multiple negation.

In a two-clause sentence, a common double negative structure—heard even from standard speakers—is potentially confusing. *I wouldn't be surprised if they didn't come* may mean the speaker expects them not to come (both negatives justified) or it may mean the same as *I wouldn't be surprised if they came.*

However, in many two-clause sentences two negatives are essential: *I didn't ask him not to go* (though I hoped he wouldn't). And occasionally a double negative occurs quite legitimately in a single clause, where in a sense the two negatives do indeed cancel each other out: *You can't not worry about it. Surely nobody has no friends* (= You have to worry. Everybody has some friends). Even here, though, like true negatives, the sentences take positive tags (*You can't not worry, can you? Nobody has no friends, do they?*).

double passive

A clause containing two verbs in the passive, the second an infinitive as in:

> *Receipts are not proposed to be issued
> Certificates are expected to be despatched next week

Usage books sometimes warn against all such structures, but their acceptability in fact varies. Verbs (like *expect* in the second example) that are also possible in the pattern, verb + object + passive infinitive (e.g. We expect certificates to be despatched) are grammatical in the double passive construction. Verbs that do not fit this pattern with a single passive (e.g. * We propose receipts to be issued) do not happily take a double passive either.

double transitive verb

The same as DITRANSITIVE verb.

dual

In some languages dual number (relating to two) is an important category (in addition to singular and plural), and there are dual forms of nouns, verbs, etc. In English *both* and to a lesser extent *either* and *neither* are the only grammatical words indicating dual number.

dummy

A dummy element is a word that has no meaning in itself but is used to maintain grammatical structure.

• **dummy *it***: used especially as subject in sentences about time and weather. This is also called *empty* or *prop it*, (but may be distinguished from ANTICIPATORY *it*):

> *It*'s five o'clock and *it* is snowing again

A similarly vague *it* also appears in various idiomatic phrases (e.g. We've made *it*; Well, that's *it*—let's go).

Other common dummy elements are *there* in existential sentences and forms of the verb *do* as *dummy operators* in questions and negatives:

> *There*'s someone at the door
> What *does* he want?
> He *did*n't say

duration

1 In phonetics, *duration* sometimes denotes the actual 'real world' time taken in articulating a speech sound, in contrast to LENGTH, which refers to the listener's subjective perception.

2 *Duration* may also be considered as part of the meaning of a word or phrase. For example, progressive tenses of verbs are usually said to imply a temporary state or *limited duration* (e.g. I am living in a hostel).

Prepositions and adverbials expressing duration include *since, for, from . . . to*, etc. (e.g. I've been here *for a month*).

dynamic

Dynamic contrasts with STATIVE in describing the meaning of verbs. Dynamic meaning is concerned with actions, events, happenings, and processes, e.g.

We've *bought* a new car
War *broke out* in 1939
They're *playing* our tune
I've *worked* hard all my life
The lights *have gone* green

It is common practice to describe verbs that can be used in progressive tenses as *dynamic verbs*, in contrast to *stative verbs*, that cannot. It is more accurate to talk of *dynamic* and *stative* meaning, because many so-called stative verbs can be used dynamically with a shift of meaning:

I have two sisters	We're *having* a party
They *are* hard-working	Do stop *being* so silly
They *look* alike	My prospects *are looking* good

Popular alternative terms for dynamic are *action* or *event* verb (with *state verb* rather than *stative*).

• **dynamic modal**: a modal verb that 'predicates something'. See p. 137 MODAL VERBS.

echo utterance

An utterance that repeats something that the previous speaker has said.

Echo utterances can take various forms, but they function as either questions:

| (A: He's a strange man.) | B: He's strange? |
| (A: Yes, he collects beetles.) | B: *What* does he collect? |

or exclamations:

| (A: Beetles. And then he sings to them) | B: He does *what*? |
| (A: He sings to them.) | B: Sings to them! You're joking! |

-*ed* form

A way of referring to either:

(*a*) The past tense form of any verb. The term includes not only regular past tenses (*looked*) but also irregular ones (e.g. *rang*, *saw*, *wrote*).

(*b*) The past tense form plus the past participle (including irregular forms). Since regular verbs have the same ending for both parts of the verb (*looked*), this usage is not unreasonable. But the existence of two different meanings is confusing. Some people use -*en form* for the past participle.

editorial *we*

The use of *we* by an individual writer, perhaps to avoid the more egotistical-sounding *I*, but possibly to sound authoritative.

elision

The omission of a speech sound or syllable. There are two main types of elision:

(*a*) *elided* word forms that are long established, where the spelling frequently reflects the earlier, fuller pronunciation;

(*b*) forms heard today in colloquial or rapid speech, but where unelided forms are also current.

Long-established elisions include the reduction of some consonant clusters   initially—*g*nome, *k*night, *w*rong

                       medially—lis*t*en, whis*t*le, san*d*wich

        and   finally—hym*n*, lim*b*

along with the loss of vowels and whole syllables, as in: Glouce*s*ter, Sali*s*bury, We*d*nesday.

In present-day speech, a consonant between two others is often elided (e.g. fac*t*s, han*d*bag, twel*f*th). Elision is particularly frequent with weak vowels, and whole syllables may be lost, e.g. *fact(o)ry*, *cam(e)ra*, *nat(u)ral*, *batch(e)lor*, *fam(i)ly*, *med(i)cine*, *p(o)lice*, *Febr(uar)y*.

Elision also occurs at word boundaries in connected speech, as in:

Nex(t), please; as a matt(e)r o(f) fact; mix (a)n(d) match

The distinction between past and present tense is sometimes lost:

I wish(ed) to help / aɪ wɪʃtə help /

See p. 157 omission.

ellipsis

Omission of a 'recoverable' word or words from speech or writing.

Words are often omitted from informal speech where they can be 'recovered' from the situation:

(Are you) coming?
(Is there) anything I can do to help?

In more formal speech and writing, words are often grammatically recoverable from the text, and in many cases it is normal to omit words in order to avoid repetition:

We're as anxious to help as you are [anxious to help]

Unless you particularly want to [buy tickets in advance] there's no need to buy tickets in advance

A: Tom's written to The Times. B: Why? [has Tom written to The Times]

A: I don't know [why he has written to The Times]. He's always writing
   letters and [he is always] complaining about something

Ellipsis may occur at different places in a clause:

initial (▲Coming?) and final ellipsis (We're as anxious as you
are▲) are commonest. Medial ellipsis or *gapping* occurs when there
is elision in a second or later clause (e.g. I breakfasted in my room,
and my cousin ▲in the restaurant).

There are rules as to what can be ellipted. Thus a subject need not
be repeated in a coordinated clause:

I telephoned my aunt and▲ told her the news

but it cannot be omitted when the link is between main and
subordinate clause:

*I told my aunt the news when▲ telephoned her

Strictly, ellipsis only exists when the missing words are exactly
recoverable. But the term is normally extended to include such
sentences as:

He wrote a better letter than I could have [written]

and often to looser examples of omission, such as

You remember that man [who, whom, that] I introduced to you?

See p. 157 OMISSION.

embedding

Embedding is the inclusion of a clause or phrase inside another, by
downgrading it in some way. For example, the sentence *Cassandra
announced the news* is embedded as a relative clause within a noun
phrase subject in

The news *that Cassandra announced* was not encouraging.

emotional *should*

The same as PUTATIVE should.

emphasis

The term is used in its general sense. Emphasis may be achieved by
marked FOCUS, by unusual STRESS (for example, on an auxiliary verb)

or by grammatical devices such as the use of *do* in declaratives (*I do apologize*) or in imperatives (*Do be sensible*).

emphasizer

1 Adverbs form such a varied word class that they are analysed in many different ways. An *emphasizer* or *emphasizing adverb* is an adverb that adds to the force of the clause or part of the clause that it applies to, as *really* and *simply* in

> I really think you might have telephoned
> I simply can't understand it

2 Similarly, some adjectives—generally in attributive use—are labelled *emphasizer* or *emphasizing adjective*, e.g. *pure* nonsense, a *real* idiot.

The term is often used with much the same meaning as *intensifier*.

emphatic pronoun

A reflexive pronoun when used for emphasis; as *himself* in *He admitted himself that the whole thing was a mistake*.

empty

Having no meaning.

- **empty *it***: the same as DUMMY *it*, as in *It is raining*.
- **empty word**: the same as FORM WORD.

end-focus

Putting the most important information in a sentence at the end.

It is normal to introduce the THEME or TOPIC of a message (often 'given' information) at the beginning of a sentence and to impart the important NEW information later. So end-focus is a normal characteristic of sentence structure. Compare END-WEIGHT.

ending

An inflected final part of a word.

In English the term applies to plural forms of nouns (cat*s*, child*ren*); to various inflections of verbs (look*ing*, look*ed*); and to some comparatives and superlatives (kind*er*, kind*est*, soon*er*, soon*est*).

end position

The same as final position (meaning after the verb), a term used in describing the position of adverbs.

end-weight

Sentences are often longer and 'heavier' at the end than at the beginning. This is because the 'new' information in the later part of the sentence may need more detailed explanation than the 'given' information at the beginning. END-FOCUS (focus on the 'new') is therefore often accompanied by end-weight, e.g.

> The bread industry and nutritionists alike (THEME)/ have been trying to get the message across *that a healthy balanced diet should include sufficient bread.*

The 'weighty' message here comes naturally at the end. Notice how the word *across* comes immediately after *message* and not at the very end of the sentence. Grammatically it could, but it would be feeble, and decidedly lightweight.

-*en* form

A way of referring to the past participle. The name is based on the fact that many irregular verbs do end this way (e.g. *broken, chosen, driven, forgotten, taken*), but it includes all past participles (e.g. *looked, hated, torn, begun, drunk*). It is a useful shorthand way of distinguishing past participles from past tense forms.

epistemic

Epistemic refers to all those meanings of modal verbs relating to theoretical possibility and necessity (e.g. whether something is likely or probable), and so contrasts with more practical DEONTIC meaning.

Out of context, sentences containing modal verbs are sometimes ambiguous. *You must love your mother* is epistemic (theoretical) if the meaning is 'I deduce, from some information or observations, that you love her.' It is deontic (relating to obligation) if the meaning is 'I am telling you to love her.' Similarly *Tom may keep the money* is epistemic if the meaning is 'He is quite likely to keep it', (but deontic with the meaning 'He is allowed to keep it').

See p. 137 MODAL VERBS.

ergative

An *ergative verb* is a particular kind of verb where the same noun can be used as subject when the verb is intransitive (e.g. The door *opened*) and object when the verb is transitive (Someone *opened* the door).

See p. 250 VERBS.

etymology

The *etymology* of a word is the history of its formation and the development of its meaning.

• **folk etymology** (or *popular etymology*): a popular alteration of a word, due to a misunderstanding about its true origin. For example, in folk etymology *asparagus* should really be 'sparrow-grass'. (But this is not true!)

• **etymological fallacy**: the mistaken belief that the 'real' meaning of a word is its original meaning—as for example that *awful* really means 'full of awe, awe-inspiring'.

event verb

The same as ACTION VERB.

exclamation

(*a*) In traditional grammar, *exclamation* is used in a classification of sentence types, based on a mixture of meaning and form. It is used in a fairly non-specialist way to cover any word or clause expressing anger, pleasure, surprise, etc. Some of these may lack normal sentence structure, e.g.

Marvellous! You poor thing! How kind of you! What a scorcher! Woe's me!

Sometimes single word INTERJECTIONS are included e.g. *Alas!*

(*b*) In some popular modern grammar, exclamation is used as a formal and more limited category, consisting only of sentences (excluding questions) that begin with *How* or *What*:

How difficult it all is

What a muddle we are in

(*c*) Other grammars that distinguish sentence forms from sentence functions label these *How* and *What* sentences *exclamatives*, and use exclamation as a general functional label that could include, for example, an exclamatory question. See p. 212 SENTENCE TYPES.

exclamation mark

The mark ⟨!⟩ used to show that a word or sentence is intended as an exclamation in function (e.g. *Isn't the weather terrible!*).

exclamatory

This term may be used as a formal or functional label, so the term *exclamatory sentence* can refer to form or function.

• **exclamatory question**: usually a sentence that is interrogative in form, but an exclamation in meaning:

Isn't it a lovely day!

exclusive

Excluding something; contrasted with INCLUSIVE.

(*a*) *exclusive we*: the meaning of the first person plural pronouns when the addressee is excluded, as in *We'll call for you tomorrow.*

(*b*) The word *or* can similarly be exclusive. *Are you going to have tea or coffee?* would often be interpreted as exclusive—you are expected to have one but not both. On the other hand *Do you take milk or sugar?* probably has an INCLUSIVE meaning—you can have both.

existential *there*

Unstressed *there* is often used as a dummy subject followed by the verb *be*:

> There is a lot to do, isn't there?
> Can there be life on other planets?
> There has been nothing in the papers about this

The usefulness of this structure is that a *new* subject can avoid an inappropriate GIVEN position (**A lot to do is*; *?Nothing about this has been in the papers*), and be presented as the new information that it is.

Existential there also occurs with some other verbs:

> There comes a time in everyone's life when . . .
> Once upon a time there lived a beautiful princess

extraposition

A special type of POSTPONEMENT, involving the use of a pro-form for the postponed words, as for example when the subject is a noun clause. The clause is moved (on the principle of end-focus and end-weight) to a position after the verb, and an anticipatory *it* is put in subject position, e.g.

> It's no use crying over spilt milk (*compare* Crying over spilt milk is no use)

> It's disappointing you can't stay longer (*compare* That you can't stay longer is disappointing)

Some examples of this structure have in fact no corresponding non-extraposed equivalents e.g. *It seems that they're not coming after all* (**That they're not coming after all seems*).

F

factual verb

A verb that is typically followed by a *that*-clause containing a verb in indicative mood. Factual verbs are contrasted with SUASIVE VERBS (where the following verb can be indicative, subjunctive, or *putative should*).

This is a syntactically based classification, so *factual* verbs include *allege*, *claim*, *suspect*, and others where the facts in reality may be otherwise. Factual verbs include *public* verbs of speaking (e.g. He *announced* that the police have arrested two youths) and *private* verbs of thinking (e.g. We *believe* that the police have arrested two youths).

fall

In the intonation of a syllable or longer utterance, a *fall* (also called *falling tone*) is a pitch change from relatively high to relatively low; contrasted with a RISE.

Phoneticians distinguish various kinds of falls—such as the *high fall*, starting near the normal high limit of the voice; and the *low fall*, with a lower start. A fall usually suggests more finality than a rise, and statements typically end with one.

fall-rise

A tone in which the pitch falls and then rises again.

This tone has various conversational functions, but often suggests only partial agreement ('yes, but . . .')

  A: Did you enjoy the film? B: Yes.

feminine

Belonging to the grammatical GENDER that mainly denotes female persons or animals. Contrasted with MASCULINE.

In some languages grammatical gender distinctions of masculine and feminine (and sometimes also neuter) apply to all nouns and related words. In English, however, such distinctions are found only in third person singular personal pronouns and determiners, where the feminine forms (*she*, *her*, *herself*, *hers*) contrast with the masculine ones (*he* etc.) and the non-personal *it* etc.

The suffix *-ess* (as in *lioness*, *hostess*) is a feminine marker in nouns, but feminism has reduced its use, so that, for example, some women who would previously have been described as *actresses* may now prefer to be called *actors*. Conversely, words that contain the suffix *-man* (e.g. chairman, fireman, fisherman, spokesman) are objected to on the grounds that they are exclusively masculine. Various unisex terms are suggested, although not everyone (whether male or female) necessarily wants to be a chair(person), firefighter, fisher, spokesperson, or whatever.

field

A range or system of words sharing some related meanings.

The meaning of a word depends partly on the other words it is related to in meaning. All these words together constitute a *semantic* (or *lexical*) *field*. Classic examples are the fields of colour and kinship. Different languages divide the spectrum differently, but in English the meaning of e.g. *blue* is limited by the existence of *green* and *purple*, the latter itself further limited by the existence of, say, *mauve*. Similarly the meanings of *brother*, *cousin*, and so on form a network of connected family terms.

• **field of discourse:** the particular subject-matter being talked or written about. In some instances different subject-matter may involve few differences other than those of vocabulary. But some fields of discourse are characterized by their own distinctive grammatical styles, e.g. legal language, football commentaries, advertisements, sermons.

figure of speech

A non-literal word, phrase, or sentence to describe something. Figures of speech can be divided into several different types, of which METAPHOR and SIMILE are the commonest.

final

At the end of a clause or sentence. Contrasted with INITIAL (or *front*) and MEDIAL (or *mid*).

Final position (also called *end position*) is a term used in relation to adverbials, and strictly means after the verb (and object). This is the typical position for many adverbs, giving SVOA as the normal, unmarked word order (e.g. They repaid the money *without question*).

Final ellipsis, ellipsis of the end of a clause, involves the omission of part of the predicate, e.g.

'Have they repaid the money?' 'Yes, they have▲'

See p. 157 OMISSION.

finite

A finite verb is a verb form that has tense, in contrast to NON-FINITE forms, which do not. Clauses and sentences containing finite verbs are also described as finite.

The third person singular *-s* form (e.g. *looks, sees*) is always finite, as is the past form (*looked, saw*), whereas the *-ing* form (*looking, seeing*) and the past participle (*looked, seen*) are non-finite. The base form (*look, see*) can be either. It is finite as a present tense (I *see*), in the imperative (*Look* out!) and as a subjunctive (The boss insisted that I *see* him). Modal verbs only have finite forms.

Although we talk of finite verb phrases, it is in fact only the first word of a verb phrase that is finite, e.g.

We *have* been wondering

It *may* be being changed

fixed

Not subject to variation.

• **fixed phrase** (also called *set expression*): a phrase where few if any variants are acceptable, e.g.

knife and fork (*fork and knife)

pay attention to (*pay attention towards/for/at)

heir apparent (*apparent heir)
from bad to worse (*from good to better)
beneath contempt (*below/under/underneath contempt)
no good, no different (*no bad, *no similar)

- **fixed stress:** in a fixed stress language, stress regularly occurs on the same syllable in each word. This is not the case with English, which is therefore a FREE stress language.

- **fixed word order**: English is, relatively speaking, a fixed word order language, because Subject–Verb–Object is normal, and a change can significantly affect meaning. *Putting the cart before the horse* is quite different from *putting the horse before the cart!*

focus

The focus of a sentence is the most important part in terms of information content, in contrast to its THEME.

In analysing a sentence as a 'message' (rather than in grammatical terms) it is common to divide the sentence into two, using such terms as GIVEN and *new* or TOPIC and *comment*.

The pair *theme* and *focus* often mean much the same as the other pairs. Thus a sentence commonly begins with a topic or theme, which may be 'given' (i.e. something already known), and the second part of the sentence presents the new information on which to focus.

Normally therefore the focus falls at the end (END-FOCUS), and in spoken English this is signalled by a pitch change, as in *The telephone's still out of* ORDER. But the focus will be shifted to earlier in the sentence if the end is predictable: The PHONE's ringing.

In speaking, focus can be marked on any part of a sentence by moving the stress:

You should phone YOUR mother (not mine)
You should PHONE your mother (not write)
You SHOULD phone your mother (it's your duty)
YOU should phone your mother (don't expect someone else to)

But when written this sentence would normally be interpreted as having the focus at the end (MOTHER), so special devices such as cleft may be used to *mark* the focus if this is different.

focusing adverb

An adverb that focuses on a particular part of the sentence; in contrast to one that belongs to the whole predicate or even to the entire sentence.

Typical focusing adverbs are *even*, *merely*, and *only*, as in

> *Even in old age*, she was immensely active
> I *merely asked them the time*
> *Only you* would say a thing like that

Focusing adverbs (sometimes called *focusing subjuncts*) and INTENSI-FYING adverbs correspond to all or part of the more traditional degree category.

See p. 11 ADVERBS.

form

The shape of a word or phrase, contrasted with its meaning or FUNCTION.

1 All lexical verbs have several forms. For example, the verb *see* has five forms—*see*, *sees*, *seeing*, *saw*, *seen*, while several verbs have two alternative past tense forms (e.g. *spelt*, *spelled*). Some nouns have two plural forms (e.g. *indices*, *indexes*).

2 On a morphological level, many words are made up of *free* and *bound* forms. For example, *seeing* consists of the free form *see*, and the bound form *-ing*.

3 Above word level, phrases can be analysed by their formal constituents. Thus, a noun phrase may consist of a single noun (e.g. *people*), but often contains a determiner and an adjective (*the best people*) and possibly postmodification too (*all these people you were telling me about*).

formal

1 Relating to form; contrasted with FUNCTIONAL.

'Noun phrase', 'verb phrase', etc. are formal categories, defined largely by their structural composition, irrespective of their meaning or their function in a sentence. For example, *last night* is formally a noun phrase, even if it functions adverbially, as in *Where were you last night?*

2 Relating to form as opposed to meaning.

Traditional grammar often defines words in NOTIONAL terms, e.g. 'A noun is the name of a person, place, or thing.' Modern grammar seeks more formal criteria and prefers to define parts of speech largely by their syntactic roles.

3 Formal language is characterized by a relatively impersonal attitude and adherence to certain social conventions. It contrasts with INFORMAL language.

Formal speech and writing is characterized by more complicated grammatical structures and the use of rarer vocabulary than informal language and by the avoidance of colloquialisms. *Patrons are requested to refrain from smoking* is more formal than *Please Don't Smoke.*

Formal and informal are, however, at the end of a continuum, and much language is not marked as either.

formula

An instance of stereotyped language. A formula usually allows few or no changes in form and may not conform to current grammatical usage.

Common formulae include:

> Thank you!
> How do you do? (*How does your mother do?)
> See you!
> No way!
> Many happy returns!

This category overlaps with FIXED phrase.

formulaic subjunctive   See SUBJUNCTIVE.

form word

A word that primarily has formal or grammatical importance rather than meaning. Contrasted with CONTENT WORD.

In some traditional grammar, word classes (parts of speech) are divided into form words and CONTENT WORDS (or *lexical* words).

Form words are mainly closed class words that glue the content words together: auxiliary verbs, determiners, conjunctions, and prepositions. The distinction is out of favour today, since all form words normally carry some meaning.

Confusingly, in view of the fact that form and function are often contrasted, form words are sometimes called *function words*. Another label is grammatical word.

See p. 165 PARTS OF SPEECH.

fossilized

Having a structure that is no longer productive.

Fossilized clausal structures in English include:

Handsome is as handsome does (*Good is as good acts)
Come what may (*Occur what will)
Long may it last (*Short may it last)
How come . . . ? (*How happen . . .)

Fossilized phrases include *kith and kin, to and fro*.

Fossilized word-formation processes include the plural -en, still present in *children, brethren, oxen*, but not possible for new words (except perhaps as a joke).

The term *fossilized* overlaps with other terms such as ARCHAISM, FIXED PHRASE, and FORMULA.

free

Unrestricted in some way; not fixed.

• **free form**: the smallest unit of language (also called a free morpheme) that can stand alone as a word. Contrasted with a BOUND FORM.

This is a term in word formation. For example, *kind* is a free form, but -*ly* and -*er* (as in *kindly, kinder*) are bound.

• **free indirect speech**: a way of reporting what someone has said that mixes features of both indirect and direct speech. Like *indirect speech* it includes backshifted verbs, changed pronouns, and changes in time and place reference words. But like *direct speech* it usually has subject-auxiliary inversion in questions, and it usually lacks a reporting verb.

It is popular in fiction and narrative writing for reporting both speech and thoughts. *Free direct speech* is also found, marked by an absence of quotation marks and also by present tenses that contrast with the past tenses of the rest of the narrative.

In the following extract the conversation is reported in a mixture of the writer's free indirect speech (shown in italics) and the old man's free direct speech:

> As our conversation continued the old man became whiter and whiter. The dust clung to his hat, his face, his moustache, his eyelashes and his hands. He did not complain.
>
> *Who was doing all the killing?*
> —Oh, the guerillas of course. If the guerillas see you and do not know you they kill you.
>
> *And what about the army?*
> —The army are all right, if you greet them and have papers.
>
> *Was there enough food?*
> There is enough food, but there is no business.
>
> (P. Marnham *So Far From God* (1985), p. 148.)

● **free stress**: the occurrence of stress on different syllables of polysyllabic words across a language as a whole.

Although individual words in English have their own fixed stress patterns, stress falls on different syllables in different words, e.g.

*ad*vertising, un*for*tunate, diplo*ma*tic, misunder*stand*ing

*pho*tograph, pho*to*grapher, photo*graph*ic, photogra*vure*

English is therefore a free stress language (in contrast to fixed stress languages).

● **free word order**: free word order, where word order can often be varied without changing the meaning, tends to be a characteristic of highly inflected languages like Latin. English has a fairly fixed word order.

free variation

Sounds which contrast with each other in such a way that meaning is affected (i.e. distinct phonemes) cannot normally be interchanged. But in some words two normally contrasting phonemes are both acceptable and are therefore said to be in *free variation*.

Among British speakers, a majority are said to prefer the word *ate* to be pronounced to rhyme with *met*; but a large minority favour a pronounciation like *eight*. The two pronunciations are therefore in free variation. Other words with two pronunciations in free variation are *economics* and *either*.

Free variation also occurs with the stressing of some words, although strong feelings are aroused over such variants as con*troversy* and con*troversy*.

Free variation occurs in the spelling of some words (e.g. *realize/realise*, *judgement/judgment*, *jail/gaol*).

frequency

1 The term is used in its everyday sense in the term *frequency adverbs*. This is a group of adverbs, such as *always, usually, often, sometimes, never*, which are related primarily by meaning. But they are also related by usage, since they often take mid-position before the verb, e.g. He *always/usually/never* arrives on time.

2 With modern technology it is possible to obtain *word frequencies* from vast collections of spoken and written texts. The word of highest frequency in English is *the*.

fricative

A consonant sound articulated by two speech organs coming so close together that there is audible friction.

There are four pairs of voiceless and voiced fricatives in standard English, plus the voiceless /h/.

The pairs are:

/f/ (as in fan, *ph*ysics, rough) and /v/ (van, of);
/θ/ (as in think, author, path) and /ð/ (as in father, with);
/s/ (as in soon, pencil, hopes, loose) and /z/ (as in zoo, easy, was, lose);
/ʃ / (as in shop, sure, machine, wish) and /ʒ/ (as in usual, presti*g*e).

The Scottish pronunciation of the final sound in the word *loch* is also a fricative, but not a regular phoneme for non-Scottish speakers.

See p. 264 THE CONSONANTS OF ENGLISH.

frictionless continuant

Several English sounds could be described as frictionless continuants, but this label for a manner of articulation is most usually applied to the southern British /r/.

See p. 264 THE CONSONANTS OF ENGLISH.

front

At or very close to the beginning of a sentence. Front (or INITIAL) position is a term used in describing adverb usage, where it contrasts with MID- and END position.

• **fronting**: putting any word or phrase at the beginning of a sentence for emphasis.

English sentences typically begin with a subject, but an object, complement, adverbial, even part of the verb phrase can be placed at the beginning to mark the THEME:

Loud music I do not like	(fronted object)
Horrible I call it	(fronted complement)
After half an hour, we walked out	(fronted adverbial)
Walk out we did	(fronted lexical verb)

full stop

The PUNCTUATION mark ⟨.⟩ used at the end of a sentence or abbreviation. Also called *full point* and *period*.

function

1 The syntactic role that a word, phrase, or clause takes in some larger unit; distinguished from its FORM.

For example, the five elements of CLAUSE structure, namely, Subject, Verb, Object, Complement, and Adverbial are defined by virtue of their functions. Although the function of verb is always realized by a verb phrase, there is no one-to-one correspondence between the other functional sentence elements and the forms they take. Thus the function of subject (like object) is often realized by a noun phrase but could, for example, be realized by a verb phrase (e.g. *To err* is human).

2 Sentences themselves may be classified in terms of their semantic (or discourse) functions, in contrast to their forms. See p. 212 SENTENCE TYPES.

function word

The same as FORM WORD.

fused participle

A fused participle is a structure containing an *-ing* form preceded by the ordinary case of a noun or by an object pronoun, when a possessive is considered correct, e.g.

> Forgive *me asking*, but . . .
> Were you surprised at *my father arriving* early?

Prescriptive grammarians consider the *-ing* form here to be a verbal noun requiring a possessive (Forgive *my asking* . . . , Were you surprised at *my father's arriving* early?). But the 'fused participle' is common in both written and spoken English, and is not wrong.

A participle construction is in fact the only possibility with longer noun phrases, and with non-personal nouns or pronouns:

> It depends on the people next door agreeing
> I don't recall such an opportunity ever arising

future

In traditional grammar, tenses formed with *shall* and *will* are called future tenses. See p. 235 TENSES.

Modern grammar sometimes uses such labels, but often points out that strictly English has no future tense as such, but has various ways of talking about future time, including also

present progressive:	*I am seeing Robert tomorrow*
present simple:	*His plane arrives at 8.33 am*
	If the plane is late, . . .
	When he arrives . . .
the '*going to*' future:	*It's going to rain.*

future in the past

A tense that from a time in the past looks towards its own future. Traditionally this label is given to a certain type of verb phrase containing the word *would* as in

They did not realize then that by 1914 the two countries *would be* at war

future perfect

A tense formed with *shall* or *will* + *have* + a past participle, expressing expected completion in the future:

I *will have wasted* the whole morning if they don't come soon (future perfect simple)

I'*ll have been waiting* three hours by one o'clock (future perfect continuous/progressive)

See p. 235 TENSES.

Future perfect passive tenses are also possible:

The best things *will* all *have been sold* by the time you get there

G

gapping See ELLIPSIS.

gender

A classification of nouns, pronouns, and related words, partly according to natural distinctions of sex.

In some languages *gender* is an important grammatical property of nouns and related words, marked by distinct forms. In French, for example, all nouns must be either *masculine* (*son livre*: his or her book) or *feminine* (*sa plume*: his or her pen), the form of the possessive being dictated by the gender of the noun, and having nothing to do with the sex of the owner. In some languages (e.g. Latin, German, and Old English) there is a third gender, neuter, for nouns denoting inanimate objects (although many nouns for 'things' in fact belong to masculine or feminine gender).

In modern English, grammatical gender hardly exists, except in third person singular pronouns (*he/him/his* versus *she/her* etc.) with *it/its/itself* often called non-personal, rather than neuter. Even here there can be some mismatch between natural and grammatical gender. Countries, ships, cars etc. may sometimes be referred to with masculine or feminine pronouns; a baby may be *it*; animals may be referred to by personal or non-personal pronouns.

Natural gender distinctions are made covertly in many English words referring to males and females. Pairs of words occasionally show a derivational relationship (e.g. *hero/heroine*, *widow/widower*), but many male and female noun pairs show no morphological connection (e.g. *brother/sister*, *duck/drake*). Some words for animate beings can refer to males and females, and are said to have *common gender* (e.g. *baby*, *person*, *bird*, *horse*).

generic

Relating to a whole class; in contrast to SPECIFIC.

(*a*) In describing the uses of the articles, a useful distinction is drawn between *generic* and *specific*, which cuts across the more obvious distinction between *definite* and *indefinite*. In English, *the* + singular count noun can have definite but generic meaning, as in

> The dodo is extinct
> Who invented the wheel?

The + certain adjectives is also used with generic (and plural) meaning—

> The poor are always with us
> I don't understand the Chinese

Some kinds of indefinite meaning are often labelled generic, as in

> *Unexploded bombs* are dangerous (plural count)
> *An unexploded bomb* is dangerous (singular count)
> *Danger* lurks everywhere! (uncount)

But such usages often indicate examples of a class rather than a class as a whole, so the label CLASSIFYING may be preferred.

(*b*) Some personal pronouns are used with the generic meaning of 'people in general' or 'mankind':

> *One* never can tell
> Man seems to think *he* rules the planet
> *You* can lead a horse to water
> *We* still have many diseases to conquer

genitive

The genitive case of nouns and pronouns indicates possession or close connection. It contrasts with COMMON case. It is sometimes called *Saxon genitive* and is typically used before a noun.

The genitive is marked in nouns by the addition of *'s* to regular singular nouns and to plurals that lack *s* (e.g. *the boy's mother, the children's mother*). An apostrophe (') only (which of course has no spoken realization) is added to regular plurals (e.g. *the boys' mothers*).

The distinct genitive forms of personal pronouns and determiners (e.g. *my, mine*) are called POSSESSIVE.

Several types of genitive are distinguished on grounds of form, meaning, or both. They include:

- **classifying** (or **descriptive**) **genitive**: sheep's eyes, a women's college, a stone's throw.

- **double genitive** (also called **post-genitive**): a structure such as *a home of their own*, *some books of Jane's*, where possession is marked twice.

- **group genitive**: a genitive form added to a whole phrase, e.g. the Prince of Wales's speech, the boy next door's car, someone else's problem

- **independent genitive**: a genitive standing alone because the headword has been ellipted, e.g.

  My garden isn't as good as Jilly's

- **local genitive** (implying someone's home or shop):

  We're going to Jilly's for the weekend
  I got it at the chemist's

- **objective genitive**: the enemy's defeat (someone defeated/will defeat the enemy)

- **partitive genitive**: this term is variously applied but can mean a genitive + noun, showing a relationship of whole to part, e.g. the Earth's surface

- **subjective genitive**: the enemy's plans (the enemy planned/are planning)

When a possessive or similar relationship is expressed by a post-modifying *of*-phrase (e.g. *the mother of the boys*), the term *of-genitive* can be used.

gerund

The gerund is the *-ing* form of the verb when used in a partly noun-like way, as in *No Smoking* (in contrast to the same form used as a PARTICIPLE, e.g. *Everyone was smoking*). (Sometimes called *verbal noun*.)

However, there are many uses that are partly noun-like and partly verb-like. For example, in *My smoking twenty cigarettes a day annoys them*, *smoking* is noun-like in being preceded by *my* and in being the head of a phrase (*my smoking twenty cigarettes a day*) which is the subject of the sentence; but it is verb-like in taking an object and an adverbial (*twenty cigarettes a day*). So the more neutral term *-ing form* is often preferred.

given and new

Given and *new* are used in some analyses of the information structure of a sentence. The given information is information already supplied in the text or 'known' in the situation. It usually receives little stress if spoken, while the important new part of the message is stressed.

The given and new distinction is much the same as TOPIC and COMMENT, or THEME and FOCUS. However, whereas the topic or theme is what the speaker chooses to begin with, *given and new* analyses an utterance from the listener's angle, the *given* being something the listener is assumed to know.

glottal

Glottal sounds are produced in the *glottis*, the opening between the vocal cords at the upper end of the windpipe.

The /h/ sound of English is commonly classified as a voiceless glottal fricative. Whispered speech is also produced with a considerably narrowed glottis.

See p. 264 THE CONSONANTS OF ENGLISH.

glottal stop

The voiceless plosive sound made when air is released after a complete closure (with vocal cords held together) of the glottis.

(*a*) This sound / ʔ / is not a phoneme of English, but nevertheless may be heard in standard RP:

  (i) emphasizing a vowel at the beginning of a syllable
  (ii) optionally to avoid a LINKING *r*, as in *overenthusiastic* /ˌəʊvəʔɪnθjuːzɪ' æstɪk/
  (iii) reinforcing the voiceless plosives /p/, /t/, and /k/, at the end of syllables or words, especially when followed by a consonant as in 'shor*t*, shar*p* shoc*k* treatment'

(*b*) In some accents of English the glottal stop is heard as an allophonic variant of /t/ at the end of syllables, so that *better butter* may be pronounced /ˈbeʔə/ ˈbʌʔə/ and *quite right* as /kwaɪʔ raɪʔ/. This was at one time considered to be almost exclusively a Cockney feature, but it is now much more widely heard and is a characteristic of the newly emerging 'Estuary English', described as 'a mixture of "London" and General RP forms'.

govern

In traditional grammar various words which have other words dependent on them are said to govern those words. For example, in Latin a particular verb or preposition requires a particular case in a following noun or pronoun, but the term is not very relevant in English. Government is usually contrasted with *concord* (now often called AGREEMENT).

gradable

Capable of being ranked on a scale.

The term is particularly applied to adjectives and adverbs. Gradable adjectives and adverbs can take degrees of comparison (*better, most northerly, soonest*) and be intensified (*very difficult, too quickly*).

They contrast with non-gradable (or ungradable) words that normally cannot (**more supreme, *very impossible, ?less unique, *most north, ?too occasionally, *less perfectly*).

Some determiners and pronouns are also gradable, e.g.

    many/much: more, most
    few: fewer, fewest
    little: less, least

gradience

The quality of indeterminancy.

Grammatical categories are not always clear-cut. Word classes, in particular, have fuzzy boundaries. At one end of a scale are words that meet all the criteria for membership of a particular class, but further down the scale are words that pass only some of the tests, or even share characteristics with another class. The word *near*, for example, even when syntactically used as a preposition, can be compared (*Stand nearer the table*). It thus shows gradience between prepositions and adjectives or adverbs.

Gradience is also found in semantics. One object may clearly be a cup and another a mug, but somewhere in between there may be an object about which opinions differ: foolproof definitions can be elusive.

grammar

1 The entire system of a language, including its syntax, morphology, semantics, phonology.

2 Popularly, the structural rules of a language, including syntax and perhaps morphology (word formation), but excluding vocabulary (the semantic system) and excluding phonology.

3 A book containing rules and examples of grammar (particularly in sense 2).

4 An individual's application of the rules, as in *This novel is full of bad grammar*.

Traditional grammar can cover many periods. It is often used—as in this book—to mean eighteenth-, nineteenth-, and early twentieth-century grammar, which was often based on Latin grammar. It is contrasted with more modern analysis that began in the nineteenth century and depends on research into actual usage.

grammatical

1 As a formal term, grammatical means relating to grammar. So we can contrast grammatical concord with NOTIONAL concord; grammatical gender with natural GENDER, grammatical SUBJECT with AGENT etc., and grammatical (or grammar) words—also called FORM words—with CONTENT words.

2 Contrasted with *ungrammatical*, grammatical means conforming to the rules.

Popularly, sentences and other utterances are grammatical if they obey the rules of the standard language or—more narrowly—the

PRESCRIPTIVE rules of usage books, and ungrammatical if they do not. Hence *I never said nothing* or *He were right angry*, though acceptable in some dialects, might be judged ungrammatical. But then so might *It's me* if judged by Latin-based traditions.

Grammatical is not synonymous with *meaningful*; a sentence can be grammatical but nonsensical (e.g. *'Twas brillig, and the slithy toves Did gyre and gimble in the wabe*). Conversely, a sentence may be meaningful but ungrammatical (e.g. **Broked he the window?*). A sentence may also be grammatical, but 'unacceptable' because it is (say) too long to be comprehensible.

greengrocer's apostrophe

The use of an apostrophe in an ordinary plural, where it is incorrect. E.g. *potato's 15p*.

group noun

Usually the same as COLLECTIVE NOUN, but sometimes more narrowly a collective noun, often a proper name, that is only found in the singular, e.g. *Whitehall believes/believe . . .*

H

hanging participle

A participle that is not related grammatically to its right noun phrase. Also called *dangling, misrelated, unattached,* or *unrelated participle.*

A participle clause usually contains no subject, but grammatically, if it is placed near the subject of the main clause, it is 'understood' to refer to this. Failure to observe this ATTACHMENT RULE results in a hanging participle, or often—more accurately—a *misrelated participle.* In this, the participle is grammatically attached to the subject, though this is not the meaning intended. For example:

> ?Speaking to her on the phone the other day, her praise for her colleagues was unstinting

The meaning may be clear enough; equally clear is that neither the lady herself nor her praise for her colleagues was speaking to her on the phone.

The same rule can also apply when the participle clause is introduced by a conjunction or preposition:

> ?When buying statuary, old or new, its impact on the garden will be strong
> ?Every afternoon, instead of dozing listlessly in their beds, or staring vacantly out of a window, there is organized entertainment

The hanging participle is generally condemned as ungrammatical, rather than as a mere error of style. But it has long been widely used—most famously by Shakespeare in *Hamlet:*

> Sleeping in mine orchard, a serpent stung me

The rule does not extend to participles that refer to the speaker's or writer's comments (*Strictly speaking,* Monday is not the first day of the week) nor to apparent participles that are accepted as prepositions or conjunctions (*following, provided that . . .*)

head

The obligatory word in some kinds of phrase, the word that determines what kind of phrase it is (also called *headword*).

In the noun phrase *the ankle-deep propaganda which I waded through*, the head is the noun *propaganda*. Similarly in the adjectival phrase *very misleading indeed* or the adverb phrase *somewhat superficially* the heads are *misleading* and *superficially*.

headed

A phrase containing a head(word) is headed. Phrases that contain no word that could by itself fulfil the same function as the whole phrase are *unheaded* or *non-headed*.

Compare:

I was *very anxious* (headed adjectival phrase)

with

I was *in two minds about it* (non-headed prepositional phrase)

headlinese

The grammar of newspaper headlines.

Newspaper headlines often contain grammatical conventions that differ from the norm. Articles and other minor words are often omitted (*Man hit by gunman 'critical'*); present tenses are used for past events (*Designer weeps in court*); a to-infinitive stands for a future tense (*UN to search for solution*); nouns are heavily stacked in noun phrases (*Monster fish mystery death*).

helping verb

A somewhat dated term for AUXILIARY.

heterograph

A word written (i.e. spelt) differently from another, but which is pronounced the same way (Greek *heteros* 'other'), e.g. *feet, feat*; *so, sew*.

If we want to emphasize the sameness of the sound, then such word pairs are HOMOPHONES (Greek *homos* 'same').

See p. 106 HOMONYMS.

heteronym

A word having a different meaning from another word that is identical to it in spelling and possibly also in pronunciation. Contrasted with SYNONYM.

Word pairs such as *bill* (statement of charges) and *bill* (beak) or *lead* (cause to go) and *lead* (metal) are usually considered together in the first place on the basis of their similarity, and are more likely to be labelled HOMONYMS (*bill/bill*) or HOMOGRAPHS (*lead/lead*). The term *heteronym* emphasizes difference. (See p. 106)

heterophone

A word having a different sound from another which is spelt the same.

Since a certain similarity is the reason for considering two words together as some sort of pair (e.g. *lead* (cause to go) and *lead* (metal) or *row* (a line) and *row* (a quarrel)), an alternative term would be HOMOGRAPH, or—more loosely—HOMONYM. (See p. 106)

historic present

The present simple tense (or sometimes the present progressive) when used with past reference (also called *narrative present*). The device is often used to make narrative more vivid and immediate. It is frequently used in newspaper headlines (e.g. *Fifty-five die in train disaster*).

See p. 237 TIME AND TENSE.

homograph

A partial HOMONYM, characterized by identical spelling but pronounced differently, e.g. *row* (line) and *row* (quarrel or loud noise), or *lead* (as in *give a lead or lead the way*) and *lead* (metal).

The same words are HETEROPHONES if we want to emphasize the different sounds. (See below)

homonym

A word that has both the same pronunciation and the same spelling as another, but is etymologically unrelated to it.

For example, *pole* (a long slender rounded piece of wood or metal) and *pole* (each of the two points in the celestial sphere about which the stars appear to revolve) are homonyms. Traditionally, homonyms of this type are treated as separate words and given distinct dictionary entries, (e.g. 'pole 1' and 'pole 2') whereas more closely related meanings are treated as offshoots of the same word, which historically speaking they are (so 'Each of the two terminals of an electric cell or battery, etc.' comes under pole 2.)

HOMONYMS AND RELATED TERMS

....

HOMONYM

A word with the same spelling and same pronunciation as another word, though usually etymologically unrelated:

   bill (statement of charges); bill (beak)
   fair (just); fair (sale, entertainment)
   pole (long slender piece of wood or metal); pole (each of the extremities of the earth's axis)
   row (line); row (propel a boat)

....

HOMOGRAPH

A word with the same spelling as another word, but with a different meaning. (Usually also with a different pronunciation, and therefore a *heterophone*)

   row (line, propel a boat); row (quarrel, noise)
   lead (cause to go); lead (metal)
   sow (bury seed); sow (female pig)

....

HOMOPHONE

A word with the same sound as another word, but with a different meaning. (Usually also with different spelling, and therefore a *heterograph*)

   feet; feat. sow (bury seed); so; sew. no; know.

....

homophone

A partial HOMONYM characterized by identical sound, but spelt differently, e.g. *feat/feet; no/know; none/nun; stare/stair*. In fact, therefore a heterograph!

Some English pairs are homophones in some accents but not in others, e.g. *pore/pour, wine/whine*.

hybrid

A word formed from words or morphemes deriving from different languages is a hybrid (or a hybrid word).

Many affixes in common use in English word formation are ultimately of Latin or Greek origin (e.g. *a-, anti-, co-, ex-, in-, non-, post-, syn-; -al, -ation*) but they are so well established that they combine easily with words of Old English or any other origin. Examples are:

> anticlockwise, disbelieve, interweave, refill, eatable, jingoism, starvation, talkative

Quite a number of hybrids were criticized when first introduced, for example *appendicitis* (Latin *appendic-* + Greek *-itis*), *speedometer* (English *speed* + Greek *-(o)meter*), and *television* (Greek *tele-* + French/Latin *vision*).

See p. 145 NEW WORDS.

hypercorrection

Using a standard form in a context where it is not standard, under the impression that this is 'correct' and grammatical usage, results in hypercorrection.

Typical instances of hypercorrection involve pronoun use:

> *That's a matter for John and I to decide [for John and me]
> *She mentioned some people whom she thought were cheating her [who . . . were cheating]

or the use of subjunctive *were* where *was* is correct:

> *Even if that were true in 1950, it isn't now [if that was]
> *We didn't know if he were old enough [if he was]

or *as* when *like* is correct:

*He drinks as a fish [like a fish]

hypernym

The more all-embracing 'umbrella' term in a set of related words, in contrast to HYPONYM.

For example, *animal* is a hypernym of *tiger* and *kangaroo*.

hyphen

The sign ⟨-⟩ has several uses. It is used to

   (i)   join words semantically or syntactically (as in *sister-in-law*, *good-natured*);
   (ii) indicate the division of a word at the end of a line;
   (iii) indicate a missing or implied element (as in *over- and underpayment*).

There is considerable variation and inconsistency in the use of hyphens in words or compounds. For example, one finds *coal field*, *coal-field*, and *coalfield*.

Basically, hyphens are meant to aid comprehension. So splitting words at the end of a line needs to be done carefully. (*Now- here* and *leg- end* are confusing!)

One useful convention is to use a hyphen to separate vowels that could otherwise be run together in a word, as in *co-occur*, but this rule is not universally followed, even though such forms as *cooccur* are rather opaque. Another useful convention is to hyphenate words that would not normally be hyphenated in order to avoid ambiguity; a *spare room-heater* is not the same as a *spare-room heater*.

hyponym

A word with a more specific, or subordinate meaning in relation to a more general, superordinate term (a HYPERNYM).

Tiger and *kangaroo* are hyponyms of *animal*; *knife* and *fork* of *cutlery*; *diamond* and *ruby* of *gemstone*. Words that are hyponyms of the same superordinate term are *cohyponyms*.

ideogram

A written character symbolizing a word or phrase without indicating the pronunciation. (Also called *ideograph*.)

Ideograms are rather marginal to the English writing system, but include numerals, and symbols such as £, $, %, &, +, −.

idiolect

An individual's knowledge and command of the language.

Speakers differ in their knowledge and use of the grammar and vocabulary of their language, so that in some ways everyone has their own idiolect. The term is modelled on the word DIALECT, using the prefix *idio-* 'own, personal, distinct'.

idiom

1 A group of (more or less) fixed words having a meaning not deducible from those of the individual words, e.g.

> over the moon, under the weather, by the skin of one's teeth, up to one's
> eyes in work, for crying out loud;
>
> kick the bucket, paint the town red, give in, take up;
>
> had better, might as well, how goes it?

Some of these phrases allow no alteration except extremely facetiously (*over the stars, *kick the pail). Others allow some changes (*up to my/his/her/their eyes in work*).

2 A phrase that is fairly fixed—not necessarily with opaque meaning—but which shows or appears to show some grammatical irregularity:

> these sort of people, come to think of it

It is not unusual to find phrases such as *by car*, *on foot*, *in prison* (i.e. a preposition + a normally countable noun, but without an article) described as idioms, though this use of a base form where number is irrelevant is a regular feature of English (compare *bookcase, street guide*—not **bookscase, *streets guide*).

In some cases there is no very clear distinction between *idiom*, COLLOCATION, and FIXED phrase.

if-clause

A subordinate clause introduced by *if*.

The term is particularly applied to clauses introduced by *if* and expressing condition. It may be extended loosely to cover other clauses of condition (introduced by *unless, provided that*, etc.).

immediate constituent analysis See CONSTITUENT.

imperative

A form or structure expressing a command. In particular it means the base form of the verb when used to issue a command, order, request etc.: the *imperative mood*, e.g.

  Listen!   Have fun!   Be sensible!

An imperative verb phrase can include *do* for emphasis (e.g. *Do listen!, Do be sensible*) or *don't* for a negative (*Don't forget, Don't be silly*).

As a verbal category, imperative contrasts with INDICATIVE and SUBJUNCTIVE mood.

Where a distinction is made between form and function in the analysis of sentence types, *imperative* is a formal category.

See p. 212 SENTENCE TYPES.

impersonal

An *impersonal verb* is a verb used with a formal subject—usually *it*. The term is particularly applied to verbs such as *rain* or *snow* expressing an action with no real-world subject (e.g. *It is snowing*).

More widely, other structures with 'impersonal *it*' as subject can themselves be called impersonal:

> It is considered bad manners to eat peas with a knife
>
> It appears that nobody knew

It is usually classified as a PERSONAL PRONOUN for syntactic reasons (e.g. it can substitute for a noun or refer to a 'thing'), but when used with an impersonal verb or in other vague ways it is referred to by such labels as *dummy* and *introductory*.

inanimate

'Not living'; contrasted with ANIMATE. Both terms are mainly used in the classification of nouns, and are meaning-based.

inclusive

Inclusive contrasts with EXCLUSIVE.

1 inclusive *we* includes both speaker(s) and addressee(s)

> Why don't we all go together? You'd enjoy it

2 Applied to the meaning of *or*, it means both alternatives are possible (e.g. Will you have milk or sugar?).

indefinite

Some words, tenses, etc. that do not indicate any particular and precise reference, but have a vaguer meaning, are labelled *indefinite*, in contrast to DEFINITE. The word is particularly used in the terms INDEFINITE ARTICLE and INDEFINITE PRONOUNS (see below), but is used to describe other items which have imprecise meaning.

(*a*) Adverbials of *indefinite* frequency (*generally*, *usually*, *always*, *repeatedly*, *occasionally*, etc.) contrast with adverbials of definite frequency (e.g. *daily*, *twice a day*, etc.).

(*b*) In the use of tenses, a simple present perfect often refers to an indefinite time, e.g.

> Have you ever read Macbeth?

in contrast to a simple past, which characteristically implies a definite, even if unstated, time, e.g.

> (When) did you read Macbeth?

indefinite article

The common grammatical name for the determiner *a/an*.

Although *a* and *an* are indefinite in meaning, reference may be general (any person or thing of that class or kind) or more particular (an actual example):

> We don't expect letters—but send us a postcard (*general*: any postcard)

> I've still got a card my grandfather sent from Kabul (*specific*: a particular card and no other)

Some grammarians label the first meaning CLASSIFYING or GENERIC, and the second SPECIFIC. But many popular grammars use terms like *general* and *specific* very loosely.

indefinite pronoun

A pronoun lacking the definiteness of reference inherent in personal, reflexive, possessive, and demonstrative pronouns.

Indefinite pronouns include compound pronouns (e.g. *everybody*, *something*, etc.) and *of*-pronouns of quantity (e.g. *all*, *either*, etc.).

Corresponding determiners (*all, some, every . . .*) have similar indefinite reference.

indicative

Indicative refers to a verbal form or mood denoting fact, and so contrasts with IMPERATIVE and SUBJUNCTIVE.

Traditional grammar follows Latin and similar models in making a threefold MOOD distinction. However, since there are few verb inflections in modern English, this is not very appropriate now.

See p. 250 VERBS.

indirect object

In clause structure, the noun phrase that 'receives' the DIRECT OBJECT.

In *Can you tell me the time?* and *They bought her a bicycle*, *me* and *her* are indirect objects. An indirect object normally precedes the direct object in SVOO sentences, though there can be exceptions (*Give me it/Give it me*).

In traditional grammar, any noun phrase with a DATIVE function is an indirect object. Typically, when placed after the direct object the indirect object requires *to* or *for* (e.g. *They bought a bicycle for Susan, and gave it to her*). Modern grammars vary as to whether they classify such prepositional phrases as indirect objects or not.

See p. 38 CASE.

indirect question

A question as reported in indirect speech.

Indirect questions are characterized by using unmarked SV word order, instead of auxiliary-and-subject inversion.

Thus

	What	do	you	want?
	[Object	+ *Aux*	+ S	+ *V*]

becomes

I asked him	what		he	wanted.
	[Object		+ S	*V*]

Indirect yes/no questions are introduced by *if* or *whether*.

indirect speech

Indirect speech is a way of reporting what someone has said without repeating the exact words (as in DIRECT SPEECH).

In real life we may rather loosely report what someone has said, but even if we report accurately, *indirect speech* usually involves changing pronouns, time and place adverbials, and tenses to our viewpoint now. Compare:

> *direct*—'Well, what do you want?' said Molly. 'Why don't you want to stay here next week? I've tried to help. I can't read your mind. Please explain what's bothering you, and don't waste my time.'

> *indirect*—Molly demanded to know what I wanted. She asked why I didn't want to stay there the following week. (She said) she'd tried to help, but she couldn't read my mind. She told me to explain what was bothering me and not to waste her time.

The term *indirect speech* is often loosely used to cover the reporting of thoughts, using an introductory 'thinking' verb and a *that*-clause.

In general, *indirect speech* and REPORTED SPEECH are synonymous and interchangeable, but some people make a distinction, and use the term *reported speech* to cover both direct and indirect reporting. FREE INDIRECT SPEECH combines characteristics of both direct and indirect speech.

infinitive

The unmarked BASE form when it is used without any direct relationship to time, person, or number.

In English the infinitive is often preceded by *to* (the *to*-INFINITIVE), e.g.

> I wanted *to help*
> *To err* is human

It is for this reason that many people object to the so-called SPLIT INFINITIVE, but the infinitive is also used alone (the BARE INFINITIVE), e.g.

> Don't *apologize*
> They can't *make* you *do* it

Some other non-finite verb phrases are analysed as complex infinitives, e.g.

> *To have made* a mistake is understandable (perfect infinitive)
> It was upsetting *to be questioned* (passive infinitive)
> I expected you *to be waiting* for me (progressive infinitive)

See p. 250 VERBS.

inflection

A word can be inflected (changed) to indicate differences of tense, number, gender, case, etc. This is usually done by adding a suffix.

English is a relatively uninflected language. Lexical verbs inflect for

> 3rd person singular, present simple tense (*looks, sees*)
> past simple (*looked, saw*)
> present participle (*looking, seeing*)
> past participle (*looked, seen*)

Nouns inflect for

> plural (*girls*)
> possessive (*girl's, girls'*)

Inflection does not (except in certain uses of *-ing* forms) change the word-class to which a word belongs, in contrast to DERIVATION, which usually does.

informal

An informal style (whether spoken or written) is characterized by simpler grammatical structure and more familiar vocabulary than FORMAL style.

The attitude of speakers (or writers) to their audience is often reflected in different levels of formality—with formal and informal style as two extremes, and a wide range of stylistically less marked language in between.

information structure

There are different ways of arranging the words of a clause or sentence so that a particular part of the 'message' receives greatest attention. This is information structure.

The term is a general one, concerned with such contrasts as GIVEN and new, THEME and focus, topic and COMMENT.

-ing form

The part of the verb that ends in *-ing*.

In traditional grammar, a distinction is made between the GERUND with its noun-like functions, e.g.

> *Seeing* is *believing*

and the present PARTICIPLE used in the formation of progressive tenses and in other verb-like ways, e.g.

> We're *seeing* them tomorrow
> *Seeing* them in that condition, I was greatly upset

But noun-like and verb-like uses sometimes merge, so this more neutral term (*-ing* form) is often preferred. See p. 250 VERBS.

The term is usefully extended to embrace borderline uses that lie between the verbal participle and the adjective. In *running water, rising standards*, the *-ing* forms resemble adjectives in standing in attributive position, but their meaning is definitely verb-like and the words would be analysed as participles if they were in predicative position (e.g. *Standards are rising*). This type of *-ing* form can be distinguished from, on the one hand, the fully adjectival-*ing* form— the PARTICIPIAL ADJECTIVE (e.g. *a very interesting book*; *the book is more interesting than I expected*) and, on the other, from a fully verbal form, which cannot be used attributively (e.g. *That man is waving*; **Who is that waving man?*).

inherent

An inherent adjective describes the quality that directly belongs to whatever it refers to—in contrast to *non-inherent*.

The meaning of most adjectives is not seriously affected by their position in a sentence, so that *rich* means the same in attributive position (*She's a rich woman*; *that rich woman*) as it does in predicative position (*That woman is rich*). Such adjectives are *inherent*.

By contrast some adjectives in attributive position have a non-inherent meaning: *you poor darling* does not mean '*Darling, you are poor*'. Other examples of non-inherent adjectives are:

> an old friend, pure invention, a complete idiot, a heavy sleeper, a real genius.

See p. 6 ADJECTIVES.

initialism

The use of initial letters as an ABBREVIATION for a name or expression, each letter being pronounced separately, as in *BBC* or *p.t.o.* Often included with other types of ACRONYM.

See p. 157 OMISSION.

initial position

Initial (or *front*) position means the beginning of a clause or sentence. The expression is used in analysing ELLIPSIS, and also the position of adverbials. It contrasts with FINAL (*end*) position and MID- (*medial*) POSITION.

Since *end* position is normal for adverbials in clause structure, initial position is a marked position. Contrast *I'm leaving tomorrow* with *Tomorrow, I'm leaving*, where *Tomorrow* is marked as topic.

An ordinary manner adverb may become a disjunct when used in initial position. Contrast *He spoke frankly* (that is how he spoke) and *Frankly, we didn't believe him* (we are telling you this as a frank opinion).

instrumental

The instrumental case or role of a noun indicates the implement or other inanimate thing used in performing the action of the verb. Old English actually had a few traces of an inflected case with this meaning. In modern English, the term often describes the meaning of a *with*-phrase, as in

> They attacked the police *with bricks*

This contrasts with an (animate) *agentive* phrase:

> The officers were attacked *by the mob* with bricks

intensifier

A word that reinforces meaning upwards, or in fact downwards, on a scale of intensity.

(*a*) Adverbs form such a broad class of words that there are many different ways of classifying them. In one very detailed classification *intensifiers* form a subgroup of SUBJUNCTS which contrast with *emphasizers*, *focusing adverbs*, and others. Traditionally, intensifiers would be classed among *degree* adverbs. They may modify the verb

> We *thoroughly* disapprove and are *bitterly* disappointed

> You worry *a lot*

> I *hardly* know them

> We were *kind of* wondering

or other parts of speech, e.g. *pretty* soon, *nearly* everybody, *quite* an occasion. See p. 11 ADVERBS.

(*b*) Adjectives too can intensify, and the term *intensifying adjective* (not always distinguished from *emphasizing adjective*) is applied to some attributive adjectives, e.g.

> *pure* joy, *downright* nonsense, a *firm* commitment, *utter* rubbish, *great* hopes

See p. 6 ADJECTIVES.

interjection

Interjections form a minor word-class. They are outside normal clause structure, having no syntactical connection with other words. Interjections are usually emotive in meaning

> aha, alas, eh?, mm, oops, sh!

Several interjections involve sounds that are not part of the regular speech sounds of English—such as those represented in writing by *tut-tut*, actually a sequence of clicks, or *ugh*, where the *gh* represents a voiceless velar fricative (as in the Scottish pronunciation of *loch*), although in these two particular cases spelling pronunciation is also heard.

See p. 165 PARTS OF SPEECH.

International Phonetic Alphabet (IPA)

A system of written symbols to enable the speech sounds of any language to be consistently represented.

The alphabet was first published by the International Phonetic Association in 1889 and, adapted in various ways, is still in very wide use today. Some of the symbols are ordinary Roman letters, having the values that English speakers would expect: for example /p/ and /b/ for voiceless and voiced bilabial plosives. Other familiar letters have values that they have in other languages: e.g. /j/ representing the initial sound of *Jaeger, you, yes*. Other symbols were specially invented or adapted from existing letters. For example /θ/, the voiceless sound in English *think*, is based on Greek theta, and /ð/, the corresponding voiced sound (as in *this*), is based on an Anglo-Saxon letter.

interrogative

A word or sentence typically used to ask a question.

Interrogative and QUESTION are often used interchangeably. Where a distinction is made between the form and function of a sentence, interrogative may be reserved for the syntactic form, in which typically there is inversion of subject and auxiliary (*Is everybody ready?/What do you think?*).

Interrogative sentences normally, as here, function as questions, but may function as statements, orders, exclamations, etc. See p. 212 SENTENCE TYPES.

Interrogative words typically begin with *wh-*, and include adverbs (e.g. *why, when, where,* plus *how*) and derived compounds (e.g. *wherever*), also determiners and pronouns (e.g. *what(ever), which(ever), who(ever), whom, whose*).

intonation

The pitch variations and patterns in spoken language.

The total meaning of a spoken utterance comes not only from the actual words and the patterns of STRESS but also from the PITCH patterns used (the rises and falls in the voice). Intonation is concerned with the 'tunes' over sequences of words (TONE UNITS), and the type of pitch change (or 'nuclear' tone) in each such unit.

Intonation has two main functions. First, it plays a part not unlike punctuation in the written language. For example a sentence such as

> You don't believe me

is a statement when said with a fall on the last stressed syllable (*-lieve*) but a question if a rise is used instead. Intonation may also indicate whether a relative clause is defining (part of the same tone unit as its antecedent) or non-defining (separated by its own tone unit in speech, just as it is separated off by commas in writing):

> My sister who lives in New Zealand is a teacher
> My sister, who lives in New Zealand, is a teacher

Secondly, intonation conveys attitude, so that the same words, depending on intonation and the different *tunes* used, may sound friendly, angry, apologetic, puzzled, etc.

intransitive verb

A verb not taking a direct object. Contrasted with TRANSITIVE. See p. 250 VERBS.

introductory *it*

1 Another term for DUMMY *it*, EMPTY *it*, or *prop it*, as in *It is raining*.

2 Another term to describe ANTICIPATORY or PREPARATORY *it*, as in *It is difficult to know what to do*.

intrusive *r*

The pronunciation of an /r/ sound between two words spoken in sequence, where there is no *r* in the spelling.

Intrusive *r* is much criticized, but is quite commonly heard in standard RP. It typically occurs where the first word ends in a vowel sound and the second begins with one

law (r) and order, umbrella (r) organization

Intrusive *r*, like the acceptable LINKING *r*, are both forms of LIAISON.

inversion

The reversal of the usual word order of subject and verb, particularly for direct questions.

This is often called 'subject-verb inversion', but in fact only an auxiliary (or a primary verb), is normally placed before the subject, and if necessary DO is used. Thus the unmarked word order of subject + (auxiliary) + verb (e.g. *I am listening, I have a complaint*) is changed to auxiliary (or primary) + subject (+ verb), e.g.

[Aux]	[S]	[V]	
Are	you	listening?	
Have	you		any complaints?
Do	you	have	any complaints?
Does	he	understand?	

Similar inversion occurs when some negative words are fronted (e.g. *Never did I imagine anything so amazing*).

Inversion of subject and main verb, without DO, occurs in certain structures involving FRONTING and the placing of a subject in end position, e.g.

> Here *comes the bride*
> Just as surprising *was their refusal to help*

inverted commas

The same as quotation marks (" ").

IPA

The INTERNATIONAL PHONETIC ALPHABET or the International Phonetic Association.

irregular

Not conforming to a rule; contrasting with regular.

The term is particularly applied to verbs that do not follow the general pattern of adding *-ed* to form past simple tense and past participle. Thus *see/saw/seen* or *put/put/put* are irregular verbs.

Among nouns, common irregular plurals include *children*, *mice*, *teeth*. Irregular degrees of comparison include *good/well*, *better*, *best*; *bad/badly*, *worse*, *worst*; *little*, *less*, *least*; *much/many*, *more*, *most*.

Irregular sentence is a vague term applied to different kinds of utterance that do not conform to standard sentence structure. See p. 212 SENTENCE TYPES.

juncture

The transition between two words or syllables and the phonetic features that mark it.

As listeners we normally distinguish the separate words of an utterance, but much speech is in fact a continuum without pauses between words. We are helped in mentally separating the words by the speaker's retention of certain phonological features that characterize the pronunciation of phonemes in different phonetic contexts.

For example, *grey day* /greɪ deɪ/ potentially has open juncture between /eɪ/ and /d/, and close juncture between /d/ and /eɪ/; whereas *grade A* /greɪd eɪ/ has the reverse. These junctures entail subtle, but important, differences: for example, differences of vowel length (/eɪ/ is longer in *grey*, where it is word-final, than in *grade*); and differences in voicing, pitch, and stress (/d/ is more forceful in *day*, where it is initial, than it is in *grade*.) Such differences may be lost in rapid speech.

L

labial

A speech sound involving the active use of one or both lips.

The term is a rather general one. The lips are of course passively involved in all speech sounds, but the term *labial* is confined to those where one or both lips actually contribute to the articulation.

English labial consonants are usually more specifically described as BILABIAL (/p/, /b/, /m/) or LABIO-DENTAL.

As far as vowels are concerned, LIP POSITION is described in terms of *lip-rounding* and *lip-spreading*.

labio-dental

A place-of-articulation label for a consonant articulated with the lower lip and the (upper) teeth.

English has two labio-dental phonemes, the voiceless and voiced pair of fricatives:

/f/ as in *f*ine, *ph*otograph, enou*gh*
/v/ as in *v*ine, ne*ph*ew, o*f*

See p. 264 THE CONSONANTS OF ENGLISH.

labio-velar

Articulated with some lip-rounding and the tongue raised towards the velum. The English /w/ (as in *w*on, *o*ne, *wh*y, *qu*ick, *su*ite) is classified as a labio-velar SEMI-VOWEL.

See p. 264 THE CONSONANTS OF ENGLISH.

language

1 In the most general sense, the method of human communication, consisting of words, either spoken or written.

2 The language of a particular community or country, as in *the English language*, *the languages of the British Isles*, *Indo-European languages*, *Romance languages*.

These are all *natural languages*, in contrast to an artificial language or a computer language.

3 The style of an utterance or text, as in *bad language*, *graphic language*, *literary language*, *poetic language*.

4 The variety of language used in a particular profession or specialized context, e.g. *legal*, *religious*, *scientific language*; *the language of the law*; *the language of advertising*.

5 The earliest language that an individual learns to speak is his/her *first language* or *mother tongue* and he/she is a mother-tongue speaker or *native speaker* (though these terms are sometimes criticized).

The language of an individual is an IDIOLECT; that of a local region or community is its DIALECT.

laryngeal

Relating to the larynx, the hollow muscular organ situated in the upper part of the trachaea (the windpipe).

The importance of the larynx in the study of phonetics is that it contains the VOCAL CORDS, which produce voiced sounds when vibrated. Hence the popular name for the larynx, the 'voice box'.

See p. 266 THE SPEECH ORGANS.

lateral

A speech sound made with air escaping on one or both sides of the tongue.

Like the terms *stop* and *fricative*, *lateral* describes the manner, not the place, of an articulation. In RP there is a single lateral consonant phoneme, /l/, which is usually voiced and non-fricative. The tip of the tongue articulates with the centre of the alveolar ridge and air escapes on both sides.

There are two main allophones:

(*a*) *Clear l*: the front of the tongue, not merely the tip, is raised towards the hard palate, giving the sound a slightly front-vowel quality. Clear *l* is heard before vowels (e.g. in *leave*, *let*, *fill it*) and before /j/ (*failure*, *million*).

(*b*) *Dark l*: the tongue-tip again articulates with the teeth ridge, but the back of the tongue is somewhat raised, giving a back-vowel quality. Dark *l* is heard word-final after a vowel (e.g. *fill*, *oil*, *pale*); after a vowel and before a consonant (e.g. *help*, *else*, *although*); and in syllabic *l* (as in some pronunciations of *apple*, *final*, *camel*, etc.).

The Welsh sound, spelt *ll*, as in *Llangollen*, is a voiceless alveolar fricative lateral.

See p. 264 the consonants of english.

length

The relative time taken in the articulation of different sounds or syllables, and a listener's perception of them.

Traditionally the twelve 'pure' vowels of English are categorized as *long* or *short*. The long vowels (in standard RP English) are:

/iː/	green, heat, machine
/ɑː/	cart, heart, father
/ɔː/	cord, caught, saw, bought
/uː/	food, route, rude, blew
/ɜː/	herd, heard, sir, nurse, worse

The short vowels are

/ɪ/	bit, women, busy, hymn
/e/	bed, head, any
/æ/	hat
/ɒ/	hot, wash, laurel
/ʊ/	good, put
/ʌ/	hunt, love, blood
/ə/	moth*er*, *a*way

The long vowels are traditionally shown, as here, with the length mark [ː]. But in fact the differences between similar long and short vowels, as for example /iː/ and /ɪ/ in *beat* and *bit*, or /uː/ and /ʊ/ in *food* and *good* are differences of quality as well as length, so that it is now common, as here, to use different symbols. And sometimes length marks are dispensed with altogether.

An added complication is that length differences in actual articulation are conditioned by phonetic context. For example, the final voiceless /t/ in *beat* has a shortening effect on the preceding long vowel, whereas the short vowel in *bid*, being followed by a voiced consonant, is not shortened, with the result that the vowel lengths in these two words may be objectively the same.

A distinction can therefore be made between 'linguistic' length, as the listener perceives it, and 'real world' length (or *duration*), as acoustically measured.

lexeme

A word in an abstract sense, consisting of all the actual forms that belong to this word in a particular meaning. In ordinary usage, *word* has more than one sense, so that it is possible to say 'The five words (i) *see, sees, seeing, saw* and *seen* are different forms of the same word (ii)'. To distinguish these two meanings, word (i) is sometimes called a *form* or *word form*, and word (ii) a lexeme.

Identical forms with unrelated meanings (i.e. homonyms) are treated as separate lexemes, just as they are treated as different vocabulary items in a dictionary. Thus *see* (the area under the authority of a bishop or archbishop) is a different lexeme from *see* (discern with the eyes).

lexical

Relating to words. The term is extensively used in a fairly general sense, as in lexical AMBIGUITY, contrasted with grammatical ambiguity; or lexical MEANING, the dictionary meaning of a word, contrasted, say, with the emotional meaning it might have in a particular situation.

lexical verb

Any verb except a MODAL, AUXILIARY, or PRIMARY verb.

Lexical verbs (also called *full verbs*) constitute the majority of verbs. Formally, they use auxiliary verbs to form questions and negatives, and themselves always function as MAIN VERBS.

See p. 250 VERBS.

lexical word

The same as CONTENT WORD.

liaison

The linking together of words in connected speech, particularly when this involves what is felt to be an unusual phonetic feature. INTRUSIVE r and LINKING r are prime examples in English. Some speakers are so anxious to avoid an intrusive r that they use a vowel glide or insert a glottal stop even where a linking r would be natural, e.g. in *more and more*.

linguistics

The scientific study of language. This is a vast area of study, so in addition to *general* (or theoretical) *linguistics*, there are various specialist areas.

Diachronic linguistics studies a language over a period of time, in contrast to **synchronic linguistics**, which is concerned with a particular point in time.

Comparative (or **historical**) **linguistics** is diachronic. It studies the evolution of a single language (e.g. the development of English from Anglo-Saxon times) or the historical connections between languages (e.g. the way in which French, Italian, Spanish, and other Romance languages have developed from their common Latin origins).

The synchronic comparison of two languages (i.e. at the same period of time), for example modern English and German, or modern Spanish and Italian, is usually termed **contrastive linguistics**.

Applied linguistics is the practical application of linguistic studies in other areas, especially in the teaching of foreign languages.

linking r

The pronunciation of a written word-final r when the next word begins with a vowel.

In standard RP a written word-final *r* is not pronounced before a pause or before a following consonant sound. However, it is usually pronounced when the following word begins with a vowel (as in *Here it is* or *far away*).

link(ing) verb

A verb that semantically joins the rest of the predicate, particularly a noun or adjective complement, back to the subject. (Also called *copular verb*.)

The prime linking verb is *be*. But other verbs are used in a similar way, e.g.

> She's become a courier
> He's looking much better

See p. 250 VERBS.

linking word

An umbrella term for:

- (*a*) co-ordinating conjunctions (*and, but . . .*);
- (*b*) subordinating conjunctions (*although, because, when . . .*);
- (*c*) conjuncts (*in addition, moreover, meanwhile, nevertheless . . .*).

lip position

The position of the lips affects the quality of speech sounds, even when the lips are not primary articulators (as they are with BILABIAL and LABIO-DENTAL consonants). In particular, every English vowel has its own characteristic lip position, which may be described with terms such as *rounded, neutral,* or *spread*. For example, English /iː/ (as in *bead*) is usually said with *lip-spreading*; /ɑː/ (as in *hard*) is pronounced with the lips neutrally open; while /uː/ as in *boot* is a rounded vowel, said with *lip-rounding*.

loanward   See BORROWING.

logical gap See CONDITION.

long vowel See LENGTH.

lost consonant

A consonant that survives in the spelling but is no longer pronounced, as in gnome, *k*nife.

M

main clause

A clause that is not subordinate to any other clause.

Main clause is traditionally contrasted with SUBORDINATE CLAUSE. Thus in *I was ten when I got my scholarship*, the main clause is *I was ten* (and *when I got my scholarship* is a subordinate adverbial clause of time).

A main clause can usually stand alone as a complete sentence. So the coordinated clauses of a compound sentence are also main clauses, as in *I was ten and I got the scholarship*.

See p. 42 CLAUSES.

main verb

This is an ambiguous term, with several common meanings.

1 As a functional label, *main* contrasts with the functional meaning of AUXILIARY. So the final word or the sole word in an unellipted verb phrase is the main verb:

> Have you been *waiting* long?
> It may have been *forgotten*
> I *know* nothing about it
> What *is* the matter?

2 As the main verb (as defined in 1) is often realized by a LEXICAL (or *full* verb), the terms *main* and *lexical* are sometimes used as synonyms. By this definition *be*, *do*, and *have* are never main verbs.

3 Loosely, 'main verb' sometimes means the complete verb phrase in a main clause (e.g. It *may have been forgotten*).

See p. 250 VERBS.

major

Major has its usual meaning of 'more important than' something else; contrasted with *minor*.

For major part of speech, see p. 165 PARTS OF SPEECH.

For major sentence type, see p. 212 SENTENCE TYPES.

manner

A semantic category of adverbs and adverbials, consisting of those that answer the question 'How?'

Adverbs are traditionally classified by meaning, a fairly standard basic division being into *adverbs of place* (answering the question 'Where?'), *time* (When?), *manner* (How?), and *degree*.

Single-word *manner adverbs* are often derived from adjectives by adding *-ly* (e.g. *brightly*, *stupidly*, *quietly*) and are felt to be central or typical adverbs.

Clauses of manner usually imply comparison

> He looked / as if he had seen a ghost
> He speaks / just as /like his father always did

and so such clauses are sometimes classified as part of a *comparison* category. See p. 13 ADVERB CLAUSES.

manner of articulation

The method by which a speech sound is made, in terms of degrees and types of closure of the speech organs.

Manner of articulation, along with PLACE OF ARTICULATION, forms a major part of the framework used in describing the production of speech sounds, particularly consonants.

Among the different manners of closure involved in the production of consonants are PLOSIVE, AFFRICATE, NASAL, LATERAL, and FRICATIVE. See p. 264 THE CONSONANTS OF ENGLISH.

marginal

Marginal contrasts with CENTRAL in describing various language features.

The term is sometimes used of word meaning, where metaphorical meanings are said to be marginal, in contrast to basic or central meaning.

More usually the term is applied to members of a word class that only have some characteristics of that class—in contrast to CENTRAL members, e.g. marginal modal verb (the same as SEMI-MODAL), or marginal PREPOSITION.

marked

Any linguistic feature that is distinguished in some way from the basic or central form to which it is related is a marked form—and the basic form is therefore *unmarked.*

With nouns and verbs and other words that can be inflected, the base forms are said to be unmarked (e.g. *look, table, nice*) while inflected forms (*looked, looks, tables, nicer*) are marked for past, plural, comparative, and so on. Similarly, active voice is unmarked, the passive marked.

The concept of markedness can be applied in many other areas of language. Thus a simple declarative sentence (*I love Lucy*) is unmarked, whereas *I don't love Lucy* is marked for negation, and *Do you love Lucy?* is marked for interrogative. Similarly, *Lucy I love* has a marked word order (OSV) compared with the more usual unmarked SVO.

Markedness also applies in vocabulary. Thus, *horse* is unmarked for sex, whereas *stallion* and *mare* are marked. This type of marking is *semantic* marking. Other words exhibit formal marking, e.g. *hostess* (marked for female) v. *host*; *widower* (marked for male) v. *widow.* In a 'neutral' context the unmarked term in a pair is used. Thus in *old* versus *young*, *old* is the unmarked term (e.g. *How old is the baby?*)

masculine

Belonging to the grammatical gender that mainly denotes male persons and animals. Contrasted with FEMININE.

Traditionally, masculine pronouns and determiners can be used generically to refer to both men and women, but feminists object to this.

There are various avoidance strategies, including the use of *he or she, him or her,* etc., or, in writing only, *he/she* or *s/he,* etc. But these are clumsy conventions if repeated, and many people prefer to use sex-neutral *they*.

The use of *they* after indefinite pronouns is long established, although prescriptivists object that this breaks the rules of AGREE-MENT:

> Everyone is ready, are they?
> When you marry someone, you expect them to be there when you need them

In fact *they* is also sometimes used with reference to a single individual whose sex is known:

> A: Who was that on the phone?
> B: They didn't say—I think it was a wrong number

Whether *they* will ever be totally acceptable as a sex-neutral singular pronoun is impossible to say, but the emergence of *themself* in recent years suggests that some people are trying to achieve this. What is certain is that for some people masculine pronouns are always masculine and not 'unmarked'.

mass

In general, *mass noun* is exactly the same as UNCOUNT(ABLE) or *non-count* noun—one of the two main classes of common nouns, the other being COUNT (or *countable*).

Many English nouns seem to belong to both classes (e.g. *beer/ a beer*; *cloth/a cloth*; *ice/an ice*; *iron/an iron*; *paper/a paper*; *war/a war*).

One solution is to consider the words in such pairs to be two separate dictionary entries, but when the two meanings are close it seems preferable to talk of a single word with both mass and count usage. Hence terms like *mass usage*, *mass meaning*, and *mass interpretation* are sometimes introduced.

See p. 151 NOUNS.

meaning

Many different types of meaning are distinguished, and different classifications are made:

(*a*) DENOTATION is a general label for objective, factual meaning. Other terms used include *cognitive, descriptive, propositional*, and *referential*.

(*b*) CONNOTATION refers to more subjective and personal meaning, also described as *affective, attitudinal*, or *emotive*.

(*c*) Meaning as particularly involving social interaction is labelled *interpersonal, situational*, or *social*.

(*d*) LEXICAL meaning is concerned with the meaning of individual words as given in the dictionary—sometimes called 'dictionary meaning' or CENTRAL meaning.

(*e*) GRAMMATICAL (or STRUCTURAL) meaning is concerned with the meaning inherent in the grammar—for example, the meaning of tenses, the relationship of subject and object, the difference between declarative and interrogative.

means

A term used in the semantic analysis of adverbials and prepositions. Adverbials of means are usually contrasted with words expressing INSTRUMENT or AGENT, for example

We came *by train*
They got in *by breaking a window*

in contrast to

They got in *with a skeleton key* (instrument)
It was stolen *by a cat burglar* (agent)

medial

In the middle of a clause or other language unit.

(*a*) The term is particularly used to describe the position of adverbs, where it contrasts with INITIAL and FINAL positions. Broadly, medial position (or MID-POSITION) means between the subject and the verb:

The train *soon* gathered speed
I *hardly* think so

With verb phrases consisting of more than one word, several positions can be called medial. A common medial position is after the first auxiliary:

I have *definitely* made up my mind

but other medial positions may be possible:

He *definitely* had intended to go

It could have been *intentionally* overlooked

(*b*) Medial ellipsis (also called *gapping*) is a relatively rare type of
ELLIPSIS.

metalanguage

A form of language used to discuss language. Many of the head-
words used in this book are examples of metalanguage.

metaphor

Describing an object or action with a word or phrase that applies imaginatively but not literally (e.g. *a glaring error*, *a dirty
trick*).

Ordinary language is much more metaphorical than is commonly
realized. Thus even prepositions of time—*at* (the weekend), *on*
(Sunday), *in* (the morning)—are metaphorical applications of prepositions of space.

In a *mixed metaphor*, incongruous and incompatible terms are used
of the same object or event:

If we want to take part in the new space frontier, we must get in on the
ground floor. We have the key to the twenty-first century.

middle verb

An apparently transitive verb that does not normally occur in the
passive.

This term usefully classifies a small but distinct group of verbs such
as *have* in its possessive meaning, *consist of*, *lack*, *possess*, *resemble*,
and some other verbs in certain of their meanings, e.g.

*A house is had by us

*You are suited by blue

*I am not fitted by this jumper

*Twenty is equalled by 4 times 5

mid-position

Between subject and verb; medial.

Mid-position is a popular alternative to MEDIAL in describing the position of adverbs, and contrasts with INITIAL (or front) and FINAL (or end).

Frequency adverbs (*always, often, sometimes, never . . .*) as in *We always watch the news*) are 'mid-position adverbs'—though they can in fact appear in other positions.

minor

Less important or occurring less frequently, contrasted with MAJOR. The term is applied in its normal sense to certain PARTS OF SPEECH (p. 165), less usual SENTENCE TYPES (p. 212), and so on.

misrelated

Grammatically joined to a word or phrase that is not the one intended by the meaning.

Although terms such as *misrelated, dangling, hanging, unattached,* etc. are most commonly applied to participles, (see HANGING PARTICIPLE) verbless phrases can also be misrelated:

?*A rock-climber of some note*, there is a story, never denied, of how he tackled the treacherous mountain ridge by moonlight, dressed in his best suit

Here the first noun phrase refers back to someone mentioned in the previous sentence, and forward to the *he* of this one, but grammatically it is entirely unconnected to anything in the sentence.

modal verb

A particular type of auxiliary verb that expresses MOOD. (Also called *modal auxiliary* or *modal operator*.)

(*a*) Modals are formally unlike other verbs. In particular they have no *s* forms, infinitives, or participles; they do not have a range of tenses formed with *be* or *have*; they make questions by inversion, and negatives by adding *not* or *n't*; and they are always auxiliaries.

MODAL VERBS AT A GLANCE

FORM:

Central modals:	can, could, may, might, must, shall, should, will, would
negation—add n't/not	can't, may not, shouldn't, etc.
questions—invert	could I?, will you?, etc.
Semi-modals:	dare, need, ought to, used to
negation and questions	some formed like modals and some like ordinary lexical verbs

MEANING: *possibility* <———————> *necessity*

1 **influencing**
   behaviour (deontic)   permission <—> (advice) <—> duty, obligation
2 **theorising** (epistemic)   possibility <–> (likelihood) <–> certainty
3 **factual** (dynamic)   *ability*   and   *willingness*
                            (can/could)   (will/would)

EXAMPLES:

Influencing behaviour (1)	**Theorizing** (2)	**Factual** (3)
Please *can* I borrow the car?	You *can't* mean that!	I *can't* run as fast . . .
Could I make a suggestion?	I *could* be wrong	. . . as I *could* when I was young
You *may* borrow it, if you promise to bring it back by midnight	If I were younger, I *could*	
	It *may* be raining tomorrow	
	That *may* be Tom on the phone	
I don't like that, if I *might* venture an opinion	It *might* be better to say nothing	
You *will* do as you're told	That *will* be Tom on the phone	Tom *will* often go swimming before breakfast
Of course I *will* help you (promise)	No good *will* come of this	
You *shall* have my reply by Friday	This time next week I *shall* be on holiday	
You *should* pay attention	The eclipse *should* be visible if the cloud lifts	
Would you just wait a minute, please!	Where *would* we be without it?	As children we *would* often hide in the old barn
You *must* repay the money	They *must* have forgotten	

There are also several SEMI-MODALS (marginal modals) which are partly like modals and partly like ordinary lexical verbs.

(*b*) Meaning. In very general terms, the central modals (plus *ought to* and *need*) express a range of meanings on a single scale, with possibility (*can*) at one end, and necessity (*must*) at the other. But this scale conceals two rather different uses. For example, out of context *Tom may keep the money* is ambiguous. Perhaps Tom's mother is giving permission, perhaps she is guessing. Most of the other modals are similarly versatile. So modal meaning can be divided into two:

1 The speaker is in some way hoping to influence behaviour—with *can* and *may* giving permission, through *should* (advice) and other expressions (about duty and obligation), to a firm order or prohibition (*must*, *mustn't*). The specialist name is DEONTIC meaning.

2 The speaker is theorizing—with *may* expressing a mild guess, through varying degrees of likelihood and probability to *must* and *can't* as near certainty (EPISTEMIC meaning).

A third modal use is called DYNAMIC, and it only applies to *can*, *could* (for 'ability') and *will* and *would* (for a sort of strong insistence and habit).

Dynamic modals make factual statements, e.g.

> She can read a novel in an evening
> A cat will sit in front of a fire for hours

Contrast

> You can borrow my paper if you like (permission)
> Can this really be true? (theorizing)
> What will your Mother say? (predict!)

Unlike other modals that are apparently past in form but that do not—except in some subordinate clauses—refer to past time (e.g. *might*, *should*, *ought to*), dynamic *would* and *could* refer to real past time:

> She could already read and write when she was four
> Even as a small child she would sit reading for hours

See p. 137 MODAL VERBS.

modification

A word that affects the meaning of another more important word in the same phrase is said to *modify* it.

Modification is particularly important in noun phrase structure, where it may be

PREMODIFICATION as in *The Third* Man
POSTMODIFICATION as in Travels *with my Aunt*
a mixture of both as in *Our* Man *in Havana*

Other sentence elements, apart from noun phrases, may be modified, and adverbs frequently function as *modifiers* of other words, e.g. *really* useful (+ adjective), *very* badly (+ another adverb), *almost* everyone (+ pronoun), *right* at the end (+ prepositional phrase).

Modifiers that come before their head are *premodifiers* (*too* warm); those that follow are *postmodifiers* (warm *enough*).

In traditional grammar an adverb(ial) in clause structure is sometimes said to be the modifier of the verb; hence the name adverb.

monophthong

A vowel in which there is no change in the position of the vocal organs during articulation, in contrast to a DIPHTHONG. English vowels of this type are usually referred to as *pure* vowels.

See p. 265 THE SOUNDS OF ENGLISH.

monosyllabic

A word having only one syllable is monosyllabic. The term is particularly used in describing the formation of the comparative and superlative of adjectives, because almost all monosyllabic adjectives (if they are gradable) can inflect, e.g. *kind/-er/-est*.

It is also a useful term to describe the pronunciation of some two-syllable words that are frequently pronounced monosyllabically—e.g. /pliːs/ for *police*.

monotransitive

Monotransitive verbs take one and only one object, in contrast to INTRANSITIVE or DITRANSITIVE verbs, e.g.

avoid the traffic, *raise* money

mood

1 One of the formal categories into which verbs forms are classified, depending on whether the verb is expressing fact, command, etc. Traditionally we speak of INDICATIVE, IMPERATIVE, and SUBJUNCTIVE moods. See p. 250 VERBS.

2 A distinction of meaning expressed by any one of the chief sentence types. In this definition INTERROGATIVE joins INDICATIVE and IMPERATIVE as a mood category. See p. 212 SENTENCE TYPES.

morpheme

Morpheme is a word with two related but different meanings.

1 The smallest meaningful unit of grammar. As a unit of meaning, the morpheme is an abstraction (comparable to the phoneme). Thus, 'the plural morpheme' is realized in regular nouns by three different ALLOMORPHS (/-s/, /-z/, and /-ɪz/) and in other ways in irregular plurals such as *men*, *mice*, and *sheep*.

2 The smallest unit in word formation and morphology. Here the morpheme has an actual physical shape. In this definition *looked* and *forgotten* each consist of two morphemes, *look* + *ed*, *forgot(t)* + *en*. But whereas in definition (1) *-ed* and *-en* are variants of the same (abstract) 'past participle morpheme', in this second definition *-ed* and *-en* are two different morphemes.

morphology

The study of word formation.

Morphology covers two main types of word formation—INFLECTION, concerned with changes to 'the same word' for grammatical reasons (e.g. number, tense) and DERIVATION, which is concerned with the formation of NEW WORDS.

multiple

More than one, several. This is a very general term and is applied in many areas of grammar.

• **multiple analysis**: grammar is not always a straightforward matter of right and wrong. Sometimes we can analyse a phrase or structure in different but acceptable ways. For example if we look at sentences containing the structure verb + preposition + noun, most people would analyse

I waited at the bus-stop

as subject + verb + adverbial (*Where* did you wait? *At the bus-stop*). On the other hand, an apparently similar sentence

I looked at the time-table

although it could be analysed like that, would probably be analysed as subject + verb (*look at*) + object (*What* did you look at? *The timetable*).

- **multiple meaning**: see HOMONYM
- **multiple modification**: more than one premodification or post-modification combined. Sometimes such multiple modification is in sequence (though there may well be a preferred order), e.g.

    the lady / *over there* / *in the green hat*

Sometimes one modifier modifies another, as in *poor quality leather*, where *poor* premodifies *quality*, and then *poor quality* premodifies leather. (Contrast *beautiful black leather* where the premodifiers are simply in sequence.)

- **multiple sentence**: an umbrella term for COMPLEX, COMPOUND, and COMPOUND-COMPLEX sentences.

multi-word verb

A verb + a PARTICLE functioning as a single verb. This is an umbrella term that covers PHRASAL VERBS, PREPOSITIONAL VERBS, and PHRASAL-PREPOSITIONAL VERBS.

multiplier

A determiner with a 'multiplying' meaning, e.g.

twice the price
three times that amount

N

name

A word or words referring to a particular and identifiable person, place, book, event, etc. (e.g. *Winston*, *Bermuda*).

The term *name* (or *proper name*) is loosely used interchangeably with PROPER NOUN, but a distinction can be made. A name can extend beyond single words (*Winston Churchill*); can include ordinary words (*the Bermuda Triangle*, *South America*); and may even contain no proper noun at all (*the North Pole*, *the Red Sea*, *War and Peace*, *the Second World War*).

nasal

A speech sound made with an audible escape of air through the nose, in contrast to an ORAL sound.

English has three nasals, all of them consonant phonemes:

> bilabial /m/, as in *more*, *whim*, *hammer*
> alveolar /n/, as in *no*, *,win*, *hand*
> velar /ŋ/, the sound represented by *ng* in wi*ng* and *n* in wi*nk* (and never word-initial in English)

Other English phonemes are sometimes pronounced with some nasal quality, under the influence of adjoining sounds, e.g. the vowel in *man*.

A 'nasal twang', as a label for an individual speaker's above-average nasal accent, is a colloquial term and not recognized in phonetics.

See p. 264 THE CONSONANTS OF ENGLISH.

nationality word

Nouns (and related adjectives) referring to members of nations or ethnic groups are to some extent treated like *proper nouns*, being written with an initial capital. But like common nouns, nationality nouns are countable and can have specific and generic reference.

The commonest type has the singular noun identical to the adjective, and adds *-s* for plural, e.g. *an Italian, Italians, the Italians*.

There are however many variations. (Think about *English, Scots, Welsh, Irish*!)

negative

(*a*) *Negative* is the opposite of AFFIRMATIVE (or positive), and means denying that something is the case. Typically an English clause or sentence is *negated* by adding *not* or *n't* to a primary verb or to the first (or only) auxiliary, or by using *do* as an auxiliary:

> This *is not* difficult
> He *couldn't* have been thinking
> It *doesn't* matter

Generally the 'scope' of the *negation* extends from the negative word to the end of the clause, so there is a difference in meaning between such pairs as:

> I didn't ask you to go; I asked you not to go
> They aren't still here; They still aren't here

Sentences may also be negated through the use of other negative words:

> There is *nothing* to do (*compare* There isn't anything to do)
> It's *no* trouble (*compare* It isn't any trouble)
> *Nobody* told me (*compare* They didn't tell me/I wasn't told)

(*b*) In general, only one negative word is needed in a clause, so a DOUBLE NEGATIVE (*There is*n't nothing* to do, *Nobody told me *nothing*) is ungrammatical in standard English.

Similarly, SEMI-NEGATIVE words (sometimes called *near negatives*) do not require a further negative word (*He barely said nothing).

(*c*) A negative affix makes a word negative, but not the whole sentence:

> Perhaps they will sign a *non*-aggression pact

● **transferred negation**: putting a negative in the main clause, when more logically it belongs in the subordinate clause. This commonly happens with verbs of opinion:

I don't think you understand (= I think you don't understand)
It doesn't look as if they're coming now (= It looks as if they are not coming)

neologism

The coining of a NEW WORD or expression, or such a word or expression itself. See p. 145.

neuter

This is a grammatical GENDER term contrasting with *masculine* and *feminine*. It is applicable in a language such as Latin or German, but not applicable in English.

neutral vowel

This is another name for the central weak vowel /ə/, which is usually referred to as SCHWA.

new word

New words (or *neologisms*) have a variety of sources, but most of them are formed in some way by *analogy* with existing patterns of word formation. Thus the majority of new words are either *derived* from existing words by the addition of affixes (e.g. *deaccession*, *fattism*) or else formed by joining two words together (*compounding*), as in *drink-driving*.

A few new words are due to *back formation*, where a word is formed from an existing word by the omission of a real or supposed affix (e.g. *ovate* from *ovation*).

Nonce words (strictly, words coined for a particular occasion) mainly follow regular patterns of word formation—whether well established in the standard vocabulary (e.g. *international*), or less likely to last (e.g. *pigeonicide*).

Words formed by joining morphemes derived from different languages, e.g. *speedometer* (English *speed* + Greek *-(o)meter*) are sometimes stigmatized as *hybrids*.

NEW WORDS

....

Analogy (with existing patterns of word formation)

derivation:

(prefix + word)   deselect, disinvest, Eurolaw
(word + suffix)   fattism, Greenery, yuppify

compounding:

cashpoint, cotton-rich, drink-driving, homeshopping, power
dressing, user-friendly

back formation:

burgle (from burglar), informate (from information), ovate (from
ovation)

hybrid:

speedometer, television

....

Abbreviation of existing words

acronym: NIMBY (= not in my backyard)

radar (= radio detection and ranging)

blend: camcorder (camera + recorder), fanzine (fan + magazine),
guesstimate (guess + estimate), televangelist (television +
evangelist)

clipping: cred(ibility), sitcom (situation comedy)

....

Conversion: a retread (noun from verb), to doorstep (verb from
noun), average (adj. from noun)

....

New meaning for old word: mouse (= small device for controlling the
cursor on a VDU screen)
wicked (= marvellous)

....

Borrowing (loanword): glasnost, intifada, karaoke

....

Onomatopoeia: bebop, gobbledygook

....

Nonce: agnostic, international, serendipity
?Eurosclerosis, oldcomer, pigeonicide, user-hostile

....

Other types of new words based on existing words are various kinds of abbreviations, such as *acronyms*, *blends*, and *clippings*.

Conversion, where one part of speech gets used as another (e.g. to *doorstep*, a verb from a noun), and even the use of an existing word with a strikingly different meaning, also count as neologism.

Borrowings (or *loanwords*) from foreign languages are the big exception to words formed by analogy, but even these may be Anglicized and given regular English inflections.

A very minor source of new words is *onomatopoeia*—the new word is meant to express the sound of what is referred to, e.g. *bebop*, *gobbledygook*.

There are also some words of unknown origin, e.g. *dweeb* (= nerd, wimp).

nominal

Nominal means 'noun-like' and can be used of any word, phrase, or clause when it is functioning like a noun or noun phrase in a particular context.

Various parts of speech sometimes have a nominal function. For example, in *The great and the good don't want to know*, *the great and the good* is nominal, functioning as the subject, but *great* and *good* are adjectives, not nouns.

nominal clause

A clause functioning like a noun, popularly called NOUN CLAUSE. See p. 152.

nominalization

A noun formed from another part of speech has been *nominalized* from it. For example: driver, from *drive*; examinee, from *examine*; shrinkage, from *shrink*; accuracy, from *accurate*; kindness, from *kind*.

Similarly, a clause can be nominalized, and turned into a noun phrase. For example, *talking heads* or *her determination to succeed* can be thought of as nominalizations of 'heads talk' and 'she is determined to succeed'.

nominal relative clause

This kind of clause is not differentiated from other kinds of nominal (noun) clause in popular grammar. Like any noun clause, it functions as a subject, object, etc. in a sentence. It gets its name because it also contains a relative *wh*-word. However, this *wh*-word not only introduces its own clause (as in an ordinary relative clause); it also stands for an antecedent absent from the preceding clause. Compare

> I don't know *why it happened* (nominal clause)
> I don't know anything *that would help* (relative clause)
> I don't know *what happened* (nominal relative clause) (= I don't know *that* [*which happened*])

Unlike other nominal clauses, a nominal relative clause can refer to people or things:

> *Whoever told you that* was wrong (= *The person* [*who* told you that] was wrong)

See p. 152 NOUN CLAUSES.

nominative

In older grammar, nouns and pronouns used as the subject of the verb were said to be in the nominative case. But SUBJECT is the preferred term today. See p. 38 CASE.

non-assertive

A word that tends to be restricted to questions, negative contexts, and other tentative statements is a non-assertive word, in contrast to ASSERTIVE words.

Non-assertive words include the *any*-series of words (e.g. *any*, *anyone*, *anywhere*) in contrast to words in the *some*-series, plus

either: Jane didn't know either (*compare* Jane knew too)
ever: Have you ever had a winter holiday? (*compare* I always have a winter holiday)
far: How far is it? Not far (*compare* It's a long way)
much: There isn't much food left (*compare* There's a lot of food left)
yet: Haven't you finished yet? (*compare* I have already finished)

nonce word

A word deliberately coined on a particular occasion, though possibly now a common word. For example, Horace Walpole coined *serendipity* (1754), Jeremy Bentham gave us *international* (1780), and more recently Dr M. Gell-Mann gave the name *quark* (1964) to a subatomic particle.

The term is sometimes loosely used for jocular-sounding words that seem unlikely to last long, e.g. *jocumentary, oldcomer, trendicrat*.

See p. 145 NEW WORDS.

non-defining

A *non-defining relative clause* gives additional information about the noun phrase to which it belongs but does not define it, because the noun phrase is already identified. (Also called *non-restrictive*.)

See p. 205 RELATIVE CLAUSES.

Other words, e.g. adjectives, that give additional information about a person or thing already defined can be described as non-defining, as in *your dear father*.

non-finite

A verb form or clause without tense is non-finite, in contrast to FINITE.

The term covers the INFINITIVE, e.g. *(to) look, (to) know*; and both PARTICIPLES, e.g. *looking, knowing, looked, known*.

A *non-finite clause* is a clause whose verb is non-finite (whether an infinitive or an *-ing* or *-en* participle), e.g.

> *To expect a refund* is unreasonable
> All he ever does is *complain*
> *Having said that*, I still hope he gets one
> *If consulted*, I would have advised against

A non-finite clause may function as an integral sentence element (as in the first two examples here), or as a separate subordinate clause (as in the third and fourth). A non-finite clause may contain its own logical subject:

> *For him to expect* a refund is unreasonable

See p. 42 CLAUSES.

non-past

This is a useful alternative term for *present* in the discussion of tenses. It emphasizes that the so-called present tenses do not necessarily refer to present time.

Present tenses sometimes actually refer to the immediate present (*Yes, I am listening*; *yes, I promise*) and often to a more extended present period (*She works in Cambridge*; *She's living with friends*). Other uses have a sort of timeless reference (e.g. *Ice melts when you heat it*; *Shakespeare says . . .*) and others clearly refer to the future (*Are you coming tomorrow? When can I see you?*).

What all these uses have in common is that they are *unmarked* for past. Compare p. 237 TIME AND TENSE.

non-personal

A meaning-based classification for describing the meaning of any noun or pronoun when it refers to any non-human being or thing or abstraction.

This is a particularly useful classification when dealing with the so-called PERSONAL PRONOUNS and the pronouns *who* and *which*. Pronouns that normally relate to people (*he/him*, *she/her*, *who/whom*) may have *non-personal* reference to animals or even things (e.g. *this ship and all who sail in her*), while *it* and *which* (usually referring to 'things') may refer to people (*A child needs its mother*; *Which of my cousins do you mean?*).

It should also be noted that the personal pronouns *they* and *them* have both personal and non-personal reference.

non-sentence

A non-sentence is a sequence of words functioning like a complete sentence, but lacking normal clause structure. This is not a clearly defined concept and other terms are *irregular sentence* or *minor sentence*.

You and your headaches!	Nice one, Norman!
You fool	Of all the daft things to do!
Whatever next?	No way .

Non-sentences include formulae and interjections.

notional

Notional essentially means 'based on meaning', but several different contrasts are made, and it can be a term of praise or abuse.

• **notional grammar** is sometimes used to describe older, traditional grammar, in which, for example, parts of speech were defined in terms of meaning ('A verb is a doing word') rather than by syntax. *Notional* in this sense contrasts with FORMAL or GRAMMATICAL (good!) and today is often used to suggest 'sloppy', 'inaccurate'.

However, when applied to syllabuses for teaching a foreign language, notional is often a term of praise, since such teaching is held to be based on communicative meaning rather than arid (and now bad!) FORMAL syllabuses.

• **notional concord** (e.g. *Neither of them have arrived*) contrasts with GRAMMATICAL concord. It is considered ungrammatical by prescriptivists, but is acceptable to modern grammarians.

noun

A word that belongs to the WORD CLASS that inflects for plural, that can function as subject or object in a sentence, can be preceded by articles and adjectives, and can be the object of a preposition.

In traditional grammar, a noun is defined notionally as 'the name of a person, place, or thing'. But this definition only partly works; abstract nouns like *criticism* or *tolerance* are hardly things, and it is syntax, not meaning, that decides that *think* is a verb in one sentence (*I must think*) and a noun in another (*I'll have a think*). Modern grammarians therefore prefer more formal syntactical definitions.

Nouns are divided on grounds of syntax and meaning into PROPER nouns and COMMON nouns. Common nouns are further divided for grammatical reasons into count and uncount nouns. The division into abstract and concrete is based on meaning and cuts across the count/uncount division.

Popular grammars often refer to what is strictly speaking a noun phrase (e.g. *a room*, *a room with a view*) as a noun.

NOUNS AT A GLANCE

....

PROPER NOUN: Elizabeth, Scotland, the Mississippi, Cairo, the Andes . . .

proper name: the United States of America, the Tropic of Capricorn, the Red Sea, the United Kingdom, *The Times, War and Peace*.

....

COMMON NOUN:

countable: *abstract*: crime, law, problem . . .
              concrete: animal, gun, mask . . .

uncount(able)   *abstract*: heritage, news, physics
  or **non-count:**   *concrete*: earth, seawater

....

PLURAL FORMS OF COUNT NOUNS

regular: hats, proofs, boxes . . .
irregular: children, mice, feet, knives . . .
  zero: deer, sheep . . .
  foreign: crises, errata, formulae, stimuli . . .

....

CASE

common case: boy, child, boys, children
genitive (or
  possessive) case: boy's, child's, boys', children's

....

OTHER TERMS USED ABOUT NOUNS

collective noun: This army/committee/family is/are . . .
        These armies/committees/families are . . .

group noun: [Usually the same as *collective noun*, but sometimes used for a noun not used in the plural]: The Treasury believes/believe that . . .

partitive noun: [The same as unit noun.]
plural-only noun   [taking only plural verbs]
  (a) (*binary*)   These scissors/trousers are . . .
  (b)   clothes, thanks . . .
        cattle, people, police
  (c)   arms (= weapons), regards (= best wishes)
'plural in form'   [but with singular verb]: physics, measles, billiards
        This news is . . .

unit noun: (or   a *blade* of grass, a *pat* of butter . . .
partitive)

....

NOUN CLAUSES AT A GLANCE

....

FUNCTION

subject:	*That you have my full support* goes without saying
	Why he did it remains a mystery
object:	He alleges *(that) he doesn't remember a thing*
	I wonder *whether the police know*
complement:	The question is *how we should proceed*
complement of adjective:	I'm not sure *if/whether we should report this*
complement of preposition:	It depends on *who else knows*
apposition:	The question, *whether this is a criminal matter*, is not easy to answer

....

FORM

that-clause:	*That you don't know* is no excuse
	I am surprised *(that) you didn't ask*
	They said *(that) it was all my fault*
	The suggestion, *that I was to blame for it*, annoyed me
wh-clause:	*Why it mattered* was not explained
	It's now a question of *how we can proceed*
	They asked me *what I was going to do next*

Nominal relative clauses:

    What happened is a mystery (= *That* [*which* happened] is a mystery)

    Whoever told you that was wrong (= The *person* [*who* told you] was wrong)

    So that's *who you were talking about* (= So that is *the person* [*who* you were talking about])

    Please do *whatever you think best* (= Please do *that* [*which* you think best])

....

NOUN CLAUSES IN REPORTED SPEECH

reported statement:	They said *(that) I was to blame*
compare:	They said: 'You are to blame'
reported questions:	They asked me *what I was going to do next*
	They wanted to know *if/whether I had any plans*
compare:	They asked: 'What are you going to do next?'
	They said: 'Have you any plans?'

....

noun clause

A clause functioning like a noun. (Also called a *nominal clause*.)

A noun clause, like a noun or noun phrase, can function as subject, object, or complement in sentence structure. It can also function as the complement of an adjective or of a preposition, or be in apposition to a noun.

Many noun clauses are introduced by the conjunction *that* or by a *wh*-word, giving rise to such terms as *that-clause* and *wh-clause*. Such clauses when they follow a reporting verb produce *reported speech*. Reported questions can begin with any *wh*-word (including *how, when, where,* and *whether*) and also with *if*.

In the NOMINAL RELATIVE CLAUSE, a *wh*-word has a double function. It is a relative pronoun and it also stands for an element not present in the preceding clause. But the distinction is not always clear, and popular grammar often ignores the difference.

noun phrase

A word or group of words functioning in a sentence exactly like a noun, with a noun or pronoun as HEAD.

A *noun phrase* (NP for short) can be a noun or pronoun alone, but is frequently a noun or pronoun with pre- and/or post-modification: *the name, an odd name, the name of the game, the name he gave.*

See p. 176 PHRASES.

nucleus

This is an important term in the analysis of intonation. The *nucleus* is the one essential element in a TONE UNIT, the place where the PITCH change occurs. Even a single-syllable tone unit (e.g. *Right!* or *Yes?*) has a nucleus. A single word without marked pitch would be interpreted as an incomplete utterance.

number

1 A grammatical classification used in the analysis of word classes which have contrasts of SINGULAR and PLURAL.

Number contrasts in English are seen in nouns (*boy/boys*), pronouns (*she/they, this/these*), determiners (*this/these, each/all*), and verbs (*say/says, was/were*).

2 A NUMERAL (e.g. *one, two, three; first, second . . .*).

numeral

As the word NUMBER is used as a grammatical category, *numeral* is often the preferred word for discussing the CARDINAL series (*one, two, three*, etc.) and the ORDINALS (*first, second, third*, etc.)

In traditional grammar, numerals (numbers) may be treated as a subclass of adjectives ('numeral adjectives') or be divided between adjectives and pronouns. Modern grammar prefers to treat numerals as determiners (strictly POSTDETERMINERS) and as pronouns.

O

object

1 By itself *object* usually means the DIRECT OBJECT of the verb, e.g.

> We've bought *a flat*, although we really wanted *a house*

It contrasts with INDIRECT OBJECT.

2 In modern analyses, object is one of the five elements in clause structure (along with Subject, Verb, Complement, and Adverbial). In this use, both *direct object* (DO) and *indirect object* (IO) may be represented by a single O. Thus the following is an SVOO sentence:

> We / have bought / Mother / a flat

A direct object may also take the form of a finite or non-finite clause:

> She / said / *(that) she was delighted*   (SVO)
> We / told / her / *not to worry*   (SVOO)

3 *Object* (or *objective*) case is the case taken by pronouns that are morphologically marked when not in subject position. In English there are only six distinct object (or *objective*) pronouns— *me*, *her*, *him*, *us*, *them*, *whom*. Contrasted with *subject(ive)* pronouns.

4 Object of a preposition: a word or words following a preposition (e.g. a bundle of *nerves*). Words following a prepositional verb (e.g. *look after*, *wait for*) are sometimes included here, but sometimes called a *prepositional object* (e.g. Look after *your wallet*).

For *object complement*: see COMPLEMENT.
For *objective genitive*: see GENITIVE.

object territory

Any noun phrase position after the verb. Contrasted with SUBJECT TERRITORY.

The term has been coined partly to explain the use of object pronouns in such contexts as

That's *him*

You were quicker than *me*

Prescriptive grammarians want subject pronouns here (i.e. after the verb *be* and where a clause with subject pronoun could follow (e.g. . . . *than I was.*) But object pronouns are normal and acceptable English here.

of-construction

The terms *of-construction* and also *of-phrase* are used somewhat loosely, and may mean a phrase consisting of a noun + *of* + another noun, or just the second (*of* + noun) part.

Some *of*-constructions have some sort of possession meaning, and are often interchangeable with the genitive case, e.g. *my grandparents' house/the house of my grandparents, the West End of London/London's West End*. This use can be called the *of*-genitive.

But the *of*-construction has other meanings and is sometimes essential, e.g. *the end of the road, a book of verse, an object of ridicule, a man of honour, few of those people.*

of-pronoun

An *of*-pronoun is a pronoun that can be followed by a PARTITIVE *of*-phrase, e.g.

few (of those people), *much* (of the time), *some* (of our problems)

omission

Leaving sounds out of words, and words out of sentences is a regular feature of language, and language might be rather tedious if we did not do this. The table shows some of the acceptable ways in which this is done.

OMISSION

OMISSION OF SOUNDS AND SYLLABLES FROM WORDS

blend:	brunch (breakfast + lunch) . . .
clipping:	ad(vertisement), sitcom (situation comedy) . . .
contraction (short form):	I've, don't, let's . . .
elision:	(1) *established*—gnome, whis*t*le, lam*b* . . .
	(2) *current*—fact(o)ry, med(i)cine, p(o)lice . . .
initialism:	BBC [= British Broadcasting Corporation]
	p.t.o. [please turn over]
	UN [United Nations]
written abbreviation:	Dr (Doctor), St (saint, street), etc. (etcetera)

OMISSION OF WORDS FROM CLAUSES AND SENTENCES

block language:		Danger: Falling Rocks
labels:		Contains no additives
instructions:		Bring to boil
headlinese:		Jailed Racing Driver's Bail Request Rejected
ellipsis	*initial*:	▲ You all right?
	medial	I had coffee, and the children ▲ ice
	(gapping):	creams
	final:	I'm all right, but Jack isn't ▲
reduction:	[a general term relating to ellipsis and substitution]	
reduced clause:		
	If ⟨it is⟩ *possible*, you should be here by six.	
	There's a man ⟨who is⟩ *waving at us over there*.	
understood: ⟨You⟩ Be quiet!		

See also SUBSTITUTION

---

onomatopoeia See SOUND SYMBOLISM.

---

operator

Operator describes the function of the first word in a verb phrase, the word that 'operates' various mechanisms, and which in particular can

add *not* (or *n't*) for negation
invert with the subject for questions
stand for a whole phrase (e.g. I hoped they would lend me the money, but they *wouldn't* ▲)

This in fact means that only a modal verb, or *be*, *have*, and *do* can be an operator, because a verb phrase consisting of a single lexical verb (e.g. He *knows*) has to use *do* as an operator:

They *could* have been imagining things

I *was* wondering

Are you sure?

Have you heard the news?

I *haven't* a clue

Does he know?

He *doesn't* know

Modal auxiliaries therefore always function as operators, and lexical verbs never do. Of the primary verbs, *be* is always an operator by this definition (whether used as an auxiliary verb or a main verb) and *have* often is, but not when it uses *do* (*He doesn't have much fun*). *Do* is an operator for other verbs, but as a main verb it behaves like any other lexical verb and needs an extra *do* as operator (**I didn't the housework. *Did you the dishes?*).

oral

Relating to the mouth, but with two different meanings.

1 As a phonetic term, oral contrasts with NASAL. All normal English sounds, except for the three nasal consonants are oral, because they are made with air 'escaping' through the mouth.

2 Oral meaning 'spoken' contrasts with 'written'. Oral competence, for example, may be contrasted with writing ability.

ordinal

Ordinal numbers relate to position in a series. E.g. *first*, *second*, *third* . . . in contrast to CARDINAL numbers.

orthography

The study or science of how words are spelt.

English spelling is largely standardized, which means most words only have one correct spelling. But there are some cases where variants are acceptable, e.g.

cipher/cypher, hallo/hello, mateyness/matiness, standardise/standardize

There are also some distinct British and American spellings, e.g.

centre/center, colour/color, sceptical/skeptical, travelling/traveling

• **orthographic word**: a word as written or printed. In general a word as commonly understood is written with spaces on either side, although there is variation with COMPOUNDS. There are also problems sometimes with the use of the apostrophe. An advertisement some years ago said:

> Four little words that can cost a tobacconist £400
>
> THEY'RE FOR MY MUM

They're for many people is two words, but it is a single orthographic word, so the advertisement is correct by the definition given here.

overcorrection

The same as HYPERCORRECTION.

palatal

The hard bony part of the roof of the mouth is the *palate*, and the *soft palate* further back in the mouth is the VELUM.

In a palatal speech sound the front of the tongue articulates with the hard palate. Standard (RP) English has one phoneme made like this—the sound /j/, which is heard at the beginning of *yes* / jes / or *useful* /juːsf(ə)l/ and before the vowel in *cure* /kj../. This is normally classified as a SEMI-VOWEL, and not as a consonant.

See p. 264 THE CONSONANTS OF ENGLISH.

palato-alveolar

In a palato-alveolar speech-sound the tip (or tip and blade) of the tongue articulates with the alveolar ridge, while at the same time the front of the tongue (the part behind the tip and blade) is raised towards the hard palate.

English has two pairs of palato-alveolar consonants, each consisting of one voiceless and one voiced phoneme:

(*a*) the palato-alveolar affricates

/tʃ/ as in *church*, na*t*ure
/dʒ/ as in *judge*, *g*eneral

(*b*) the palato-alveolar fricatives

/ʃ/ as in *shop*, ma*ch*ine, *s*ugar
/ʒ/ (never word initial in English) as in u*s*ual, presti*g*e

See p. 264 THE CONSONANTS OF ENGLISH.

paradigm

1 A set of word forms produced by inflection from a single base form. For example, *see, sees, seeing, saw, seen*, constitute a paradigm.

2 Any set of words or phrases that are in an *or-relationship* (or *choice* relationship) with each other can also constitute a paradigm, in contrast to members of a SYNTAGM, which are in an *and-relationship* or CHAIN.

Thus the English article system and the pronoun systems are both paradigms. We can say *a book* or *the book*, but not **a the book*. Similarly we can grammatically substitute one pronoun for another in *I told the truth* (e.g. I/You/He/She/We/They/Somebody, etc.) but we cannot choose more than one pronoun unless they are coordinated (*You and I told the truth*).

paragraph

A distinct section of a piece of writing, beginning on a new, and often indented, line.

Although the way a text is set out on the page may be an important factor in its intelligibility, the paragraph as such has no grammatical status comparable to that of a phrase, clause, or sentence.

paraphrase

A sentence (or other piece of text) that expresses the 'same' meaning as another in a different way is a paraphrase of it. But although objective (denotative) meaning may be preserved, most paraphrases change the emphasis of the message in some way.

parenthesis (plural parentheses)

A word, clause, or sentence inserted as an explanation or afterthought into a passage which is grammatically complete without it. In writing, parentheses are usually marked by a pair of round brackets ( ), which can also be called parentheses, or by dashes or commas.

parse

To *parse* means to describe each word in a sentence grammatically, stating what part of speech it is, and its relation to the sentence as a whole. Parsing as an exercise is unfashionable, but analysing clause and sentence structure is the basis of grammar.

participial adjective

An adjective having the same form as the participle of a verb, e.g. *loving* friends, *exciting* times, *alarming* symptoms, *frozen* assets, *hurt* feelings, a *knitted* suit.

Participial adjectives also include words formed with a participial ending, but which lack a corresponding verb. These are called *pseudo-participles*, e.g.

half-hearted effort, *three-cornered* hat
talented musicians, *wooded* slopes, *unexpected* pleasure
breathtaking views, *unconvincing* excuses

Some *-ing* forms are of course noun-like, and not participles or adjectives at all, e.g. *dining room*, *planning permission*.

Participial forms with complete adjectival status can, if they are gradable, take *very* (which verbs do not).

Contrast

They are very loving (adjectival)
They are loving every minute of it (verb + object)

The distinction between adjectival and verbal use is not, however, always clear. Occasionally an attributively used past participle may be analysed as verbal and active. For example, an *escaped prisoner* is 'a prisoner who has escaped' rather than one who 'has been escaped by someone'. And in some contexts the status of a participle-like form is ambiguous. *I was annoyed* can be interpreted verbally (e.g. *I was annoyed by their behaviour*) or as an adjective (*I was* (or *felt*) *very annoyed*) or even as both (*I was very annoyed by their behaviour*).

participle

A non-finite form of the verb. There are two kinds, which traditionally are labelled:

1 *present participle*: this always end in *-ing*, e.g. *being*, *doing*, *drinking*, *looking*

2 *past participle*: This ends in *-ed* (the same as the past tense) in regular verbs, but may end in *-en* or some other way in irregular verbs, e.g. *been*, *done*, *drunk*, *looked*.

Neither name is accurate, because both participles are used in the formation of a variety of complex tenses and can be used for referring to past, present, or future time (e.g. *What had they been doing? This must be drunk soon*).

A more relevant distinction is that the *-ing* participle is usually active in meaning and the 'past' participle is usually passive.

See p. 250 VERBS.

participle clause

A non-finite clause with an *-ing* or *-en* form as its verb, e.g.

> *Looking to neither right nor left*, he marched out
> *Treated like that*, I would have collapsed

A participle clause is sometimes introduced by a conjunction: *If treated like that*, . . .

A participle clause that contains its own subject is a type of ABSOLUTE clause. A participle in a clause which does not grammatically attach itself to the intended noun phrase in the adjoining clause is a HANGING PARTICIPLE. Also criticized is the FUSED PARTICIPLE.

particle

1 *Particle* is a neutral term to cover any adverb or preposition used in a MULTI-WORD VERB. Most particles are high-frequency words which can function both as adverbs and prepositions. Compare:

> She looked up the word
> She looked   it/the word up   in her dictionary   } (*up* = adverb)

> She looked up the road   (*up* = preposition)
> *She looked   it/the road up

2 The word *to* when used before an infinitive.

To is generally a preposition (as in *ten to six, go to Oxford*) and less frequently an adverb (*Brandy might bring him to*). So traditionally the *to* before an infinitive is called a preposition, but its grammar is different—most notably in that the preposition *to*, if followed by a verb, needs this verb to be an *-ing* form. Contrast

> We *look forward to* your visit
> We *look forward to seeing* you   } (*to* = preposition)

> We hope *to see* you soon   (*to* = particle)
> *We look forward to see you

partitive

A partitive word or phrase denotes part of a whole.

(*a*) The partitive construction is basically *X of Y*. It refers particularly to quantity or amount—*a piece of paper, two pieces of paper, a bit of a problem, an item of clothing*; but also to quality—*a sort of clown, different kinds of cheese, that type of person.*

Count nouns that can act as the first noun in this structure are *partitive nouns* (or UNIT NOUNS). Many are specific to particular items, e.g. a *blade* of grass, a *loaf* of bread, a *speck* of dirt; and they enable us to count uncount nouns:

three *rashers* of bacon (*three bacons)

an interesting *piece* of information (*three informations)

(*b*) When the second noun in this sort of construction is plural, the first one may denote not a part but a larger group

a *bunch* of flowers

a *flock* of sheep

Some *partitive* nouns (e.g. *crowd, flock*) can also be classified as COLLECTIVE nouns. Partitives can also denote containers (e.g. a *packet* of cigarettes, a *teaspoon(ful)* of sugar).

The term *partitive genitive* is used in various ways, but particularly to indicate a 'whole to part' relationship rather than strictly possession, e.g. *the baby's eyes, the Earth's surface.*

part of speech

This is the traditional term for different classes of words that are distinguished largely by syntactic criteria, though traditionally they were often defined by meaning (e.g. 'a verb is a doing word'). The preferred term today is WORD CLASS.

There is no single correct way of analysing words into parts of speech and the boundaries between different groups are not always clear. Generally recognized parts are nouns, verbs, pronouns, adverbs, adjectives, conjunctions, prepositions, and interjections. Today determiners are usually recognized as a distinct class, which includes articles.

These classes are sometimes grouped into *major* and *minor* classes on the basis of how much they are presumed to contribute

PARTS OF SPEECH
....
MAJOR AND MINOR PARTS OF SPEECH

MAJOR   (sometimes called *content words*, *lexical words*, *full words*):

adjective:	beautiful, nice, nasty, strange . . .
adverb:	beautifully, nicely, often, perhaps, since, soon, very . . .
noun:	alligator, country, food, intuition, oddity, hopelessness . . .
verb:	be, choose, get, lose, put, would . . .

MINOR   (sometimes called *form words*, *grammatical words* or *structure words*):

determiner:	(including *articles*): a, all, any, both, each, every, much, several, some, this, these . . .
conjunction:	and, or, although, because, if, since, provided that, so that, when, as soon as . . .
preposition:	at, for, from, into, out of, to, with, by, down, up, in, on, after, since . . .
pronoun:	I, her, it, us, they, himself, all, any, both, each, much, several, some, none . . .
interjections:	ah! alas! eh! mm! oops! . . . .

....
OPEN AND CLOSED CLASSES

OPEN CLASS (a class to which new words can be added)
= the same as the major parts of speech, except
(*a*) only lexical verbs (not auxiliaries) are open class
(*b*) numerals, often classified as determiners, are also perhaps open class, as both cardinals and ordinals can go on to infinity.

CLOSED CLASS (to which new words are never or only rarely admitted)
= the minor parts of speech, plus
primary verbs (*be, do, have*), and
modal auxiliaries
....
OTHER WORDS FOR PARTS OF SPEECH

adjunct:	(*a*) any adverb or (*b*) only a 'central' adverb, e.g. of manner (*nicely*), place (*here*), time (*today*)
article:	indefinite *a, an* } now often classified definite *the* } as determiners
conjunct (or **connector**):	a member of a subgroup of adverbials (e.g. *however, nevertheless* . . .)
coordinator:	a coordinating conjunction (e.g. *and, but, or*)
correlatives:	pairs of joining words (e.g. *both . . . and, either . . . or, so . . . that, hardly . . . when*)
disjunct:	a member of a subgroup of adverbials (e.g. *to be frank, undoubtedly, understandably*)

emphasizer:	a subtype of both *adjective* (e.g. a *real* challenge, *pure* nonsense) and *adverb* (I *simply* can't understand it)
focusing adverb:	e.g. I *only* asked
intensifier:	a subtype of both *adjective* (e.g. *utter* rubbish) and *adverb* (e.g. We were *bitterly* disappointed)
nationality word:	a noun or adjective denoting a member of a nation or ethnic group (e.g. *English, French*)
particle:	a small word that is sometimes an adverb and sometimes a preposition (e.g. *by, down, in*)
subjunct:	an adverbial with a subordinate role (e.g. *very* hot, *too* quickly)
subordinator:	a subordinating conjunction (e.g. *although, if, because*)

....

to meaning. Another grouping is into *open* classes that admit new words (e.g. nouns, verbs, adjectives) and *closed* classes (e.g. modals, prepositions) that do not. At the same time, individual word classes may be further subdivided in various ways.

Many words belong to more than one class, e.g.

Some *like* it hot (verb)
It was just *like* old times (preposition)
He looks just *like* his father did at that age (conjunction)
I don't want to hear of any *likes* and dislikes (plural noun)
. . . in *like* manner (adjective)

See p. 165 parts of speech.

passive

When a verb is in the passive, the grammatical subject 'suffers' or 'experiences' or 'receives' the action of the verb. Passive contrasts with active.

(a) **Form**. Formally, passive tenses consist (minimally) of a form of the verb *be* plus a past participle, as in

Dinner is served
Trespassers will be prosecuted
Mistakes cannot afterwards be rectified

Contrast (active voice)

Someone is/We are serving dinner
We will prosecute trespassers
We cannot rectify mistakes afterwards

Only transitive verbs can have passive forms, because the grammatical subject of a passive verb corresponds to the object of an active verb. Even so, not all active structures have a passive counterpart:

Blue suits you. *You are suited by blue
Those people lack confidence. *Confidence is lacked by those people

If an agent is mentioned with a passive verb, this is usually by means of a by-phrase (*Dinner was served by uniformed staff*). In some cases, mention of an agent is unlikely or impossible (*Churchill was born in 1874*). A passive construction with no agent mentioned is labelled a *non-agentive passive* or *agentless passive*.

(b) **Meaning**. Choice of a passive rather than an active tense depends on context and other factors. A passive may be used to ensure that the TOPIC comes first as subject (e.g. *Dinner, Trespassers, Mistakes*) and that the message gets END-FOCUS (e.g. *is served, will be prosecuted*, etc.). Or a passive may be used to avoid mentioning who is doing the action (e.g. *cannot afterwards be rectifi*ed etc.).

But if the agent is important, then a passive puts the agent in the 'focused upon' end-position (e.g. *Could the loch really be inhabited by a monster?*).

(c) When a clause contains two verbs in the passive (e.g. It *was said to have been sighted* several times), this is a DOUBLE PASSIVE.

• **pseudo-passive**: a structure that looks like a passive, but does not have an exact active counterpart and cannot take an agent, e.g. *My homework is finished now*. An active sentence with this meaning would be 'I have finished my homework now', and not 'I finish my homework now'. Also unacceptable is *'My homework is finished now by me'.

• **semi-passive**: this is closer to a true passive. For example, *I was impressed* can have an agent, and has an active counterpart:

I was impressed by his fluency
His fluency impressed me

but the participle has adjective-like qualities (e.g. *I was very impressed, I was impressed and happy, You didn't seem impressed*).

past

The grammatical sense relates essentially to the usual meaning of 'time gone by'—in contrast to PRESENT. But it is more accurate to say that past tenses are MARKED as 'non-present'. While they refer primarily to past time, they can also be used for *hypothesis*, i.e. as tenses marked for unreality:

> I wish I *knew*
> If I *had* my way, I would . . .

and for *social distancing*

> *Could* you lend me some money?
> I *wanted* to ask you something

With no further label, the past of a verb is the *past simple tense*, which in regular verbs always end in *-ed*, and whose form is normally listed second when verb forms are given (e.g. see, *saw*, seen; drive, *drove*, driven). As a more general term, past tenses include other 'tenses' that begin with a past form (e.g. past perfect, past progressive).

See p. 235 TENSES and p. 237 TIME AND TENSE.

past participle

This is the form of the verb usually given third in dictionaries (e.g. see, saw, *seen*). It is used in perfect and passive tenses and sometimes adjectivally, e.g.

> Have you *looked*? Were you *seen*? *lost* property

In regular verbs the past participle ends in the same *-ed* inflection as the past tense, and is called the *-ed* form (or *-ed* participle) by some grammarians; while other prefer the label *-en* form (compare *spoken, driven*) to distinguish it more clearly.

The past participle has a meaning of 'perfectiveness' or completion, but is not restricted to past time (e.g. *You'll have forgotten by this time next year*). It also can have a 'passive' meaning—contrast *bored* (passive) and *boring* (active).

See p. 250 VERBS.

past perfect

A tense (sometimes called *before-past*, *pluperfect*, or *past-in-the-past*) formed with *had* + a past participle. With no further label, the past perfect tense refers to a simple active tense: *I had forgotten* (until you reminded me).

Past perfect progressive tenses and *past perfect passive tenses*, and combinations of the two, also occur:

> We *had been wondering* about that, when the telegram arrived
>
> The matter *had been overlooked*
>
> It *had been being compiled* by hand

In general, past perfect tenses refer to a time earlier than some other past time. But like other so-called past tenses, in a subordinate clause past perfect may signify hypothesis, something contrary to fact

> If you *had told* me before now, I could have helped
>
> If you *had been coming* tomorrow, you would have met my mother

Past perfect may also stress 'perfectiveness' (completion), e.g. They waited *until I had finished*.

See p. 235 TENSES.

past progressive

The tense formed with a past form of *be* + an *-ing* form.

e.g. We *were waiting*, It *was raining*.

See p. 235 TENSES.

past subjunctive   See SUBJUNCTIVE.

pattern

The (possible or necessary) ways in which words and phrases combine can be described as patterns.

At the level of syntax, clause structure can be analysed in terms of a comparatively small set of overall patterns, which primarily depend on the type of verb involved, e.g. SV (with an intransitive verb), SVO (with a transitive verb), and so on. See p. 42 CLAUSES.

Looked at another way, individual verbs have their own verb patterns. For example, both *want* and *wish* can be followed by (object) + *to*-infinitive—*I want (you) to go, I wish (you) to go*. But only *wish* can be used in the pattern verb + *that* clause; so *I wish that you would go* but not **I want that you (would) go*. Similarly we can talk of noun patterns (some can be followed by a *to*-infinitive, e.g. *determination to succeed*; others by prepositions, e.g. *love of money* etc.) and adjective patterns (e.g. *keen to help, thoughtful of you, sorry (that) I spoke*).

perception verb

A verb relating to a physical sense of the body (e.g. see, hear, feel, taste, smell).

This is a meaning-based label, but grammatically a subset of perception verbs are unusual in sharing the following two verb patterns:

I heard him sing   (verb + object + bare infinitive)
I heard him singing (verb + object + -ing form)

Other verbs that fit both these patterns are *feel, notice, observe, see, watch*, and (not a perception verb) *have*.

See p. 250 VERBS.

perfect

Linguists talk about *perfect* (or *perfective*) ASPECT, but commonly we talk about *perfect tenses*, *perfect infinitives*, etc. *Perfect* verb forms contain part of the verb *have* plus a past participle, e.g.

He has/had won
I will have finished by next week
Having said that . . .

In meaning, perfect tenses express an action or state completed (or partly completed) before some stated or implied time. With present perfect this is usually before now (*I have been at this school for three years*), and with past perfect before some past 'then' (*I had not been to school before*). But in subordinate clauses even future time is possible (e.g. *I'll lend you my book, when I have finished it*).

See p. 235 TENSES.

perfect infinitive

An infinitive formed with have + a past participle, e.g. *(to) have wanted, (to) have forgotten.*

Like other infinitive forms, the perfect infinitive may be used in a non-finite clause (e.g. *To have forgotten was unforgivable*) and as part of a finite verb phrase (*You can't have forgotten*). Passive perfect infinitives are possible (e.g. (to) *have been forgotten*).

performative verb

A verb that simply by being uttered performs an action, e.g.

I *advise* you to reconsider
I *name* this ship . . .
I *declare* the meeting closed
Patrons *are advised* not to leave valuables in their cars

Other performative verbs include *apologize, beg, confess, promise, swear, warn.* As performatives, such verbs are typically used in the first person of the present tense. In other uses they may be merely reporting a performative act without constituting one (e.g. *She advised him to reconsider*).

periphrasis

Periphrasis is the use of separate words to express a grammatical relationship that is also expressed by inflection. It is a common feature of adjective and adverb comparison, where periphrastic phrases with *more* and *most* are an obligatory alternative to forms with *-er* and *-est* for longer adjectives and most adverbs (*more beautiful, most oddly*).

A choice between inflection and periphrasis is possible with some two-syllable adjectives (*It gets lovelier/more lovely every day*).

person

A category used, together with NUMBER (singular and plural) in the classification of pronouns, related determiners, and verb forms. There are three persons—

first person: the speaker (I) or
                the speaker and others (we)
second person: the person(s) addressed (you)
third person: some other person(s) (he, she, it, they)

Be is unique among English verbs in having three distinctive forms in the present tense (including a special form, *am*, for the first person singular) and two in the past (*was, were*).

Most verbs only have a distinctive form for the third person singular of the present tense (*has, does, wants*, etc. v. *have, do, want*), and for 'tenses' formed with *be* and *have*.

personal pronoun

A pronoun belonging to a set that shows contrasts of person, gender, number, and case—though not every pronoun shows all these distinctions.

The personal pronouns are

1st person   I, me, we, us
2nd   you
3rd   he, him, she, her, they, them, it

Reflexive pronouns (*myself, ourselves*, etc.) and possessive pronouns (*mine, ours*, etc.) and possessive determiners (*my, our*, etc.) are sometimes included.

pharyngeal

The pharynx is the cavity behind the nose and mouth, and a pharyngeal sound is articulated with the root of the tongue pulled back into the pharynx. There are no pharyngeal consonants in standard English. (Arabic has pharyngeal fricatives.) The English vowel /ɑː/ could be called pharyngeal, but we do not describe vowels by place of articulation, so this phoneme is usually described simply as an *open back vowel*.

See p. 266 THE SPEECH ORGANS.

phoneme

A speech sound which contrasts meaningfully with other sounds in the language.

For example, /p/ and /b/ are separate phonemes in English, because they distinguish such words as *pan* and *ban*, *dapple* and *dabble*, *hop* and *hob*.

Actually, the *phoneme* is an idealized abstraction, because it includes variants (ALLOPHONES) that do not change meaning. Thus the actual articulations of /p/ and /b/ are conditioned by their syllable positions: initial /p/ is aspirated in *pan*, but completely unaspirated in *span*.

Phonemes and the ways in which their allophones are conditioned vary from language to language. Standard (RP) English is currently analysed as having 22 consonants, 2 semi-vowels, 12 pure vowels, and 8 diphthongs, making a total of 44 phonemes. See p. 265 THE SOUNDS OF ENGLISH.

Phonemic, concerned with meaning-related sound distinctions, contrasts with PHONETIC.

phonetic

Relating objectively to actual speech sounds.

A phonetic alphabet, such as the INTERNATIONAL PHONETIC ALPHABET, is a set of symbols based particularly on place and manner of articulation, so that each symbol has one characteristic sound.

The term phonetic is contrasted with *phonemic*, as in a phonetic versus a phonemic transcription of a piece of spoken or written language, a transcription being the use of phonetic symbols instead of ordinary letters. A phonetic transcription aims to represent speech sounds objectively, and a high degree of accuracy (a narrow transcription) can be achieved with the use of special marks (diacritics) to indicate aspiration and so on. Theoretically anyone who understood the symbols could read a phonetic transcription aloud accurately.

A phonemic transcription is more 'broad brush': each phoneme symbol stands for all its allophones, so an accurate reading-aloud is only possible if you know the phoneme values of that language.

phonetics

The science or study of speech sounds.

Articulatory phonetics deals with how speech sounds are actually made, what the tongue and lips and other speech organs are actually doing. *Acoustic phonetics* uses instruments and electronic equipment to measure the speech in terms of air vibrations. *Auditory phonetics* studies how speech sounds are received by the listener.

phonology

Phonology is the study of how speech sounds are used in any particular language. It is concerned with (*a*) the meaningful contrasts (the PHONEMIC system); (*b*) the regular ways in which the phonemes are actually articulated (the predictable allophonic variations); and (*c*) the possible combinations of phonemes, the CONSONANT CLUSTERS.

Many single phonemes, as well as consonant clusters, are restricted in their positions. The consonant /ŋ/, usually spelt *ng* never starts an English syllable, while several vowels (/e/, /æ/, /ʌ/, /ɒ/) are never syllable-final.

phrasal-prepositional verb

A multi-word verb containing a verb + an adverb + a preposition, e.g.

> We're *looking forward to* the holidays
> You shouldn't *put up with* that sort of treatment

phrasal verb

1 A multi-word verb operating as a single unit—and often having a metaphorical (or idiomatic) meaning. Thus defined, phrasal verb is an umbrella term for different kinds of multi-word verbs (including *prepositional verbs* and *phrasal-prepositional verbs*).

2 More narrowly, a phrasal verb consists of a verb + an adverb, in contrast to PREPOSITIONAL verbs and phrasal-prepositional verbs.

In this narrower definition, phrasal verbs are of two main types:

(*a*) intransitive:

> The plane *took off*
> I don't know—I *give up*!

(*b*) transitive, where the particle can follow the object:

> *Take off* your coat. *Take* your coat/it *off*
> I've *given up* chocolate. I've *given* chocolate/it *up*

phrase

A phrase is a level of structure between a word and a clause. In both traditional and more modern grammar a phrase often consists of two or more words that 'go together', e.g. *in the end, very odd indeed*. But there are differences.

(*a*) In traditional grammar (where a clause must contain a finite verb) phrases include what are now often classified as non-finite clauses (e.g. *having said that*) or verbless clauses (e.g. *if possible*).

(*b*) In modern grammar phrases are still defined in terms of form. But a phrase can consist of a single headword; it could also contain a finite clause if that is dependent on the headword.

Various kinds of phrases are distinguished:

A *verb phrase* (VP) always contains a main verb as its head. It can be a single word (e.g. *went*) or it may also contain one or more auxiliaries (*must have been going*). A finite verb phrase always functions as the verbal element (V) in finite clause structure.

An *adverb phrase* similarly has an adverb as its head (e.g. *quickly*) and may be expanded with pre- and post-modification. Adverb phrases usually function as the Adverbial (A) in clause structure.

Noun phrases and *adjective phrases* similarly contain a noun (or pronoun) or an adjective, respectively, as head—with or without modification. A noun phrase (NP) may contain a relative clause in some modern analyses (e.g. *the man I love*).

But—unlike verb and adverb phrases, which function as verb and adverbial in clause structure—noun phrases and adjective phrases function differently.

Noun phrases can function as any element of clause structure except Verb. That is, a noun phrase can be S(ubject), O(bject), C(omplement), or A(dverbial). Adjective phrases can also function as Complement in clause structure, but often function at a lower level as part of a noun phrase. Noun phrases, too, can function at a lower level (e.g. as part of a prepositional phrase).

PHRASES AT A GLANCE

FORM

VERB PHRASE

auxiliaries	+	main verb
has		went
may	have	left
must	have	taken
	have	been	waiting

ADVERB PHRASE

	adverb
rather	hurriedly
quite	strangely
very	long
as	quickly
	often
	enough
	indeed
	as I could

NOUN PHRASE

	noun/pronoun	
all	political	lives
		vanity
		us
the		art	of the possible
last		night
a		man	who has everything

FUNCTION

Verb [V] in clause structure

They *went* [SV]
He *has just left* [SAV]
He *may have taken* my umbrella [SVO]
You *must have been waiting* for ages [SVA]

Adverbial [A] in clause structure

They left home *hurriedly* [SVOA]
She was acting *rather strangely* [SVA]
He spoke *quite long enough* [SVA]
They left *very quickly indeed* [SVA]
I visited them *as often as I could* [SVOA]

in clause structure

Subject [S]: *All political lives* end in failure
Object [O]: All politicians have *vanity*
Indirect Object [O]: Give *us* the tools...
Complement [C]: Politics is *the art of the possible*
Adverbial [A]: Who were you with *last night?*

object of preposition

What can you buy for *a man who has everything?*

ADJECTIVE PHRASE

adjective

	fascinating	
	easy	to read
	amazing	
utterly	good	
very		indeed

Complement [C] in clause structure

This biography sounded *fascinating*
And it proved *easy to read*
The photographs are *utterly amazing*
It's really *very good indeed*

part of noun phrase

These are *utterly amazing photographs*

PREPOSITIONAL PHRASE

preposition

at	home
in(to)	the garden
out of	reach
after	dinner

Adverbial [A] in clause structure

Will you be *at home* this evening?
Come *into the garden*
Put it *out of reach*
They left *after dinner*

part of noun phrase

Don't forget *the old folks at home*
Everything in the garden is lovely
Vegetables out of the garden are so good
Have you any *after-dinner mints*?

Prepositional phrases are rather different from the other four types of phrase. In form they are non-headed, and must contain at least two words—a preposition plus its object (or complement), usually a noun. Prepositional phrases have two main functions. They can be the A(dverbial) in clause structure (Please put that *in the box*) or they can operate at a lower level as part of a noun phrase (a Jack-*in-the-box*).

pitch

Pitch is the 'height' of the human voice, which depends on how rapidly the vocal cords vibrate. The slower the frequency of vibration, the lower the pitch; the higher the frequency, the higher the pitch. Various typical pitch changes (or TONES) are identified by phoneticians, e.g. *fall*, *rise*, and *level*.

place

A semantic category used in the classification of adverb(ial)s and prepositions.

This is one of the traditional categories—along with *time* and *manner*—that is still used today. For example, *here*, *there* are place adverbs; *at*, *in*, *on* are among prepositions of place, as in *at the front*, *in the garden*, *on the pier*; and *where you are* is an adverbial clause of place in *Stay where you are!* An alternative label is 'space'.

place of articulation

Place of articulation, along with MANNER, is a major part of the framework for describing the production of speech sounds, especially consonants.

For this purpose, the vocal organs are diagrammatically divided up and the places labelled BILABIAL, LABIO-DENTAL, ALVEOLAR, PALATAL, VELAR, GLOTTAL, with some other terms for places in the mouth not relevant to English speech sounds. See p. 264 THE CONSONANTS OF ENGLISH.

Places of articulation as such are not used in describing vowels, where tongue-height and lip-rounding are more relevant. Stylized diagrams of the mouth are, however, used, with scales from the

back (of the mouth) to the front, and close to open. See p. 266 THE
SPEECH ORGANS.

plosive

A plosive is a speech sound made with a total closure at some place
in the vocal organs, followed by a 'hold' or compression stage and
then a third and final 'explosive' release stage. (Also called a stop
consonant.)

The English plosives consist of three pairs of corresponding voiceless and voiced sounds:

> /p/ and /b/ as in *poor*, *bore*; *tap*, *tab* (bilabial plosives)
>
> /t/ and /d/ as in *true*, *drew*; *cat*, *cad* (alveolar)
>
> /k/ and /g/ as in *cold*, *gold*; *whack*, *wag* (velar)

The glottal stop /ʔ/, which is not an RP phoneme, is a voiceless
plosive.

A plosive sound made with a slow release stage involving friction
is an AFFRICATE.

See p. 264 THE CONSONANTS OF ENGLISH.

pluperfect

The same as PAST PERFECT or before-past.

plupluperfect

This is a newish name for a verb phrase heard colloquially,
and occasionally written, and which is generally considered non-
standard. It contains an extra auxiliary, and is used as an alternative to the past perfect.

The tense in full is *had have* + past participle, but it is commonly
used in shortened form:

> If we'd have found an unsafe microwave oven, we would have named it
> (advertisement)

plural

Plural refers to more than one, and contrasts with SINGULAR.

1 In English, *plural* applies to certain nouns, pronouns, and determiners and to verbs. In general, COUNT NOUNS have distinct plural forms, which in regular nouns end in *-s* or *-es*. Irregular plurals include some words of Old English origin (*feet*, *children*, etc. and ZERO PLURALS such as *sheep*, *deer*) and some *foreign plurals* (*crises*, *errata*, etc.).

A few nouns are *plural-only*: that is, they must take plural concord. There are various kinds:

(*a*) words for tools or articles of clothing that are in two joined parts (*binary nouns*), e.g. these scissors/trousers are . . .

(*b*) words that refer to some sort of group (but not to be confused with GROUP NOUNS). Most of these nouns end in *-s* (e.g. *clothes*, *riches*, *thanks*), but some plural-only words are 'unmarked' (e.g. *cattle*, *people*, *police*).

(*c*) words that with a particular meaning are plural in form and use (e.g. *arms* = weapons, *regards* = best wishes), though there may be a singular form with a different meaning.

2 Confusingly, some grammarians, and many dictionaries, label any word ending in *-s* as 'plural' or 'plural in form', even though such a word may never be plural in syntax (e.g. This *news* is . . .). Similarly *measles*, *physics*, etc.

See p. 151 NOUNS.

polysyllabic

A polysyllabic word is a word with more than one syllable, in contrast to MONOSYLLABIC.

portmanteau word

This is another term for BLEND, a word formed from parts of two words. The term comes from Lewis Carroll's explanation in *Through the Looking Glass* (1872) of the invented word *slithy*, which he said was a combination of 'lithe' and 'slimy': 'It's like a portmanteau—there are two meanings packed up into one word.'

See p. 145 NEW WORDS.

position

The position of a word or phrase in a clause has a considerable effect on meaning.

The position of adverbs is defined as INITIAL, MID-, or FINAL. The position of words in a sentence is dealt with as WORD ORDER and INFORMATION STRUCTURE.

positive

1 A clause or sentence with no negative word is positive. (Sometimes called AFFIRMATIVE.)

2 Positive also means the unmarked DEGREE in the three-way system of comparing adjectives and adverbs (sometimes called ABSOLUTE degree), e.g. *good, beautiful, soon* (as contrasted with *better, best; more/most beautiful; sooner, soonest*).

possessive

Possessive describes a word or case indicating possession or ownership.

With nouns, possessive case is also called GENITIVE case, e.g. *boy's, boys', Mary's, the Smiths'*.

Pronouns in the possessive case are the *mine, yours* series and the corresponding possessive determiners are *my, your . . .* Possessive pronouns do not have apostrophes. (*It's* means 'it is' or 'it has'.)

The basic meaning of the verb *have* is sometimes described as possessive (e.g. *We have a house*) in contrast to other meanings, especially dynamic ones such as *have a bath, have dinner, have an operation, have a holiday, have fun*.

postdeterminer

1 A particular type of determiner that must follow any central determiner or predeterminer, e.g. *few, many, much, little* and numbers, as in *these few tokens*; as in *both these two books*.

2 A few adjectives behave like determiners in that they must precede more ordinary adjectives, e.g. *certain* or *other*, as in *certain important new ideas, the other big red cardboard box*.

See p. 66 DETERMINERS.

postmodification

When dependent words affect the meaning of a preceding HEAD word they are said to 'postmodify' it.

Postmodification thus contrasts with *premodification*.

See MODIFICATION.

Postmodification can occur in different kinds of phrases, e.g. in an adjective or adverb phrase, and may take the form of a single word or sometimes a clause:

> Is that warm *enough*?
>
> He speaks too quietly *for me to hear*

Postmodification is, however, particularly discussed in relation to noun phrase structure. Postmodifiers include

> a prepositional phrase: A Question *of Upbringing*
> a relative clause: The Way *we Live Now*
> a non-finite clause: Virgin Soil *Upturned*, a book *to read*
> an adjective (especially after an indefinite pronoun): Nothing *Sacred*

postponement

When words are placed later in a clause than they would normally be they are said to be *postponed*.

A word or words may be postponed to give end-focus to a particular part of the message. Grammatical devices for postponement include:

discontinuity, which often postpones part of a noun phrase—

> *Everyone* was delighted *except the chairman*

extraposition, often to postpone a clausal subject—

> It is hardly surprising *that he did not like the architect's original plans*

passive structures, which postpone the agent (subject of the active verb) to the end—

> The building is to be opened *by the Prince*

postpositive

Postpositive means 'immediately following', and is particularly used in describing the position of adjectives. Postpositive position (or *postposition*) thus contrasts with ATTRIBUTIVE and PREDICATIVE positions.

Postposition is obligatory for adjectives modifying indefinite pronouns and adverbs (e.g. *nobody special*, *somewhere quiet*); in certain set expressions (e.g. *heir apparent*, *the body politic*); and with some adjectives in particular meanings (e.g. the *members present*, the *parents involved*).

pragmatics

Pragmatics is the branch of linguistics concerned with how users use language to communicate, and particularly how they use it socially—for example how people take turns in conversation, whether there are any 'rules' about interrupting, what assumptions or implications are made. So pragmatics concentrates on the communicative functions of language, in contrast to the more precise grammatical or syntactical meaning of the text. Thus '*I've borrowed this book from the library*' in different contexts might have the pragmatic implication '*so I don't want to watch TV*' or perhaps '*so I don't want to go out*' or even '*I wasn't going to buy it.*'

predeterminer

A determiner that has to come before other determiners, e.g. *all*, *both*, *half*, *double*, *such*, *what* (as in *both my brothers*, *what a surprise*). See p. 66 DETERMINERS.

predicate

Traditionally, sentences are divided into two parts, the *subject* and the rest, the *predicate*, which is whatever is 'predicated' or said about the subject:

subject	predicate
All good things	must come to an end
Attack	is the best form of defence
Familiarity	breeds contempt

The division is grammatically valid, but the terms *subject* and *predicate*, being notionally based, can be misleading. The subject is not necessarily what the sentence is about, and the rest is not always 'what is predicated about' the subject. For example, the grammatical subject in *It is raining* has no meaning.

Modern grammarians tend to analyse predicate structure in terms of functional components (Verb, Object, Complement, and Adverbial), and as elements of information structure such as *new* (versus *given*) or *comment* (versus *topic*).

predicative

Predicative means 'occurring in the predicate'. It contrasts with ATTRIBUTIVE, and is particularly used in the classification of adjectives that are used after *be* or some other linking verb.

Most adjectives can be used in both attributive and predicative positions (e.g. *a fine day*, *the day was fine*). But some adjectives are only used in one of these positions.

Among predicative-only adjectives are a group beginning with *a-* (*afraid, alone*, etc.) and adjectives that usually or always require complementation (e.g. *answerable, conducive, devoid, loath*, etc.).

Adjectives that can be predicative can also take postposition (e.g. *anybody aware of these facts*, *those people impatient with the slow progress*).

prefix

An affix added before a word or base to form a new word is a prefix, in contrast to SUFFIX.

Prefixes are primarily semantic in their effect, changing the meaning of the base. Common prefixes include:

> *counter* (productive), *de* (frost), *dis* (connect), *hyper* (active), *inter* (national), *mal* (function), *mini* (skirt), *non* (event), *sub* (zero), *un* (natural), *under* (nourished)

See p. 145 NEW WORDS.

premodification See MODIFICATION.

preparatory *it*

Another term for ANTICIPATORY or INTRODUCTORY *it*, as in

> *It* is difficult to know what to do [= To know what to do is difficult]

preposition

Prepositions form a traditional word class. A preposition relates two other words or phrases to each other, and generally precedes the word it 'governs'.

Prepositions are predominantly short words (e.g. *at*, *by*, *down*, *of*, *from*, *in(to)*, *to*, *up*), some of which also function as adverbs (see PARTICLE). But prepositions also include some longer words (e.g. *alongside* the quay, *throughout* the period). COMPLEX prepositions consist of two- and three-word combinations that function in the same way (e.g. *according to*, *regardless of*, *in front of*, *by means of*, *in addition to*).

Because of the name *pre*position (based on Latin grammar) there was at one time considerable prejudice against putting a preposition later than the word it belongs to (!). Rewording is sometimes possible (e.g. *the word to which it belongs*) but in some contexts a later position, with a *deferred* or *stranded* preposition, is the only natural one:

> What did you do that *for*?
> The problem is difficult to talk *about*
> It's not to be sneezed *at*

A *marginal preposition* is a preposition which has some characteristics of another word class, e.g.

> He's wonderful, *considering* his age

See p. 165 PARTS OF SPEECH.

prepositional object

Some grammarians reserve this term for the object of a prepositional verb, e.g.

> Listen to *this*. James has come into *a fortune*
> We were hoping for *a breakthrough*

But others use it loosely to include any word 'governed' by a preposition (e.g. *dinner* in *after dinner*), making the term interchangeable with *object* (or *complement*) *of preposition*.

prepositional phrase

This is a formal label for a preposition plus its object (or complement). Prepositional phrases function mainly as (*a*) adverbials:

Who has put this umbrella *on the table*?

(*b*) as post-modifiers in noun phrases:

Is *this umbrella on the table* yours?

prepositional verb

A two-part verb that includes a preposition.

As the particle here is (by definition) a preposition, it generally comes before its object:

I am looking after the children/looking after them

not

*looking the children after/*looking them after

But in certain structures the particle may be deferred (e.g. *They need looking after*).

prescriptive

Prescriptive grammar is concerned with prescribing rules of usage, in contrast to DESCRIPTIVE grammar.

Prescriptive grammar is often used as a term of abuse, because some old-fashioned grammar or usage books prescribe Latin-based rules that do not apply to English. (e.g. 'Don't end a sentence with a preposition'; 'Say *It's I*'; 'Never split an infinitive'; etc.).

Descriptive grammar, by contrast, tries to establish how people actually speak and write. Nevertheless, most descriptive statements about language are based on some value-judgement of what is acceptable and normal, however objectively descriptive they try to be.

present

Present tenses of verbs contrast with past tenses, but the term can be misleading. Although present tenses predominantly refer to some sort of present time (e.g. *I want to help, I am looking forward to the holidays, She lives in Cardiff*) they would more accurately be described as UNMARKED for time, tenses that can be used when we are not deliberately excluding present time. Thus the *present simple tense*, which is the basic unmarked tense in English, is used for

general or 'timeless' truths (e.g. *The earth goes round the sun*);
and present tenses are also used for instances where past time
is unimportant or irrelevant (e.g. *Shakespeare says ...*); and
with reference to a future event that is certain or taken-for-
granted now (*We are leaving tomorrow, If you come next week, we
can ...*).

See p. 235 TENSES and p. 237 TIME AND TENSE.

present participle

The *-ing* form of the verb when used in a verb-like way (in contrast
to its noun-like use).

This participle is used in the formation of progressive tenses and,
alone, in non-finite clauses:

> We are/were listening
> Sitting here, I haven't a care in the world

See p. 250 VERBS.

present perfect

A tense formed with *have* or *has* + past participle.

Present perfect tenses generally refer to some state or event or series
of events already achieved in a period up to the moment of
speaking and often relate them in some way to the present. With
no further label, *present perfect (tense)* means the present perfect
simple tense:

> I *have known* her since she was twenty
> James *has come* (i.e. he is here now)

Contrast the simple past:

> My father *knew* Lloyd George
> James *came* (but is perhaps no longer here)

Present perfect progressive and *present perfect passive* tenses are
also possible:

> He has been working hard today/recently
> She has been told

See p. 235 TENSES.

present progressive

The tense formed with the present tense of *be* + an *-ing* participle, e.g. I *am wondering*, We *are listening*. (Also called *present continuous*.)

See p. 235 TENSES.

present simple

The tense that is identical to the base of the verb (except in the case of *be*) and that adds *-s* for the third person singular (sometimes just called *present tense*):

    I know and he knows too.

See p. 235 TENSES.

present subjunctive   See SUBJUNCTIVE.

primary verb

The primary verbs are *be*, *do*, and *have*.

Verbs are traditionally divided, according to function, into main verbs and auxiliaries. But as *be*, *do*, and *have* can function as both, it can be useful to make further distinctions. *Primary* is used as a label for these verbs, however they are functioning.

See p. 250 VERBS.

private verb

A verb expressing 'thinking'. Contrasted with a PUBLIC VERB of 'saying'.

Private verbs (like public verbs) often take a *that*-clause (e.g. They *believe/know/realize/understand* that three prisoners have escaped).

productive

A linguistic process that is still in use is productive. Many kinds of affixation are highly productive. For example, dozens of new words are formed with *anti-*, *Euro-*, *dis-*, *un-*, *-ee*, *-ness*, and so on. On the other hand few new words are formed with *-dom* or *-hood*, while the plural suffix *-en* (as in *children*, *brethren*) is completely *unproductive*.

pro-form

A word, phrase, etc. that can be used in place of another.

Pronouns, as the name implies, are commonly used as pro-forms for nouns. But pro-forms also include

adverbs (e.g. *here*, *there*, *then*)

phrases with the 'pro-verb' *do* (e.g. *do it*, *do so*, *do that*) replacing a predicate, e.g.

> They said they would *do it/do so*

so and *not* replacing object *that*-clauses: e.g.

> Are there any survivors? I hope *so*/I fear *not*

progressive

The *-ing* form of the verb has an ongoing, durative meaning, expressing activity in progress. Linguists talk of progressive ASPECT, rather than tense, and contrast it with PERFECT(IVE) aspect.

But commonly we refer to progressive tenses. They are formed with a part of the verb *be* plus an *-ing* form, e.g.

> I am staying with friends until the 30th (*present progressive*)
> I was wondering what to do (*past progressive*) when this job cropped up
> We will have been waiting two whole hours ('*future*' *perfect progressive*) by the time their train arrives

Passive progressive tenses are also possible (e.g. *It's being repaired*).

See p. 235 TENSES.

pronoun

Pronouns are a word class (or part of speech), with a noun-like function.

Traditional grammar defines *pronoun* as a word that can replace or stand for a noun. But this is not strictly accurate. For example in *I asked my neighbours if they would cut their hedge*, *they* certainly replaces *my neighbours* (a noun phrase, note, not just a noun) but

I can hardly be said to replace a noun. Secondly, a pronoun (e.g. *that*) often replaces a clause as in *Why did you ask that?*

Pronouns basically constitute a closed class, which can be sub-divided in various ways. They overlap with determiners, many words (e.g. *this*, *some*, *neither*) being used as both. See below.

PRONOUNS AND DETERMINERS COMPARED

	PRONOUNS	DETERMINERS
Articles		a, an, the
[definite reference]		—
Personal	I, me, he, him, it etc.	—
Reflexive	myself, yourself etc.	—
Possessive	mine, yours etc.	my, your etc
Demonstrative	this, that,	these, those
Relative	who, whom, which, that	whose
Interrogative	whose, what, whatever, which, whichever	
[indefinite reference]		
Quantifier	all, both, half	
	each, either, neither	
	(a) few, (a) little, many, much	
	fewer, less, least, more, most	
	some, any	
	enough, several	
	none	no, every
	everyone/ everybody, everything	—
	anyone, someone, nobody etc.	—

Notes:

Reflexive pronouns are called *emphatic pronouns* when used for emphasis, e.g. I don't believe that *myself.*

Quantifiers, when used as pronouns, are also called *of-pronouns* and *partitive pronouns* (e.g. *many* of these people).

Anyone, everybody, something etc. are sometimes called *compound pronouns.*

pronunciation

The sound system of British English is usually described in terms of its PHONEMES, and in particular the phonemes of RECEIVED PRONUN-

CIATION, a somewhat idealized standard model. See also SPELLING PRONUNCIATION.

proper noun

A noun referring to a particular, unique person, place, etc.; in contrast to a COMMON noun.

The traditional distinction between common and proper nouns is both grammatical and semantic. Proper nouns do not freely allow determiners or number contrasts (e.g. **my Himalaya*, **some Asias*), and article usage tends to be fixed (e.g. *the Hague, the Alps, the (River) Thames, Oxford*—not **a Hague, *Alps, *Thames, *the Oxford*).

However, the categories are not watertight. More than one person or place may share the same name, so names may in some circumstances be treated like common nouns (e.g. *The Smiths, a Mr Smith*). Nationality words and names of days are also distinctly borderline (*three Scots, an Australian, three Mondays in succession*).

The terms *proper noun* and *(proper) name* are often used interchangeably. But a proper noun, strictly speaking, is a single word (e.g. *Dorchester, Elizabeth, England*), whereas names can include ordinary dictionary words (e.g. *New York*) and may contain no proper noun at all (e.g. *the United States, the Daily Telegraph*).

See p. 151 NOUNS.

prop *it*

The same as DUMMY *it*, an *it* used for grammatical reasons but having no meaning, as in *It is raining*.

proportional clauses

A pair of balanced clauses that express a proportional relationship. As well as covering such fairly standard sentences as:

As he grew older, (so) he worried less

it also covers the more unusual pattern exemplified by:

The more he thought, the less he spoke
The more, the merrier

See p. 13 ADVERB CLAUSES.

pseudo

'Not real'. *Pseudo* is applied to various constructions that are not quite what they seem, as in pseudo-CLEFT, pseudo-COORDINATION, pseudo-PARTICIPLE, pseudo-PASSIVE, and pseudo-SUBJUNCTIVE.

public verb

A verb with some meaning of 'speaking', contrasted with a PRIVATE verb. Public verbs (e.g. *affirm, announce, boast, confirm, declare*) are often followed by a *that*-clause expressing a factual proposition.

punctuation

A system of marks which are used in order to make written text easier to understand. Punctuation is primarily based on grammatical structure, marking sentences, clauses, and some types of phrase. Broadly speaking, it has the function either of linking items (e.g. *three potatoes, two carrots, and an onion*) or of separating them (e.g. *I don't know. Ask someone else*).

The purpose of punctuation is to help the reader, and certain conventions, for example for indicating the end of a sentence, are obligatory. Elsewhere, the writer has some stylistic choice.

- A **full-stop** ⟨.⟩, **question mark** ⟨?⟩, or **exclamation mark** ⟨!⟩ is normally obligatory at the end of a complete sentence. These marks may also be used at the end of smaller word sequences, or even single words, if these are felt to be a complete utterance (e.g. *No. Everything all right? Alas!*). Full-stops are also used with some abbreviations (*a.m., i.e.*).

- The **comma** is a light punctuation mark, representing a short break in phrasing or meaning. It is used

(*a*) between words, phrases, or clauses in a list

a large, neglected, old-fashioned farm . . .
Our lives are miserable, laborious, and short . . .
He set his ears back, shook his forelock several times, and tried hard to marshall his thoughts.

(*b*) to indicate, if necessary, where one phrase or clause ends and another begins

Four legs good, two legs bad!

In spite of the shock that Snowball's expulsion had given them, the animals were dismayed by this announcement.

The animals had their breakfast, and then Snowball and Napoleon called them together again.

(*c*) to separate off words or phrases that are in some way not integral to the basic sentence. For example,

words in apposition

After the horses came Muriel, the white goat, and Benjamin, the donkey.

(Brackets or dashes could alternatively be used here.)

vocatives

Comrades, you have heard already about the strange dream that I had last night.

non-defining relative clauses

The work of teaching and organizing the others fell naturally upon the pigs, who were generally recognized as being the cleverest of the animals.

question-tags

You would not rob us of our repose, would you?

sentence adverbials

Unfortunately, the uproar awoke Mr Jones.

(*d*) to introduce direct speech

When they said, 'That's your toe!'

He replied, 'Is it so?'

• The **semi-colon** ⟨;⟩ marks a more important break than a comma. It may be used to link parallel statements, e.g.

I wasn't going to leave; I'd only just arrived.

It is also useful in some lists where simple commas could be confusing, e.g.

He was accompanied by his mother-in-law, Mrs Simmonds; his doctor; Mr Robinson, a neighbour; Tom Pertwee; and both his sons.

• The **colon** ⟨:⟩ is stronger than a semi-colon. It is particularly used to point forwards to a list, e.g.

The price of £775 includes: scheduled flights, three-star hotel accommodation, breakfast and dinner, three concerts and one opera, excursions, admissions.

or to an explanation, e.g.

> The past is a foreign country: they do things differently there.

A colon is also sometimes used to introduce direct quotations, e.g.

> Another famous novel begins: *Last night I dreamt I went to Manderley again.*

See also APOSTROPHE, BRACKET, HYPHEN.

purpose

The term is used in its usual sense, particularly in describing the meanings of adverbials and conjunctions, e.g.

> They only do it *to annoy* (infinitive of purpose)

Similarly *in order (not) to, so as (not) to.*

A finite clause of purpose, introduced by *so (that)* or *in order that* normally requires a modal verb, e.g.

> They shredded the evidence so that no one would discover the truth

Contrast a clause of result:

> They shredded the evidence, so that no one ever discovered the truth

Negative purpose is suggested by *lest* and *in case.*

See p. 13 ADVERB CLAUSES.

pushdown

A type of embedding in which a word or phrase etc. that is part of one clause operates indirectly as part of another, e.g.

> What do you think happened? [*What* do you think? / *What* happened?]
> He earns a lot more money than he admits. [*He earns* a lot more money than . . . / He admits *he earns* . . .]

Confusion over pushdown with a relative clause is a common cause of hypercorrection:

> *He was searching for his parents whom he hoped were still alive. [He was searching for his parents *who* . . . were still alive / He hoped *they* were still alive]

putative *should*

Putative *should* (also called *emotional should*) occurs mainly in subordinate clauses. It does not express obligation, but emphasizes an emotional reaction to a situation (sadness, pleasure, surprise, etc.), e.g.

It is a pity/It is sad that you should be so angry
It is wonderful that he should have got the job

An ordinary indicative tense is a possible alternative, because the reference is to a presumed fact (. . . that you are angry, . . . that he has got the job). But whereas an indicative objectively asserts the fact, putative *should* emphasizes the speaker's reaction.

Putative *should* also occurs as an alternative to the subjunctive after expressions of suggesting, advising, etc.:

They insisted that I (should) stay the whole week

Putative *should* also occurs as a main verb in a few expressions of the type *How should I know?* and *Who should walk in but James?*

Q

qualify

Broadly speaking, a word that in some way affects the meaning of another word, qualifies that word.

At one time *qualify* (along with *qualifier* and *qualification*) were particularly used to describe the way adjectives affect nouns, while MODIFY etc. was used for the way adverbs affect verbs.

In much modern grammar, however, no such distinctions are made, and the terms *modify, modification, modifier* have largely extended their meaning to include and replace *qualify* etc. In particular, the structure of a noun phrase is generally analysed in terms of the modification of the head word.

quality

Adjectives are categorized in various ways. One way is to distinguish a **qualitative adjective** from a CLASSIFYING *adjective*. In this system, a qualitative adjective describes a quality and is gradable, e.g. *happy, nice, pretty, small*. Such adjectives are then contrasted with *classifying adjectives* (e.g. *Indian, wooden, mental*), which are ungradable.

In describing partitive nouns and phrases a distinction is sometimes made between a **quality partitive**, e.g.

a *sort* of menu, two *kinds* of pudding

and the more usual *quantity partitive* (e.g. a *piece* of cake, a *lot* of food).

quantifier

Quantifying is concerned with numbers and amounts. So indefinite determiners and pronouns that quantify are sometimes classified as *quantifiers*. For example, *much, many, (a) few, (a) little, several, enough, a lot (of), lots (of)*.

See p. 190 PRONOUNS AND DETERMINERS.

quantity

Quantity is concerned with numbers and amount, so there is a meaning connection with *quantifying*.

The term *quantitative* is sometimes used more widely than quantifying, as a cover term for (indefinite) QUANTIFIERS (*few, several,* etc.) plus definite CARDINAL numbers (*one, two, three*) and also measurement terms such as *a couple of, half . . .*

question

In general, sentences that are questions in form are also genuine questions in meaning. Formally there are three main types. In all of them (except when *What* or *Who* is a subject, as in *What happened? Who says so?*) there is operator-subject inversion:

• *yes-no questions*, so-called because they can be answered with a simple *yes* or *no*, e.g. *Is it raining?* These questions usually end with a rising intonation.

• *wh-questions* (also called *information questions*) begin with a wh-word, e.g. *Where have you been? How did you discover?* They tend to end with a falling intonation.

• *alternative questions*, e.g. *Should I telephone now or later?* These also typically end with a fall, indicating that there is no further option.

Some sentences, however, are questions in form only, or in meaning only:

• **Exclamatory questions** are interrogative in form, but are not used to ask genuine questions:

Isn't it a lovely day! (= it is)

• **Rhetorical questions** similarly do not seek an answer:

What's that got to do with me? (= It has nothing to do with me)

• **Declarative questions** are declarative in form but seeking information:

You've already spent the money?

• **Echo questions** take various forms but are asking for something to be repeated (e.g. You've done what?).

Some grammarians try to distinguish between questions-in-form (INTERROGATIVE) and questions-in-meaning (QUESTION). But the labels may be reversed! See p. 212 SENTENCE TYPES.

question-mark

A punctuation mark ⟨?⟩ mainly used to show that the preceding sentence or phrase is a question in meaning. A question-mark is not, therefore, normally used after an exclamatory question, but may possibly be used with a rhetorical one. Nor is a question-mark generally used after a sentence containing an indirect question (e.g. *He asked me if I knew*).

question-tag

A question phrase, consisting of an operator + a pronoun, tagged on to the end of a declarative sentence. The whole sentence plus tag is sometimes called a *tag-question*.

In the most usual type of sentence, a negative tag is added to a positive statement, and a positive tag is added to a negative one:

> It's been cold this week, hasn't it?

> You're not really going to walk all the way, are you?

Said with a falling tone on the tag, the whole sentence is more like an exclamation, assuming the listener's agreement; with a rising tone the tag becomes a question inviting a response.

Less usual are positive statements + positive tags (e.g. *So that's what you think, is it?*). Tags can also be added to imperatives and exclamations:

> Keep in touch, won't you?

> What a wonderful thing to do, wasn't it!

question word

A *wh*-word (including *how*) when used to ask a question.

The main question words are *what, which, who, whom, whose; when, where, why,* and *how*. They are sometimes reinforced by adding (-) *ever*, as in *What ever did you do that for?*

quotation marks

A pair of marks used at the beginning and end of a word or phrase etc. to show that this bit of text is being quoted by the writer from some other context. Quotation marks may be single ⟨' '⟩ or double ⟨" "⟩. Also called *inverted commas*.

R

reason

Reason is one of the meaning categories used in the analysis of adverb clauses. An alternative term is CAUSE.

See p. 13 ADVERB CLAUSES.

Received Pronunciation (RP)

The pronunciation of British English in a way that is considered to be least regional; originally the pronunciation used by 'educated' speakers in southern England.

In recent years RP has lost some of its prestige, and a wide variety of accents are heard and accepted on British radio and television, for example. 'Pure' RP was never spoken by more than a small minority of the population, and today—as ever—many 'educated' speakers in fact use some sort of modified RP, while some younger speakers in particular strive for a more 'classless' accent.

In any case, changes in pronunciation occur over time, so that RP is not a static system. But it underlies the accepted analysis of English phonemes. It is sometimes popularly described as 'standard English', but that is a wider term embracing standards of grammar also.

reciprocal

The pronouns *each other* and *one another* are reciprocal pronouns, because the meaning is 'A does something or other to B, and B does the same to A'. There is no real difference in usage, despite a prescriptive rule that *one another* should be used when the reference is to more than two.

recoverability

If a word or phrase, though not present, can be deduced or retrieved from the context, it is recoverable.

Recoverability, enabling us to make sense of otherwise incomplete utterances, is essential to the use both of ELLIPSIS and PRO-FORMS. Thus in

> The man said he would telephone this morning but didn't

we can 'recover' *the man* from the pro-form *he*, and we can also recover the elliptic words

> but (*he*) didn't (*telephone this morning*)

recursion

The repeated use of a particular type of word or phrase. This is an important feature of language, making it possible for some structures to be repeated endlessly. For example there is theoretically no limit to the length of an adjective string:

> What fascinates them is his maddening, engaging, dotty, intelligent, charming . . . and humourless personality

or to the number of prepositional phrases that can follow each other:

> The ring was in a bag in a box in the corner of a drawer in a chest in the corner of the room in (etc.)

or to the number of relative clauses:

> This is . . . the mouse that lived in the house that Jack built

reduce

1 A clause or phrase is *reduced* when some of it is left out. Grammatical *reduction* therefore includes both ELLIPSIS and SUBSTITUTION. Thus, in reply to

> You should write to your bank manager

a reduced response could be *I have* (ellipsis) or *I've done so* (with a substitute phrase).

• **reduced relative clause**: a non-finite or verbless postmodifying structure can often be interpreted as a relative clause with its pronoun and verb omitted:

> Anyone *scared of heights* is advised not to attempt this climb (= anyone *who is scared of heights* etc.)

See p. 205 RELATIVE CLAUSES.

2 In the pronunciation of words, sounds are often reduced (or WEAKENED), e.g. the second vowel of *photo* is reduced to a weak vowel in the word *photograph*.

redundancy

Redundancy—having more linguistic features than are strictly necessary—is to some extent a normal and important characteristic of language, enabling the 'message' to be more easily understood.

Some redundancy is firmly built into the syntax. For example, in *The sun rises* there are two markers of singular, where one might be sufficient (as indeed it is in the simple past, *The sun rose*). On the other hand, there is a counter-tendency to avoid tedious redundancy by the REDUCTION of easily RECOVERABLE features, although there are grammatical limits on what is allowable.

reference

Language must refer to something, but there are different ways it does this. An expression may refer to

1 something 'out there in the real world' (its *referent*).

2 another expression in the 'text'.

Thus the phrases *the daughter of Alderman Alfred Roberts of Grantham* and *Britain's first woman Prime Minister* refer to the same person, and therefore have the same *referent*, although these expressions are not formally related and the 'sense' is different.

Reference to another expression within a text, however, often depends on PRO-FORMS or other words which are substituted to avoid repetition. Reference may be back (in anaphoric reference) or forward (in cataphoric reference):

> Mrs Thatcher was pleased when *she* was elected MP for Finchley in 1959
>
> Three years after *she* left office, Lady T published *The Downing Street Years*

In each sentence here there is *co-reference*. The two related items share both 'real world' reference (to the same person), and also textual reference (with the pronoun *she* used as a SUBSTITUTION pro-form for another expression).

reflexive

1 *reflexive pronouns* end in *-self/-selves*, e.g. *myself, themselves*. They refer back to the subject of the same clause, sometimes for emphasis:

> *He told me about it himself*

and sometimes as the object of the verb:

> *She's always hurting herself*

A reflexive pronoun is not usually considered acceptable as a subject in standard English (e.g. **James and myself intend to help*), but can be used for emphatic reinforcement (*I myself believe that he is telling the truth, despite what the others say*).

2 English only has a few verbs that have to be reflexive, e.g. *absent oneself, perjure oneself, pride oneself*.

Other verbs may be understood reflexively but a reflexive pronoun object is optional (e.g. *He washed, shaved, and dressed*).

register

A particular register is a particular variety of language (recognizable by syntax, vocabulary, and possibly pronunciation) used in particular circumstances. Different registers can relate to

(*a*) levels of formality, ranging from the very formal to the colloquial or even slangy;

(*b*) language varieties that are especially related to a particular subject or occupation, e.g. advertising language or the language of the law.

regular

A word etc. is regular if it follows the general rules for its class, in contrast to IRREGULAR.

Regular verbs form both past tense and past participle by adding *-ed* to the base (or *-d* if the base ends in *-e*). E.g. *look, looked, looked, race, raced, raced*.

Similarly, regular noun plurals are formed by adding *-s* (or *-es*), as with *books, boxes*.

relative

Relative words introduce relative clauses, which typically have an adjectival function in relation to an earlier noun phrase. The best-known relative words are the *relative pronouns—who*, *whom*, *whose*, *which*, and *that*.

When and *where* can be used as *relative adverbs*:

> That was the day when he had to climb the drainpipe
>
> I remember, I remember, the house where I was born

Relative clauses (also called adjectival clauses) are of two main kinds:

1 defining relative clause—so called because the clause follows a noun phrase and uniquely defines or identifies it. *Who*, *whom*, *whose*, *which*, and *that* are used:

> The person *who/that told me* swore me to secrecy
>
> It was someone *whose bike I borrowed*
>
> The bike *which/that I borrowed* was almost new

A *contact* clause (with no relative pronoun) is possible if the pronoun would be the grammatical object, or object of a preposition, in the relative clause:

> the woman /—/who/whom/that I love
>
> this person /—/who/that I told you about
>
> the bike /—/that/which he lent me

A defining clause is not separated from its noun phrase by a comma.

2 A non-defining relative clause gives additional information about its noun phrase, which is in some way already identified. A *wh*-pronoun must normally be used, and the clause is separated from the rest of the sentence by a comma or commas. Contact clauses are not possible.

> Algernon, whom I greatly admire, ...

Two other non-defining relative clauses are:

—the *sentential relative clause*, which refers back to the whole of the previous clause. It is introduced by *which*:

> It is very expensive. Which is a pity.

—the *continuative relative clause*, which continues a narrative:

Bob had told Edwin, who passed the news to Henry, who came and told me

A non-finite postmodifying structure where a relative pronoun and the verb *be* could be inserted is a *reduced relative clause*, e.g. Can you see that man [who is] *waving at us*?

A *nominal relative clause* contains a relative pronoun (*what*), but functions like a noun, and is often treated as a NOUN CLAUSE.

RELATIVE CLAUSES AT A GLANCE

defining (or restrictive or identifying) clause:

        the people *who/that sold me the car*
        the car *that/which I bought*
        the people *whose car I bought*
        the people *that/who I bought it from*
        the people *from whom I bought it*

contact clause:

        the people ▲ *I bought it from*
        the car ▲ *I bought*

non-defining (non-restrictive, non-identifying) clause:

        Mr Smith, *who sold it to me*, said . . .
        My Rolls, *which I bought in 1990*, is . . .
        I was talking about my mother, *whom you have never met*

sentential: She hasn't got a car, *which is really rather sensible*

continuative: Mrs X sold it to Mr Smith, *who sold it to me*

reduced relative clause:

        Do you know that man *waving at us*?
        Anyone *afraid of ghosts* would hate it
        The man, *waving frantically*, was obviously terrified

reported speech

1 Usually the same as INDIRECT SPEECH, that is, the reporting of speech using an introductory reporting verb (He *says* . . . She *told* us . . .).

2 Sometimes a more general term to cover any way in which a speaker or writer reports what someone else has said. In this sense, reported speech includes both DIRECT and INDIRECT SPEECH.

Reporting verbs are verbs used to report speech in these ways, e.g. *remark, say, tell.*

restrictive

Limiting or defining.

A *restrictive relative clause* is another name for a DEFINING relative clause. *Non-restrictive* is the same as non-defining.

A *restrictive adjective* (also called a *limiting* adjective) is a particular type of attributive adjective. This is a meaning-based label, because restrictive adjectives restrict or limit the following noun in some way, e.g. *a certain person*, *the main chance*, *an only child*.

result

The meaning of result is shown in various ways.

Result clauses are introduced by *so . . . that*, *such . . . that*, and *so*:

> It was so hot *(that) I nearly fainted*
> It was such a hot day *(that) I nearly fainted*
> The weather was too hot, *so I cried off*

Result clauses are often contrasted with those of PURPOSE. See p. 13 ADVERB CLAUSES.

An *infinitive of result* is an infinitive that has this meaning, e.g.

> He arrived to find the place on fire

Contrast an infinitive of purpose (e.g. *He hurried to help*).

retrospective

Verbs such as *forget*, *regret*, *remember* are sometimes singled out as having a retrospective or 'looking back' meaning, when they are followed by an *-ing* form:

> I'll never forget hearing Sutherland
> I remember wondering how she did it
> I regret missing her final performance

This is then contrasted with a 'looking to the future' meaning when these same verbs are followed by an infinitive (*Don't forget to/remember to lock the door, I regret to say . . .*)

But in fact this difference in time reference is a feature of many other such verb combinations. An *-ing* form is usual when the second verb refers either to an event earlier than the first verb (e.g. He admitted borrowing the car) or to an existing state or a habitual action (She enjoys driving). A *to*-infinitive by contrast often refers to a later time than the first verb (e.g. He decided/hoped/planned/wanted to borrow the car).

rhetorical

Rhetorical language is spoken or written for effect, and not meant to be taken literally.

A rhetorical conditional clause may look like an open condition, but is actually strongly assertive:

> If he wins, I'll eat my hat (= He will not win)
> She's sixty, if she's a day (= She is at least sixty)

A *rhetorical question* is similarly assertive:

> What's that got to do with you? (= It has nothing to do with you)

rhotic

A rhotic accent is an accent where the consonant sound /r/ is always pronounced. Scottish, Irish, General American, and a number of regional English accents are rhotic.

By contrast, RP, Australian, and New Zealand accents and most varieties of 'English English' have lost the /r/ before another consonant sound (as in *bird, are fine*) and when final before a pause (e.g. *Come here!*). These accents are *non-rhotic* or *r-less*.

rise

A nuclear pitch change from relatively low to relatively high in the intonation of a syllable or longer utterance, in contrast to a FALL. (Sometimes called a *rising tone*.)

Various kinds of rise are distinguished, such as the *low rise*, starting near the bottom of an individual speaker's pitch range; and the *high rise*, starting higher, and of course going higher. Yes-no questions usually end on a rise.

rise-fall

A tone in which the pitch rises and then falls. This tone often conveys feelings of surprise, approval, or disapproval.

r liaison

An umbrella term for both intrusive *r* (e.g. /lɔːr ən(d) ɔːdə/ law and order) and linking *r* (/mɔːr ən(d) mɔː/ more and more).

root

A core element from which another word can be derived.

(*a*) A root is commonly a morpheme which cannot be further analysed. For example *go* is the root of *goes*, *going*, *goer*, etc. and also of *undergo*.

(*b*) A root in this sense may be less than a complete word but an element which with an affix added makes a word. For example, *-duce* (as in *conduce*, *deduce*, *reduce*) or *jeal-* (as in *jealous*).

However, the terminology of word formation is inconsistent.

Some people prefer STEM for (*a*) and (*b*), while others use BASE for bound forms such as *-duce* and *jeal-*.

royal *we*

The use of *we* by a king or queen to mean 'I' is called the *royal we*, as in Queen Victoria's 'We are not amused.' The style is now restricted to formal documents.

RP

The abbreviation for RECEIVED PRONUNCIATION.

rule

It is perhaps worth pointing out that terms such as *grammatical rule* or *rule of grammar* are used with two somewhat different meanings. In an ideal world a *descriptive rule*, describing objectively how some feature of the language works, would be the same as a *prescriptive rule* for a user or foreign language learner. In reality, some prescriptive rules are based on misunderstanding, while other prescriptive rules, though useful guide-lines, are oversimplifications and inaccurate if taken to be a complete description.

S

schwa (Also shwa)

The weak unstressed central vowel of English /ə/, heard at the beginning of *ago* and the end of *mother*.

This is a very common sound in English and is sometimes called the neutral vowel, because other vowel phonemes are often reduced to this sound when in unstressed position. Compare *photo* /ˈfəʊtəʊ/, *photograph* /ˈfəʊtəgrɑːf/ and *photography* /fəˈtɒgrəfɪ/.

semantics

Semantics is the study of meaning. It is sometimes contrasted with grammatical meaning (the meaning of the syntax). It also contrasts with pragmatics (the meaning of language in social use).

Traditionally there is a division between syntax and word meaning, which is shown by the separation of information about language into grammar books and dictionaries.

Semantics goes beyond 'word meaning' in viewing words as part of a structured system of interrelationships.

- **semantic field**: an area of related 'things' or other referents, where the definition of each member depends on, and to some extent may overlap with, the others, e.g. *cup*, *mug*, *beaker*. See FIELD.

- **semantic shift**: a change over time in the meaning of a word. For example, *meat* once meant any food—a meaning still preserved in the word *sweetmeat*.

semi-modal

A *semi-modal* verb (also called a *marginal modal* or a *marginal modal auxiliary*) is formally partly like a modal verb and partly like a full (lexical) verb.

Verbs included here are *dare*, *need*, *ought to*, *used to*. All of them use inversion and an added-on *not* (like modals) and also *do*-support (like ordinary verbs), for questions and negatives, though often there is no choice as to which form is possible. Additionally *dare* and *need* have present tense third person singular forms with and without -*s*:

> It was—dare I say it?—a success
> You ought not to boast
> I used not to play/I didn't use to play
> I don't think he need take any action/I don't think he needs to take any action

semi-negative

A word that is almost negative in meaning, and that grammatically often has the same effect as a negative word. (Sometimes called *near negative*.)

A number of adverbials, e.g. *barely, hardly, little, scarcely,* are so nearly negative that they function much like true negative words. Thus they take positive question tags:

> It's barely/scarcely possible, is it?

Similarly, fronted semi-negative adverbs require subject-operator inversion in the same way that true negatives may do:

> *Hardly* had they arrived when the lights went out
> *Only then* did we realize our mistake

semi-passive See PASSIVE.

semi-vowel

A sound which is phonetically vowel-like because it is a glide, but which is consonant-like in being marginal to a syllable.

In English the phonemes /j/ as in *you, use, view,* and /w/ as in *way, suave, choir* are semi-vowels. Traditionally they are classified as consonants because they function marginally: it is noticeable too that like consonants they are preceded by *a,* not *an* (e.g. *a youth, a window*).

See p. 264 THE CONSONANTS OF ENGLISH.

sentence

The sentence is the largest unit of language structure treated in traditional grammar. It usually has (minimally) a subject and a predicate containing a finite verb, and (when written) begins with a capital letter and ends with a full stop or equivalent.

Traditional definitions of the sentence are often in notional terms, e.g. 'a set of words expressing a complete thought', but this is too vague to be useful. Modern attempts at more rigorous structural definitions (as above) are not entirely satisfactory either. For example, imperative sentences usually lack an expressed subject; full-stops and grammatical sentence boundaries do not always coincide; and, in any case, with spoken language, it is often impossible to say where one sentence ends and another begins.

For such reasons as these, modern grammar prefers to analyse syntactic structure in terms of the CLAUSE, although recognizing that pro-forms, connectors, and other cohesive devices in fact operate over stretches of language larger than the sentence.

Sentences are themselves categorized in modern grammar, as in traditional grammar, into simple, compound, and complex sentences on the basis of the number and type of clauses they contain. See p. 212 SENTENCE TYPES.

sentence adverb(ial)

This popular term is not consistently used. Sometimes it covers both CONJUNCTS (which, broadly speaking, connect one sentence to another) and DISJUNCTS (which in a sense may relate to the whole sentence).

In other grammars, however, the term *sentence adverb(ial)* is reserved for DISJUNCTS, and some other term such as *connector* is used for conjuncts. Consider:

> Sadly, this is a problem. However, there is no need to worry too much about it

In some grammars both *sadly* and *however* are sentence adverbs. In others, only *sadly* = sentence adverb (or disjunct), and *however* = connector (or linking adverb or conjunct).

SENTENCE TYPES

MAJOR (OR FULL OR COMPLETE) SENTENCE TYPES

FORM	FUNCTION
1 **Declarative**	
You are making a mistake	Statement
You don't believe me?	Question
You will apologize immediately	Command/Directive
You're joking!	Exclamation
2 **Interrogative** (or **question**)	
What actually do you want?	Question
Are you really going to resign?	Question
What does he think he looks like!	Exclamation
Isn't that just typical!	Exclamation
Haven't we all done silly things in our time	Statement
Will you shut up!	Command/Directive
3 **Exclamative** (or **exclamation**)	
How silly this all is!	Exclamation
What a muddle we're in!	Exclamation
4 **Imperative** (or **command**)	
Be sensible. Forget it	Command/ (advice)
Let us know how you get on	Command/ (request)
Have some more—do help yourself	Command/ (invitation)

MAJOR AND MINOR SENTENCES

MAJOR (or full or complete) sentence

A subject and finite verb are essential, except with *Imperative*, where the subject can be '*you* understood'.
[See above 1–4]

MINOR (or irregular or incomplete) sentence
(In some way lacking complete clause structure, or only having the form of a subordinate clause), e.g.

How about a swim?
Why not forget it?
As if you didn't know
To think it should come to this
Out with it!
The sooner, the better
Not to be taken   etc.

SENTENCES BY CLAUSE COMPOSITION

simple sentence—generally having only one (main) clause and only one finite verb, e.g.
    The Handbook *gives* details of specialist libraries open to the public.

compound sentence—having two or more coordinated clauses, e.g.
    Details *are* correct at time of going to press/ *but are* subject to revision.

complex sentence—having a main clause and at least one subordinate clause, e.g.
    Please *telephone* the librarian in advance/*if* you *have* any queries about your visit.

compound-complex sentence—having at least a main clause, one coordinated (main) clause, and one subordinate clause.

In the following sentence the last two subordinate clauses are not subordinate to main clauses, but to other subordinate clauses (the sixth clause to the fifth, and the fifth to the fourth).

    Please *telephone* the librarian in advance [main] / *if* you *have* any queries about your visit [subordinate]/, but *note* [coordinate with main]/ that libraries *can provide* a better service [subordinate]/ *if* telephone calls *are made* on weekday mornings on days [subordinate]/ *when* the library *is* open to visitors [subordinate]

sentence type

Sentences are traditionally analysed into four major types such as 'statement', 'question', and so on.

However, there is sometimes a mismatch between form and function. For example, *Isn't it a lovely day!* is a question in form, but functions as an exclamation. So it is useful sometimes to distinguish form and function. One grammatical model uses the terms *declarative*, *interrogative*, *exclamative*, and *imperative* as formal categories, reserving the terms *statement*, *question*, *exclamation*, and *command* (or *directive*) as function labels. But there is little consistency in usage. In any case, terms such as *command* or *directive* quite inadequately indicate the pragmatic meaning of many formal imperatives, which often serve as requests (*Remember to send us a postcard*) or invitations (*Do drop in any time you're passing*).

In addition to these four sentence types, primarily recognized on formal grounds as the commonest types and therefore *major*, other acceptable patterns may be recognized as *minor* or 'irregular' or 'incomplete'. Some lack the basic 'subject + finite verb'; others are abbreviated or ellipted in some way. Opinions differ as to what should be included here, some grammarians describing certain types of utterance not as merely irregular but as NON-SENTENCES. (Some possibilities are shown in the table, p. 212.)

sequence of tense rule

The tendency of the verb tense in a subordinate clause to be *backshifted* under the influence of a past tense in the main clause, even though a present tense would be logically acceptable.

The sequence of tense rule applies particularly, but not exclusively, to reported clauses, e.g.

> What did you say your name was?
> I didn't apply for the job although I was female and had the right degree

short form

The same as CONTRACTION (*contracted form*). Most short forms consist of a pronoun plus a primary or modal verb (e.g. *I'm*, *they've*, *we'll*) or such a verb plus the shortened negative (e.g. *hasn't*, *can't*, *won't*).

short vowel See LENGTH.

sibilant

A sibilant sound is a sound that the listener hears as 'hissing'. In English four fricative phonemes are sibilants—/s/, /z/, /ʃ/, and /ʒ/ plus the affricates /tʃ/ and /dʒ/. They contrast with non-sibilant fricatives.

See p. 264 THE CONSONANTS OF ENGLISH.

silent letter

A letter in the spelling which is not sounded in speech.

Arguably, with the vagaries of English spelling, many letters could be said to be silent. The term, however, tends to be applied particularly to *silent e*, as in *infinite, corpse, have*, although in many cases, such as *hope, rate*, the *e* indicates the pronunciation of the preceding vowel (compare *hop, rat*)—it is children's 'magic *e*'. Also silent are such 'lost consonants' as are seen in *(g)nat, (k)nife, ha(l)f*, and *croche(t)*.

simile

A figure of speech in which one thing is openly compared to another. Contrasted with METAPHOR, e.g.

    as dead as the dodo   as flat as a pancake
    as thick as two short planks   as white as a sheet
    like a bull in a china shop   like greased lightning

simple

Not COMPOUND or COMPLEX.

The term is very generally applied. At word level, a word (e.g. *cream*) may be described as simple in contrast to a compound (*icecream*) or to a complex word (*creaminess*). Or a single-word preposition (e.g. *from, before*) may be described as a *simple preposition* in contrast to a complex preposition (*out of, in front of*).

• **simple sentence**: traditionally, and still generally, a single independent clause containing a single finite verb phrase (e.g. *The matter needs careful thought*). Simple sentences contrast with compound and complex sentences. However, in some analyses, a sentence containing a relative clause that is part of a noun phrase is still a simple sentence, e.g. *This / presents / a choice which will affect every aspect of your life and future* has a 'simple' SVO structure.

• **simple tense**: a tense which in its positive form consists of a single word form. English has two simple tenses—the *present simple* (e.g. *look/looks*) and the *past simple* (*looked*). In traditional grammar, the *'shall/will'* future is sometimes called the simple future, but in more modern grammar a phrase such as *will look* is analysed as a complex verb phrase. A *simple verb phrase* is a single verb form without ellipsis (e.g. *'Look!'* he said. 'I *know*').

simplification of tenses

The use of 'simpler' tenses than might somehow be expected. (Also called *tense simplification*.)

This term is particularly applied to tense usage when talking about the future. For example, provided the main clause makes the future reference clear, a present tense is common in many subordinate clauses, e.g.

> If he *is* at the meeting on Friday, I'll tell him
> You will have to wait until he *comes*
> Let me know what he *says*
> Anyone who *isn't* there will have no right to complain
> I hope he *does* come

The term 'simplification' is rather misleading, implying that really we ought to use a 'future tense' (e.g. *will*) in such cases. But *will* often suggests prediction or willingness, so if neither meaning is intended, an *unmarked* 'present' tense is entirely appropriate.

Similarly, a simple past tense is often used in a subordinate clause dependent on a main clause containing a complex verb phrase, e.g.

> Would you do whatever I *asked*? (not *would ask)
> He had already told us what (had) *happened*

singular

(*a*) *Singular* contrasts mainly with PLURAL in the description of nouns, pronouns, and verb forms, e.g.

The *girl/She is/looks*   confident (singular)
The *girls/They are/look*   confident (plural)

(*b*) Uncount nouns are sometimes described as singular because they take singular verbs. But this is misleading, since singular count nouns and uncount nouns do not share all the same determiners (e.g. *a/one* roll, but *some/much* bread).

(*c*) nouns that lack an -*s* but always take a plural verb (e.g. *police*, *cattle*) are also sometimes described as singular on grounds of form.

(*d*) The term *singular noun* is sometimes used as a label for a type of noun which, at any rate in a particular meaning, has no plural form but can be preceded by *a/an* (e.g. *What a shame!*).

slang

Words, phrases, and uses that are regarded as very informal and are often restricted to special contexts or are peculiar to a specified profession, class, etc. (racing slang, schoolboy slang).

slot-and-filler

A once popular method of analysing sentence structure.

Various functional slots are identified, and the words and phrases (fillers) that can fill them are further analysed. For example in

I can resist everything except temptation

there are three slots:

Subject *filled by*   (I)
Verb   (can resist)
Object   (everything except temptation)

The system underlies today's analysis into clause *elements*. It also links up to some extent with the functional (rather than notional) methods used in defining parts of speech. Thus the subject slot could be filled by a vast variety of noun phrases (e.g. *you, the neighbours, everyone I know,* etc.), but all would contain a noun or pronoun as head. Similarly, anything that can fill the second slot must be a verb.

social distancing

Social distancing is the explanation given for a use of past tenses which is connected neither with past time nor with hypothetical meaning, and where a present tense could well be possible, e.g.

Did you want to see me?

I was wondering whether you could spare me a minute?

We were hoping you would help

Sometimes the usage is polite: it may be easier for the addressee to say no than to a blunter request (e.g. *We are hoping you will help*); but at other times the 'distancing' may sound over-formal or cold.

See p. 237 TIME AND TENSE.

soft *c* and soft *g*

This is a popular description of the pronunciation of the letters *c* and *g*, when they represent the sounds /s/ (as in *cell, civil, icy, ace*) and /dʒ/ (as in *gentle, gin, gypsy, age*).

They contrast with *hard c* and *g*, which represent the plosives /k/ and /g/, heard in (*camera, come, curl, sac* and *game, go, gun,* and *fig*).

soft palate

This is another name for the VELUM. See p. 266 THE SPEECH ORGANS.

sound change

Changes over time in pronunciation (as in syntax and vocabulary) are part of the dynamic of a living language. Old English is so different from modern English that it is like a foreign language.

Middle English exhibits quite different sound patterns from our own. Shakespeare's English looks deceptively more like ours than it really was because we have preserved the spelling of his time relatively unaltered. And many of the apparently arbitrary spellings of modern English are explainable in terms of earlier pronunciations.

Changing sound patterns are discernible in our own time. Daniel Jones in his *Outline of English Phonetics* (1918) included a diphthong /ɔə/ heard in such words as *coarse*, *score*, and *four*, and distinct from the monophthong /ɔː/ used in *cork*, *short*, and *fork*, though he noted that many RP speakers used /ɔː/ for both. Present-day descriptions of English (RP) no longer include /ɔə/ as a phoneme, since virtually no RP speakers make this distinction. At the same time, /ɔː/ is also frequently heard in words such as *tour* (traditionally /tʊə/); but it is now virtually never heard, as it once was, in words such as *off* and *cloth* (pronunciations which were old-fashioned even in Jones's day).

Another noticeable kind of sound change is the shifting of stress patterns within the word. One fairly systematic change in British English is a tendency in polysyllabic words for stress to move from earlier or later in the word to the third syllable from the end; hence such changes as 'controversy—con'troversy, ' primarily—pri'marily, prome'nade—'promenade.

sound symbolism

The sounds or syllables of some words are said to relate directly to the meanings. Where whole words imitate 'real-world' sounds (e.g. *miaow*), the relationship is often termed ONOMATOPOEIA.

Sound symbolism also occurs with such phenomena as the many unpleasant words beginning with *sl-* (*slag, slattern, sleazy, slime, sluggard, slurp, slop*) and with nose-related nastiness indicated by *sn-* (*sneer, sneeze, sniff, snigger, snivel, snog, snore, snort, snot,* etc.).

sound system

The phonemic system of a language. The 44 PHONEMES of standard English are shown in the table, THE SOUNDS OF ENGLISH, p. 265.

space

Space (alternatively *place*) is used in its usual sense in describing the meaning of adverbials and prepositions, including both position and direction. Many *spatial* adverbials and prepositions have both meanings, e.g. *abroad, beneath, downstairs, outside,* etc. as in

They are abroad (position)
They have gone abroad (direction)

specific

(*a*) The term is used by some grammarians in relation to article usage, and a distinction is made between *specific* and GENERIC (or CLASSIFYING) meaning. *Specific*, in this usage, means 'that particular person/thing and no other', but may be either *definite* or *indefinite*, e.g.

I met an interesting man on holiday (specific indefinite)
The man told me . . . (specific definite)

(*b*) In other grammars, *specific* is contrasted with *general*, but the distinction made is very different. Here all determiners are either one or the other but not both, and specific refers to *the* in all its meanings, to demonstratives (*this* etc.) and possessives (*my* etc.), while 'general determiners' include *a/an* (whatever its meaning). Thus *specific* includes definite, and *general* roughly equates with indefinite.

The word is often used loosely in popular grammar books, with no specialized meaning at all.

speech organ

Any part of the mouth, nose, throat, etc. involved in the production of speech sounds is a speech organ. See p. 266 THE SPEECH ORGANS.

spelling pronunciation

The pronunciation of a word according to its written form, when its traditional pronunciation is different.

Such pronunciations are considered 'incorrect' by many speakers, but may eventually supersede the traditional pronunciations. Thus spelling pronunciations of *ate*, *forehead*, and *often* /eɪt/, /fɔːhed/, and /ɒftən/ are commonly heard, rather than the traditional (RP) /et/, / fɒrɪd/, and /ɒf(ə)n/. Spelling pronunciations now fully established are *humour*, *hotel*, and *hospital* with initial /h/, replacing the older *h*-less forms.

Spelling variants are dealt with at ORTHOGRAPHY.

split infinitive

A *to*-infinitive with a word or words inserted between the *to* and
the actual infinitive, regarded as incorrect usage.

Prescriptive grammar is against the split infinitive because in Latin
the infinitive is a single indivisible word.

Avoidance may at times be wise since a split infinitive can be
stylistically clumsy and anyway may distract a prescriptively minded
reader from the message. However, avoidance has its pitfalls, as
the offending word(s) if moved may become attached to another
part of the sentence and change the meaning; avoidance can also
result in stylistic awkwardness. A split infinitive may be the best
option in:

> He has promised to be the first president to really unite the country
> (?*really to unite*, *to unite really, **to unite the country really*)

standard English

The variety of English employed by educated users; the English
defined in dictionaries, grammars, and usage guides.

Standard English is a wider term than *Received Pronunciation* (RP).
It primarily refers to a system of grammar (which can be spoken
in a variety of accents), and it includes written English.

Standard English enjoys greater prestige than dialects and non-
standard varieties, but linguists insist that non-standard English is
not linguistically substandard.

In addition to the basic 'common core' standard, many national
standards are recognized, including American English (Am. E) and
British English (Br. E), which have few grammatical differences but
much lexical divergence.

statement

See p. 212 SENTENCE TYPES.

state verb

State verbs refer to relatively permanent situations, e.g.

> They *own* their own house
> It *has* four bedrooms
> The garden *is* huge
> I *dislike* bats

State verbs contrast with ACTION VERBS (referring to actions, events, happenings). *State* is a popular label for STATIVE (just as *action* is for *dynamic*). Normally state (or *stative*) verbs are not used in progressive tenses (**They are owning their own house*); in practice some state/stative verbs are used with dynamic meaning (*We're having a party*, *You're being difficult*).

stative

Expressing a state or condition. Contrasted with DYNAMIC.

Stative (popularly *state*) is particularly used in the classification of verbs. In addition to *be* and *have* in their fundamental meanings, verbs of stative meaning include *appear, believe, concern, consist of, know, matter, own.*

stem

An element in word formation.

The terms *stem, root,* and *base* are used in contrasting (and conflicting) ways.

(*a*) Some linguists use the term *stem,* rather than ROOT for the most primitive element in word formation, to which various affixes can be added. Such a stem may be free (i.e. a word in its own right, such as the first syllable in *self*-ish) or bound (as in *jeal*-ous).

(*b*) For others, a stem (as the metaphor perhaps suggests) may be more complicated than a simple root, and something from which another word grows. For example, *self-conscious* is clearly not a primitive form. But it is the stem (or compound stem) for *unselfconscious,* because we can only add *un-* to *self-conscious* and not to some smaller part (e.g. *unself). However, some analysts refer to a form such as *self-conscious* in this context as a BASE.

stop

A stop or stop consonant is a speech sound in which there is a complete closure somewhere in the vocal organs.

The terms by itself normally means a PLOSIVE. It can, however, be extended to NASALS, in which case plosives can be distinguished as oral stops and nasals as nasal stops.

stranded

A word is stranded when it is left on its own because of ellipsis, or because it has been moved.

Ellipsis frequently leaves an operator stranded:

> She promised to send us a card, but she *didn't*

Similarly, a subject may be stranded in a comparison:

> You play the flute so much better than *George*

Stranded prepositions (What ever were you thinking *of*? The boiler needs seeing *to*) are also described as *deferred* prepositions.

stress

The terms *stress* and *accent* are often used interchangeably. Phoneticians who use the terms more precisely relate stress to the force or energy used in the articulation of a syllable, which the listener perceives in terms of loudness. They then reserve the term *accent* for this plus a pitch change.

• **word stress** (also called *word accent* or *lexical stress*): the stress patterns of words. In English these are for the most part fixed for each word, though the stress occurs on different syllables in different words, e.g. 'yesterday, to'morrow, under'stand. This makes English a *free stress* language. (Word stress may also change over time, e.g. 'controversy versus con'troversy.)

Some word pairs, involving two different parts of speech, are distinguished by stress. Contrast

> 'Exports (noun) rose in the second quarter. But we still need to ex'port (verb) more.

Some words have both *primary* and *secondary* stress. Primary stress potentially allows a pitch change (which would normally accompany the word if said in isolation.) Secondary stress involves less energy and is heard as less loud, e.g.

'microcom,puter (primary, secondary)
,anti-'aircraft (secondary, primary)

• **shifting stress** (*stress shift*): a phenomenon of connected speech. Words containing secondary stress may change their stress patterns, as a way of 'balancing' a phrase or sentence, e.g.

The ,prin'cess is now the ,Princess 'Royal

• **sentence stress**: the way which some words in an utterance are stressed and others not. In general, lexical words (nouns, verbs, etc.) are stressed, and form words (articles, prepositions, etc.) are not.

• **contrastive stress**: marked stress on a word that would not normally be stressed, in order to imply a contrastive meaning, e.g.

WHAT are you doing? (= did I hear correctly?)
What ARE you doing? (= it's very surprising)
What YOU are doing? (= never mind the others)

• **nuclear stress** (or *tonic stress*): the stress that accompanies a pitch change in a TONE UNIT. In unemphatic speech, the nuclear stress occurs on the last stressed syllable (e.g. What are you DOing?).

stress-timed

In a *stress-timed* language the stressed syllables occur at regular intervals, irrespective of how many unstressed syllables there may be. English is predominantly stress-timed, in contrast to syllable-timed languages (such as French) where the syllables (whether stressed or unstressed) occur at more or less regular intervals. Thus in the sentence.

'Both of them are ,mine

the unstressed syllables (*of them are*) are compressed, while the monosyllable *mine* takes roughly as much time as the preceding *Both of them are*.

strong form

1 Many FORM WORDS (GRAMMATICAL words) have two pronunciations: a *strong form* and a *weak form*. The strong form, containing

a *strong vowel*, is used when the word is said in isolation or when stressed for emphasis, or when it occurs in a prominent position (e.g. at the end of a sentence). The weak form, containing a weak vowel, is its usual pronunciation. Thus articles *a*, *an*, and *the* usually have weak forms (/ə/ and /ðə/ before a consonant sound; /ən/ and /ðɪ/ before a vowel sound). Their strong forms are /eɪ/, /æn/, and /ðiː/.

strong vowel

A *strong vowel* is a vowel that retains its pronunciation even when it is in a weak, unstressed position. All vowels in stressed syllables are clearly identifiable and therefore strong. In unstressed syllables, vowels often become weak, but may remain strong. All the vowels in the following words, whether stressed or unstressed are strong:

anarch /'ænɑːk/, armrest /'ɑːmrest/, fatstock /'fætstɒk/, obese /əʊ'biːs/, photo /'fəʊtəʊ/, unlike /ʌn'laɪk/

structure word

The same as FORM WORD. See p. 165 PARTS OF SPEECH.

suasive verb

A verb with a 'persuading' meaning, which is often followed by a *that*-clause.

Suasive verbs contrast both semantically and syntactically with FACTUAL VERBS. Unlike factual verbs, which take an indicative in the subordinate clause, suasive verbs allow a choice:

She demanded that {
he return the money
he should return the money
he returned the money
}

subject

1 Traditionally a sentence is divided into two parts, the subject (which usually comes first, and is what the sentence 'is about') and the PREDICATE, which is what is 'predicated' or stated about the subject.

In modern grammar, sentence (or rather clause) analysis is strictly formal. The subject is defined grammatically as whatever 'governs' the verb. It is symbolized as S, while the predicate is analysed in more detail into four further possible elements—Verb, Object, Complement, and Adverbial.

A grammatical subject is normally essential in English sentence structure and a dummy subject may be introduced if there is no other one (e.g. *It is raining*).

Although this subject is typically a noun phrase (which can, of course, be a single noun or pronoun) it can also be realized by a clause or even a prepositional phrase, e.g.

That you could do such a thing really shocks me

After nine o'clock would be more convenient

2 To overcome the ambiguity of the word *subject*, traditional grammar sometimes qualified the word. So in addition to a (grammatical) subject we may have a *logical subject*, particularly with a passive verb. Thus in

The building was designed by my favourite architect

the grammatical subject is *The building*, but the logical subject (the doer, or in today's terminology the AGENT) is *my favourite architect*.

Traditional grammar also sometimes introduced a *psychological subject*, possibly equivalent to today's THEME or TOPIC, e.g.

That question, I cannot answer. [= grammatically the object]

• **subject** (or **subjective**) **case**: the distinctive CASE forms taken by six pronouns when in grammatical subject position (i.e. *I, he, she, we, they, who*).

• **subject** (or **subjective**) **complement**: a COMPLEMENT that refers back to the subject (e.g. *I felt foolish/a fool*).

subject-attachment rule See ATTACHMENT RULE.

subject territory

The position of the grammatical subject, before the verb—in contrast to OBJECT TERRITORY. This term is particularly used in seeking to explain the ungrammatical use of pronouns. Thus in

That was the reason for my wife and I leaving the club

it can be argued that *my wife and I* is in subject territory relative to *leaving*. But this is irrelevant to the sentence's grammar, which requires 'for my wife and me . . .'.

subject-verb inversion See INVERSION.

subjunct

An adverb(ial) with a subordinate role in clause structure, and contrasting with other adverbials such as ADJUNCT, CONJUNCT, and DISJUNCT.

This is a category not recognized as such in more traditional grammar, where many of today's subjuncts would be included in some wider degree category.

In general, a subjunct (*a*) expresses a 'viewpoint' (e.g. *Politically, the idea is suicidal*), (*b*) is used as a courtesy marker (*Kindly be seated*), or (*c*) is more narrowly linked to a single word or phrase (e.g. *really odd, hardly possible, too dreadful*).

See p. 11 ADVERBS.

subjunctive

The subjunctive is a verbal form or MOOD expressing hypothetical or non-factual meanings. It contrasts particularly with the indicative.

Modern English (unlike, say, French) has few distinct verb forms that differentiate subjunctive from indicative, so there is no formal justification for describing as subjunctive the use of ordinary indicative tenses to express hypothesis (e.g. *If you came tomorrow . . .*).

Modern grammar therefore restricts the term to two distinct tenses, somewhat misleadingly labelled *present* and *past*:

1 The **present subjunctive** is a finite verb form identical with the base of the verb. This means that it is exactly the same as the present indicative tense, except in the third person singular which lacks an *-s*, and in the verb *be*, where the subjunctive is *be* (instead of *is, am, are*). The tense, despite its name, can be used when the reference is to the past. It is used in three ways:

1a The *mandative subjunctive* is used in subordinate clauses following an expression of command, suggestion, or possibility, e.g.

I recommended he write and apologize

She requested that she not be disturbed

This subjunctive has made a considerable comeback in British English in recent years, probably under American influence.

1b Rather formally, the present subjunctive can be used in subordinate clauses of condition and concession, but not with past reference, e.g.

If that be the case . . .

1c The *formulaic subjunctive* is used in independent clauses, mainly in set expressions, e.g.

God save the Queen

Some such clauses have unusual word order, e.g.

Perish the thought!

2 The **past subjunctive** (also called the *were*-subjunctive) is used in clauses of hypothetical condition. It differs from the past indicative of *be* only in the first and third person singular, which popularly replaces it:

If I were you, I'd own up (If I was you . . .)

If only my grandfather were alive today (If only my grandfather was . . .)

A hypercorrect use of *were* when an indicative *was* is preferable is a *pseudo-subjunctive*, e.g.

?If he were there yesterday, why didn't he telephone?

subordinate clause

A clause that forms part of a sentence and is dependent on some other clause, phrase, or word.

Traditional grammar recognized three types of subordinate clause: *adverb*, *noun*, and *relative*. Some modern grammar distinguishes the *nominal relative clause* from the noun (or nominal) clause, and also treats *comparative* clauses and *comment* clauses separately. Some non-finite and verbless structures may also be classed as clauses. See p. 42 CLAUSES.

subordination

Subordination is the dependence of a clause on some other part of the sentence. It is often formally indicated.

A *subordinator* (or *subordinating conjunction*) introduces an adverbial clause. Most subordinators are single-word conjunctions (e.g *although*, *because*, *before*, *if*, *since*, *whereas*), but there are also multi-word subordinators (e.g. *in order that*, *provided (that)*, *as long as*, *in case*).

Wh-words introduce some noun clauses, relative clauses, and even some adverbial clauses (e.g. Whatever happens, don't panic).

That introduces some noun clauses and some relative clauses, and forms part of some multi-word subordinators.

Some subordinate clauses have no subordinating word, e.g.

> I thought *(that) I had told you*
> It's not easy, *you know*
> What happened to that book *I lent you*?

Non-finite and verbless clauses are sometimes introduced by a preposition, e.g.

> *On* hearing this, she rushed to the bank
> *With* the money under her belt, she felt better

substitution

Substitution is a grammatical device, involving the use of pro-forms to avoid tedious repetition.

Substitution is not the same as co-*reference*. In substitution, pro-forms simply replace other words, e.g.

> I like your golf umbrella. Where can I get *one* like it?

In co-reference, the pro-form refers to another word or phrase but also to exactly the same person or thing in the 'real world', e.g.

> I like your golf umbrella. May I borrow *it*?

Substitution also differs from reference in being able to use pro-forms to replace clauses and so on:

If you'll contribute £20,   {   I'll *do so* too.
                              {   I'll *do the same*.

suffix

A suffix is an affix added at the end of a word or base to form a new word, in contrast to a PREFIX.

Suffixes, unlike prefixes, usually have a grammatical effect on the word or base to which they are added. There are broadly two kinds:

1 *inflectional*, adding an inflection, e.g.

   look + *-s* or *-ed*; *kind* + *-er* or *-est*

2 *derivational* forming a new word, e.g.

   (nouns)   book*let*, kind*ness*, play*er*
   (adjectives)   care*less*, hope*ful*, manage*able*
   (verbs)   idol*ize*, wid*en*
   (adverbs)   pretti*ly*

See p. 145 NEW WORDS.

superlative

Gradable adjectives and adverbs have superlative forms that express the highest degree of comparison, above POSITIVE and COMPARATIVE.

The superlative is formed either by adding *-est* to the positive form or by using *most*: *happiest, soonest, most beneficial, most energetically*.

suppletion

Suppletion is the occurrence of unrelated forms to supply gaps in conjugation. *Went* as the past of *go*, or *was/were* as the past of *be* are obvious suppletive forms.

syllable

The syllable is difficult to define in universally valid phonetic terms, but easier to define in terms of an individual language. In English a syllable contains one, and only one, vowel sound. This may be a pure vowel (long or short), a diphthong, or a *syllabic* consonant. Consonants which can be syllabic in English are /m/, /n/, and /l/, as in some pronunciations of *mm*, butt*on*, and app*le*.

Some syllables consist of a vowel sound alone (as in the single-syllable words *eye* /aɪ/ or *ah* /ɑː/). Consonants are marginal to a syllable. English syllable structure can be quite complicated with as many as three consonants before the vowel and up to four after, symbolized (CCC) V (CCCC). See CONSONANT CLUSTER.

An *open syllable* is a syllable ending in a vowel.

Syllables, rather than individual phonemes, carry stress and pitch patterns. In a *syllable-timed language* (e.g. French) each syllable is pronounced with roughly the same duration. This contrasts with a language like English, which is STRESS-TIMED.

Phonetic syllables (the division of a word by sound) and written syllables (division by spelling) do not necessarily correspond. For example, the word *syllable* itself is phonetically a three-syllable word, but in writing it across two lines this word could only reasonably be split at one place, *syll- able* (whatever modern typography might do to it).

synonym

A synonym is a word that means the same or almost the same as another word (in the same language). Strictly speaking there are few, if any, 'true' synonyms, that is words that are completely and always interchangeable. But pairs of words such as *close* and *shut* are sufficiently alike to rank as synonyms, even though they are not substitutable for each other in, for example, *I'm going to close my bank account*, *The meeting closed with a vote of thanks*, or *The water supply was shut off*.

syntagm

A syntagm is a serial relationship, a set of linguistic forms in an *and*-relationship, a CHAIN relationship, with each other. A syntagm contrasts with a PARADIGM.

Syntagms operate at all levels of language. Thus phonemes join into syntagms to produce words (/b/ + /ʊ/ + /k/ = *book*; morphemes too join into syntagms to produce words (*book* + *s* = *books*). And words in a chain relationship form clauses (e.g. *Books + do + furnish + a + room*).

syntax

Syntax is the grammatical arrangement of words in sentences, and the rules explaining such a system.

Traditionally *syntax* (the structure of sentences) is one of the two main branches of language study, along with MORPHOLOGY (the structure of words).

T

tag

A tag is a short phrase or clause added to an already complete utterance. Different types of tag are distinguished, for example:

(*a*) a noun phrase referring back to an earlier one for emphasis

> They use some confusing terms, *these grammarians*

or to add an exclamatory comment

> He's won another prize, *clever man*

or—perhaps more colloquially—with a verb

> They baffle you, *do those long words*
> That was the week, *that was*

(*b*) A QUESTION-TAG usually takes the form of an auxiliary verb + pronoun which are syntactically related to the sentence to which they are added (e.g. It's cold today, *isn't it*?). The complete sentence including the tag is sometimes called a *tag question*. Syntactically unrelated question tags are also found, e.g.

> It cost £1,000, *did you say?*
> That's not exactly cheap, *would you think?*
> Tell him to take it back, *why don't you?*
> Suppose I tell him, *shall I?*

(*c*) Some grammarians include among tags short responses by another speaker when these too consist of a subject + an auxiliary verb relating to the verb of the previous utterance:

> It costs £1,000. *Does it?/It doesn't!*
> That's not cheap. *Nor are the other ones.*
> Shall I tell him? *Yes, do.*

temporal

Temporal is used in its usual sense of 'relating to time', particularly in describing the meaning of some adverbs and prepositions (e.g. *then, meanwhile, before*). Temporal meaning is often contrasted with SPATIAL meaning, but many words have both meanings (*in* a box, *in* July).

tense

A form taken by a verb, particularly to indicate time. Traditionally, tense is defined in terms of time. But labels such as PAST, PRESENT, and FUTURE tense are misleading, and the relationship is more complicated. Past and present tenses can be used in some circumstances to refer to future time (e.g. *If he came tomorrow . . ., If he comes tomorrow . . ., We leave next Sunday*), present tenses can refer to the past (as in newspaper headlines, e.g. *Minister resigns*) and so on. See p. 237 TIME AND TENSE.

Some grammarians define *tense* narrowly by form—which gives English only two tenses: the *present tense*, which in lexical verbs is the same as the base (except for the -*s* ending in the third person singular); and the *past tense*, which in regular lexical verbs has the -*ed* inflection.

In terms of meaning, the present tense is then defined as the unmarked tense, which is timeless in the sense that it can embrace any time that does not exclude the speaker's time (hence its use for general truths) and any time that the speaker does not want to distance himself from. The past tense is then defined as the marked tense—marked for separation from the speaker's 'now', or to indicate hypothesis, or to indicate SOCIAL DISTANCING.

More generally, many verb phrase combinations that incorporate features of ASPECT, MOOD, and VOICE are treated as part of the tense system, giving such tenses as past subjunctive (e.g. *If I were you . . .*), present progressive passive (*Are you being served?*), and so on.

For tense usage in subordinate clauses see SEQUENCE OF TENSE RULE and SIMPLIFICATION OF TENSES.

text

Text is used as a neutral term for any stretch of language, long or short (including transcribed spoken language), that constitutes some sort of meaningful unit.

TENSES

THE TWO TENSES
(narrowly defined)

Present	Past
am/are/is	was/were
have/has	had
do/does	did
look/looks	looked
see/sees	saw

TENSES AS POPULARLY DEFINED

(using perfect and progressive aspect)

Present	simple:	I *work*/he *works* in a bank
	progressive:	I *am*/she *is*/we *are working* hard
	perfect:	I *have*/he *has worked* hard this year
	perfect progressive:	You *have*/she *has been working* all the morning
Past	simple:	We *worked* long hours
	progressive:	They *were*/He *was working* on a secret project
	perfect:	I *had worked* long hours
	perfect progressive:	They *had been working* all that night
'Future'	simple:	I/We *shall/will work* harder in future
		She/He/You/They *will work* better for this
	progressive:	I/We *shall/will be working* this evening
		She/He/You/They *will be working* on Sunday
	perfect:	I *shall/will have worked* there over thirty years when I retire
	perfect progressive:	They *will have been working* for 48 hours without a break

VOICE

Active	Passive
(transitive verb)	(same tense of *be* + past participle)

e.g.

They *speak* English there	English *is spoken* there
They*'re mending* the road	The road *is being mended*
We *won't* forget you	You *won't be forgotten*
They*'ve paid* everybody	Everybody *has been paid*
They *took* all my jewellery	All my jewellery *was taken*

MOOD

Indicative	He *insists* that I *wasn't listening*
Imperative	*Listen! Own up! Try* to remember
Subjunctive	They demanded that she *tell* them
	She insisted that she *be allowed* a solicitor
	Heaven *help* us all!
	Perish the thought!
	If I *were* younger, and he *were* richer . . .!

....

that-clause

Primarily a nominal clause beginning with *that* or where *that* could be inserted, e.g.

That you believe such nonsense amazes me
It amazes me *(that) you believe such nonsense*

Relative clauses with *that* are sometimes included, e.g.

What's all this nonsense *that you're repeating*?

theme

Theme is contrasted with FOCUS as a way of analysing the information structure of a clause. The theme states the subject-matter or viewpoint, about which more important information (the focus) will be stated.

In general, *theme* and *focus* make the same distinction as *topic and comment*. The theme (or topic) comes at the beginning (the front), and there are various grammatical devices available in English to *thematize* different elements if the grammatical subject is not the theme. One device is using the passive to thematize an object:

Trespassers / will be prosecuted
Mistakes / cannot afterwards be rectified

Thematizing is also called FRONTING or topicalization.

three-part verb

This is another term for a phrasal-prepositional verb, e.g. *look down on* (= despise), *put up with* (= endure).

TIME AND TENSE

Tense (form)	Time (meaning)
PRESENT (SIMPLE AND PROGRESSIVE)	
Of course, I *promise*	present moment
The phone's *ringing*	
They *live* in Cambridge	present period
I *catch* the 8.15 most days	
He's *living* in a hostel	
Water *boils* at 100˚C	timeless
We *leave* next Friday	future
We're *returning* on the 18th	future
If anyone *calls*, say I'm *designing* St Paul's	future
Famous pop star *dies* (news headline)	past
Shakespeare *says* . . .	
So I'm just *sitting* there and this chap *comes* up to me . . .	
PRESENT PERFECT	
This is the first time I *have* ever *flown* in a helicopter	present
I've always *wanted* to try it	past-to-present
I *have* only once *flown* in Concorde	past
I'll lend you my copy when I've *finished* with it	future
PAST (SIMPLE AND PROGRESSIVE)	
We *flew* there in 1990	past
I *promised* to help	
They *lived* in Cambridge	
I *caught* the 8.15 most days	
He *was living* in a hostel at the time	
I wish you'd told me you *weren't coming* tomorrow	future
I wouldn't ask if I *knew*	present (hypothetical)
If I *won* the pools, I'd give up my job	future (hypothetical)
Did you want something?	present (social distancing)
I *wondered* if you'd like a ticket?	present (social distancing)
PAST PERFECT	
I realized I *had forgotten* my passport	'before-past'

If only I *had known* in time!	past (hypothetical)
I *had been wondering* if you could help?	past-to-present
	(social distancing)

....

time

Time adverbs, prepositions, and so on are the same as TEMPORAL adverbs etc. Time adverbs are often subdivided under such categories as duration and frequency.

• **time clause:** an adverbial clause relating to time, and introduced by a temporal (time) conjunction such as *when*, *while*, *after*, *until*, *since*, *as long as*, and *once* (e.g. *Once we receive the money, we will send out the order*).

Some time clauses are non-finite, e.g.

While smoking in bed, he had fallen asleep

He awoke *to find the bedclothes on fire*

or verbless:

He should fix a smoke alarm, *as soon as possible*

to-infinitive

The infinitive preceded by *to*, in contrast to the BARE INFINITIVE. The *to*-infinitive (or a *to*-infinitive clause) is used:

after many catenative verbs: I want *to know*

as (part of) a nominal: *To know* all is *to forgive* all

as (part of) an adverbial clause: Pull tab *to open*

as a post-modifier: a book *to read*, nothing *to do*

as an adjective complement: nice *to know*, hard *to imagine*

tone unit

The tone unit is the basic unit in the analysis of intonation, rather like the clause or sentence is in the analysis of syntactic structure. A tone unit contains one, and only one, marked PITCH change (or nuclear tone).

A tone unit may consist of a single syllable (e.g. in an utterance such as *No!* or *Right?*), but often covers a longer phrase or even a sentence when said with no special emphasis. The different intonation patterns that are possible over a tone unit are called TUNES.

tongue

The tongue is involved in some way in the production of most speech sounds.

Vowel articulations are described in terms of tongue height, and whether the front or back or centre of the tongue is highest.

For consonants, the tongue is theoretically divided into various parts, so that whichever part is important in the articulation can be named. Sometimes the *root* is named, then slightly further forward is the *back*, then the *front* (note), then the *blade* and, farthest forward of all, the *tip* (or *apex*). The sides are called the *rims*. (Note that unfortunately this labelling is not universal, so that sometimes the blade is called the front, and the area behind that (front in other systems) is called the centre or top.) See p. 266 THE SPEECH ORGANS.

topic

The topic is that part of a sentence about which something is said, in contrast to the COMMENT.

The *topic* and *comment* distinction, like THEME and FOCUS or GIVEN and NEW is a way of analysing the information structure of a sentence. The topic frequently coincides with the subject and the comment with the predicate, as in

The land / lies in the Green Belt

but the topic can be some other grammatical element, e.g.

At Layhams Farm, it is now proposed to construct a double artifical ski slope (*place adverbial* as topic)

Recreational it may be, but no development could be more inappropriate (*adjective complement* as topic)

More building we do not want (*object* as topic)

Topic is similar to *theme,* so putting the topic (or theme) at the front is variously described as *topicalization, thematization,* or FRONTING.

transcription

Transcription is the representation of speech sounds using phonetic symbols. The aim is to indicate speech sounds consistently. This is partly to overcome the vagaries of spelling; many dictionaries give standard pronunciations of a word and common variants. But transcription also makes it possible to represent accurately the assimilations and elisions of an individual's actual speech.

The most widely used script is the International Phonetic Alphabet, usually with adaptations according to the level of accuracy required, and according to the particular purpose of the transcription.

Transcriptions may be PHONETIC or PHONEMIC. A phonetic transcription aims to represent actual speech sounds objectively and accurately. A high degree of accuracy can be achieved with additional symbols if necessary. A very detailed transcription is a *narrow* transcription; one with few details is *broad*.

A phonemic transcription is the broadest of all. It only uses one symbol for each phoneme of a particular language, regardless of actual variations. So it looks simple, but it requires a knowledge of the allophonic conventions to be reproduced aloud with approximate authenticity.

transitive verb

A transitive verb takes a direct object, in contrast to an *intransitive* verb.

The division of verbs into transitive and intransitive is long established. Some verbs are virtually always transitive (e.g. *bury*, *deny*, *distract*). Others are always intransitive (e.g. *arrive*, *come*, *digress*). But many can be both, e.g.

I was cooking (breakfast)
He lodged in Cambridge   He lodged a complaint

Even verbs that seem to be strongly transitive (e.g. *He made a cake/a mistake/a good job of it*) can have intransitive uses (*She made towards the river*) and similarly an intransitive verb such as *live* can be used transitively (e.g. *She lived a good life*). So for many verbs it is more accurate to talk of transitive and intransitive use.

Transitive verbs can be grammatically divided into three main types:

MONOTRANSITIVE, simple transitive verbs, taking one object, e.g. *I've bought a new suit* (SVO)

COMPLEX TRANSITIVE, with an object plus a complement or adverbial, e.g. *I found the story unreadable* (SVOC), *I put the book down* (SVOA)

DITRANSITIVE (double transitive), with an indirect + a direct object, e.g. *I've bought myself a new suit* (SVOO)

tree diagram

A diagram to show the syntactic structure of a clause or sentence.

A tree diagram does not have to be tied to any particular theory of grammar. Thus the sentence *He looked up the words in his dictionary* could be diagrammed as

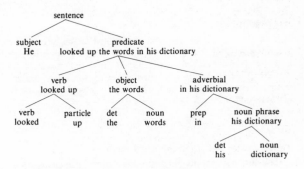

or the traditional division into subject and predicate could be omitted and the first split could be fourfold

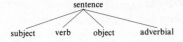

trigraph

Three letters representing one speech sound as in *manoeuvre*, where the *oeu* is pronounced /uː/.

triphthong

A single vowel sound involving three positions of the vocal organs. There are no triphthongs among the English phonemes, but such sounds occur when a closing diphthong is followed by /ə/. At least, they theoretically occur in a careful pronunciation of such words as:

player /pleɪə/, shire /ʃaɪə/, royal /rɔɪəl/,
slower /sləʊə/, hour /aʊə/

However, the sounds actually articulated and heard may often be more like diphthongs or even single long vowels.

trisyllabic

Having three syllables. As with the related terms, MONOSYLLABIC and disyllabic, the term is particularly used of adjectives and adverbs. Trisyllabic or longer adjectives and adverbs must take periphrastic comparison, e.g. *more delicious, most extraordinary, more hastily.* (Hence the oddity of Lewis Carroll's *curiouser and curiouser.*)

tune

The intonation pattern heard over a TONE UNIT.

A tone unit, by definition, has only one nuclear pitch change (a rise, fall, rise-fall, etc.), which must occur on the last stressed syllable, but this change could, for example, be a high or low rise, and this, combined with the relative 'heights' of other syllables in the unit, produces different tunes, which in their turn convey different attitudinal meanings.

two-part verb

A verb consisting of a verb plus a preposition (e.g. a PREPOSITIONAL verb such as *look after*) or a verb plus adverb (a PHRASAL verb, e.g. *take off*).

U

unattached participle

The same as HANGING PARTICIPLE.

uncount noun

An uncount noun has no plural form and therefore cannot be counted. (Also called *uncountable* and non-count, and generally synonymous with *mass noun*.) Contrasted with COUNT.

Grammatically, uncount nouns are distinguished by the fact that they can be used without any determiner or article and also with certain determiners that are exclusive to them (e.g. *much*). Uncount nouns often refer in a rather general way to substances and abstract qualities, processes and states (e.g. *china*, *petrol*, *poverty*, *rain*, *welfare*) rather than discrete units. But the *uncount* versus *count* distinction is grammatical, not semantic, and a number of English uncount nouns (e.g. *information*, *luggage*, *traffic*) have countable equivalents in other languages.

See p. 151 NOUNS.

understood

The term '*you*' *understood* is sometimes used to describe the subject that is missing from most imperatives, although clearly implied, as is shown by the fact that it can be added, e.g.

(You) do as you're told
(You) be quiet
Don't (you) forget
Sit down, (won't you)

Understood is not entirely synonymous with RECOVERABLE. The latter is usually applied to words that could, with little or no change of form, be inserted in the text. 'Understood' may relate more abstractly to underlying meaning. Thus sentences such as *They tried to telephone us* or the colloquial *We said not to worry* contain 'understood subjects' for the non-finite verbs, but in neither case can we grammatically insert the understood words (**They tried they to telephone. *We said they not to worry*).

ungrammatical

Grammaticality is judged in relation to what is considered a standard, but standards vary. *I never said nothing to nobody* is ungrammatical in standard English, but conforms to the rules of its own dialect.

uninflected

English is relatively uninflected compared with many other languages. The verbs have few INFLECTIONS, and nouns merely the plural inflection.

unique

The term *unique reference* is used to explain the use of the definite article (*the*) in various contexts where, although the referent has not been mentioned before, its definiteness is assumed. Sometimes the referent really may be unique (e.g. *the Earth*); more often it is unique in the context of a particular place or time (e.g. *the Pope, the Queen, the moon*), or even in some much smaller situational context (e.g. *I'm going to the post office—please shut the windows*).

Uniqueness may also be due to grammatical or logical factors, e.g. *the day after tomorrow*; *May the best man win.*

unit noun

Another name for PARTITIVE NOUN, e.g. a word that allows us to break up an uncountable noun into countable parts, e.g. a *pat* of butter, two *pieces* of toast.

See p. 151 NOUNS.

unmarked

A linguistic form is *unmarked* when it is more basic than the MARKED form to which it is related. This is a distinction which applies to many areas of grammar. For example, the so-called 'singular' form of a count noun is actually the unmarked form. Hence we say a *bookcase* (not a *bookscase); *we came on foot* (not *on feet), because the number of books or feet is irrelevant. But if we want to mark for number we can use *a* to mark for singular (*a book*, *a foot*) or say *books* or *feet* to mark for plural.

usage

Usage is a somewhat wider and vaguer term than *grammar* or *syntax*. In one sense, usage is what people generally say and write, how they actually use their language. So ideally, *usage* should (*a*) include grammar and (*b*) be objective and descriptive, rather than prescriptive.

In practice, usage guides tend to deal fairly briefly with core grammar and to pay more attention to areas of disputed usage, giving guidance that veers towards prescription (which is probably what most users of such books want). Grammatical usages discussed include such matters as *If I were* versus *If I was* or *used not to* versus *didn't use to*. Other areas are word formation and spelling (e.g. *blamable* or *blameable?*); pronunciation (haʀassment or HAʀassment?) and vocabulary (e.g *flout* versus *flaunt; disinterested* versus *uninterested*; and the meaning of *decimate*).

Questions of usage are complicated by the fact that accepted usage may vary from one speech community to another, according to different national, regional, or social varieties, and such factors as who is writing or speaking to whom about what.

Some dictionaries add *usage labels* to some entries, to indicate whether particular words or phrases are formal, informal, British, American, dialectical, dated, slang, offensive, euphemistic, and so on.

utterance

An uninterrupted sequence of spoken language. *Utterance* is intended to be a more neutral term than the grammatically defined clause or sentence. *Utterance* is sometimes contrasted with TEXT, and sometimes included in it.

uvula

The fleshy extension of the soft palate hanging above the throat. Uvular plosive consonants are heard in Arabic, and a uvular *r* is the standard pronunciation of this sound in French. Uvular sounds are not a feature of standard RP, though they may be heard in some northern accents.

See p. 266 THE SPEECH ORGANS.

V

velar

Velar sounds are sounds made with the back of the tongue against the *velum* (or soft palate). Standard English has three velar phonemes: the voiceless and voiced plosive pair /k/ and /g/ and the nasal /ŋ/, the sound at the end of *sing*.

See p. 264 THE CONSONANTS OF ENGLISH.

The sound heard in the Scottish pronunciation of *loch* is a voiceless velar fricative.

The so-called 'dark *l*' allophone of the English /l/ is a velarized sound—that is, it has a secondary, velar element, with the back of the tongue raised towards the velum.

velum

The velum (or soft palate) is the back part of the roof of the mouth, lying behind the bony hard palate, with the UVULA at its own back extremity. The velum is raised for oral sounds, and lowered for nasal sounds.

See p. 266 THE SPEECH ORGANS.

verb

1 Verbs are a major WORD CLASS, and a verb is normally essential to clause structure. Verbs inflect, and can show contrasts of aspect, number, person, mood, tense, and voice. In traditional grammar, the verb is sometimes defined notionally as a 'doing' word, but modern grammar prefers a more syntactical definition.

Verbs are usually subdivided first into:

(i) LEXICAL (or *full*) verbs

(ii) AUXILIARY verbs

Regular lexical verbs have four different forms—the base (e.g. *look*), the third person singular present (*looks*), the *-ing* form (*looking*) and the *-ed* form (*looked*). Irregular verbs may have an extra form because past and past participle are often different, so these are both given in addition to the base when the 'parts' of an irregular verb are stated (e.g. *see, saw, seen; take, took, taken*). Some of the five possible verb forms are finite, some non-finite, and some both.

Lexical verbs are classified in various ways, according to both syntax and meaning. Classification that is dependent on what words can or must follow a verb leads to such categories as TRANSITIVE, INTRANSITIVE, and LINKING. Another meaning-based distinction with grammatical consequences is STATIVE versus DYNAMIC.

Auxiliary verbs are sometimes divided into PRIMARY and modal, because *primary* verbs can also function as *main* verbs.

2 In a description of the functional elements of clause structure, V stands for the whole VERB PHRASE. Thus both *I bought oranges* and *I have been buying oranges* are SVO sentences.

- **verbal adjective:** another name for a PARTICIPIAL (or PARTICIPLE) ADJECTIVE, as in *the listening bank*.

- **verbal noun:** the same as a GERUND, as in *seeing is believing*.

Linguists usually try to avoid using the word *verbal* when the meaning is ORAL, or when the meaning is 'relating to a word or words'.

verbless clause

A clause without a verb. *Verbless clauses* are not usually recognized as such in much traditional grammar, where they are more likely to be dealt with as phrases. Some verbless structures, however, have some of the semantic and structural features of clauses. For example, some are introduced by a conjunction, e.g.

> *When in Rome*, do as Rome does
> Come early *if possible*

Others have a subject introduced by *with* or *without*

> *With the exam behind her*, she felt able to enjoy the holiday (compare *the exam being behind her . . .*)

> *Without you here*, I don't know what I'd do (compare *if you were not here . . .*)

VERBS AT A GLANCE

FORM	FUNCTION
1 **Lexical** (or full) verb: e.g. *arrive, give, take*, etc.	**Main** They *arrived* yesterday They were *given* instructions Tom must *take* his medicine
2 **Modal auxiliary** e.g. *can, must, will*, etc.	**Auxiliary** *Can* I help you? Tom *must* take his medicine Why *won't* he? [i.e. take it]
3 **Primary** [*be, do, have*—only]	(i) **Main** *Is* he ready? What are you *doing*? *Do* your homework I *have* an idea; let's *have* a party (ii) **Auxiliary** Yes, he *is* waiting I *don't* like this *Have* you thought of the consequences? She *hasn't* decided who to invite

THE PARTS OF THE VERB AND THEIR USES

finite

1 **base** (i) *imperative*
Give us the tools . . .
Be sensible!

non-finite

infinitive
and we will *finish* the job
To *be* or not to *be* . . .

(ii)	*present simple* I *know* that . . . and they *know* too		What you don't *know* . . . . . . can't *hurt* you
2	**-s form**	History *repeats* itself	—
3	**past simple**	I *came*, I *saw*, I *conquered*	—
4	**-ing form**	—	(i) *participle* We are *waiting* for the long promised invasion An appeaser is one who feeds a crocodile—*hoping* that it will eat him last (ii) *verbal noun* *Seeing* is *believing*
5	**past participle**	—	An iron curtain has *descended* across the Continent History is too serious to be *left* to the historians It is a riddle *wrapped* in a mystery inside an enigma

VERBS ACCORDING TO COMPLEMENTATION

intransitive:	Harry's *arrived*. Don't just do something—*sit* there!
linking:	This *is* silly. It's *becoming* a nightmare
transitive: (=monotransitive)	*Do* something! By the time you *reach* my age, you've *made* plenty of mistakes if you've *lived* your life properly
ditransitive: (=two objects)	*Make* / me / an offer *Ask* / him / the time / and he'll *tell* / you / how the watch was made
complex transitive:	Don't *make* / me / a scapegoat (object + complement) They *sent* / him / away (object + adverb)

reflexive:	I've *hurt* myself
catenative:	*want* (you) to go, *enjoy* swimming
(+object) + verb	*go* swimming, *get* (it) accepted, *help* (me) (to) do this
causative	*Get* your hair cut
perception	I *watched* them go, I *watched* them going
factual (+ indicative clause):	He *knew* (that) it was wrong
	They *realized* (that) they had made a mistake
suasive:	They *insisted* { he apologize he should apologize he apologized }

MULTI-WORD VERBS

phrasal verb:	The plane *took off*. *Look out!*
	Take off your hat; *take* it *off*: *take* your hat *off*
prepositional verb:	*Look after* your wallet; *look after* it
phrasal-prepositional verb:	I won't *put up with* that sort of behaviour; I won't *put up with* it

OTHER TERMS RELATING TO VERBS

stative (or state) verb versus dynamic (or action or event) verb:	
stative:	They *own* a chain of hotels (*They are owning . . .*)
	They also *have* a travel business (*They are having . . .*)
	I *dislike* large hotels (*I am disliking . . .*)
dynamic:	They *are having* problems with cash flow
	I'm *enjoying* this
ergative verb:	The door *opened*, Someone *opened* the door
performative verb:	I *apologize*, I *declare* the meeting closed
public ('speaking'):	He *announced/boasted/declared* that . . .
private ('thinking'):	They *imagined/thought* that . . .

Others have neither conjunction nor subject, yet a paraphrase suggests a clausal rather than a phrasal interpretation, e.g.

> *Unhappy at the result*, she decided to try again (compare *because she was unhappy . . .*)

See p. 42 <small>CLAUSES</small>.

verb phrase (VP)

A group of words which functions in the same way as a single-word verb or a single-word verb on its own, e.g.

> has been thinking, must be leaving, was forgotten, having been urged, went

In a finite verb phrase the first word is in fact the only word that is finite and indicates tense. The last word in any verb phrase is the lexical verb. If a finite verb phrase consists of a single word then lexical word and tense are combined (e.g. *goes*, *went*).

See p. 176 <small>PHRASES</small>.

vocabulary

All the words in the language or a set of some of these. Vocabulary as such does not feature very much in traditional grammar, which tends to concentrate on syntax and morphology, leaving word meanings to the dictionary. But there is an increasing trend to recognize the relationship between vocabulary and syntax, and many modern dictionaries noticeably give a considerable amount of grammatical information.

Vocabulary size: it is not easy to say how many words there are in the English language, partly because <small>WORD</small> itself is difficult to define, partly because there are problems such as: do we include obsolete words? Or words in other national varieties of English (e.g. Indian English, New Zealand English)? Do we count slang or dialect words? And so on.

A typical 'desk dictionary' may define about 100,000 items, while the *Oxford English Dictionary* lists more than 500,000.

As for how many words an individual English-speaking adult might know, estimates vary greatly, but it is unlikely to be less than 50,000.

vocal cords

The vocal cords, which are situated in the larynx, are not actually cords at all, but folds or bands of muscle and tissue. When they are held closely enough together for them to vibrate when subjected to air pressure from the lungs, the result is VOICED sounds.

When the cords are held rather wider apart they do not vibrate, and *voiceless* sounds are produced. Holding tightly together and then releasing the vocal cords produces a GLOTTAL STOP.

vocal organs

The same as SPEECH ORGANS.

vocative

An optional element in clause structure, denoting the person (or being) addressed.

In some inflected languages nouns have a distinct vocative case to denote an addressee. In English the vocative is marked not by inflection but by intonation.

Vocatives can include names (e.g. *Mary, Grandpa, Fido*), titles (e.g. *Sir, Mr President, Doctor, Waiter, Nurse*), epithets and general nouns, both polite and otherwise (e.g. *darling, chums, bastard, friends, liar, mate*). Some of these can be expanded (e.g. *Mary dearest, my dear friends, you stupid idiot*).

Inanimate 'things' can also be addressed, e.g.

I vow to thee, my country . . .
Come, friendly bombs, and fall on Slough ... .

voice

Voice is the name of a grammatical category which in English provides two different ways (ACTIVE and passive) of viewing the action of the verb.

Voice is applicable to verbs, verb phrases, and to entire clauses or sentences. The names, *active* and *passive*, are meaning-linked in that with an active verb the subject is often the 'actor' or 'doer' of the verbal action, as in

The early bird caught the worm

while its passive counterpart shows the subject 'passively' being acted upon

The worm was caught by the early bird

But essentially this is a distinction of grammar, not meaning.

See p. 235 TENSES.

voiced

A speech sound made with the vocal cords vibrating is a voiced sound, and contrasts with *voiceless* sounds.

In standard English, all the vowels are voiced, as are thirteen consonants and both the semi-vowels. The remaining nine consonants are voiceless.

See p. 265 THE SOUNDS OF ENGLISH.

vowel

1 (*a*) A speech sound made with the vocal cords vibrating, but without any closure or stricture, in contrast to a CONSONANT.

(*b*) A speech sound that is central to a syllable and therefore SYLLABIC.

2 Any of the letters *a, e, i, o, u*.

As with the word *consonant*, the term *vowel* suffers from ambiguity. Vowel sounds, defined as in (1*a*) and (1*b*) are usually represented by vowel letters as in (2). But there are discrepancies. Vowels (or vowel-like sounds) in modern definition can include syllabic consonants, such as the second syllable of *muddle*. At the same time many vowel sounds are sometimes represented in writing by a combination of vowel and consonant letters, e.g. *ah*, k*ey*, h*al*f, p*ar*t, l*aw*, n*ew*, d*ay*, while the letter *y* represents vowels (as in *by*, *city*) or a semi-vowel (as in *year*).

• **vowel system**: the vowel system of English RP is usually analysed in terms of 12 pure vowels (or MONOPHTHONGS), some long and some short; and 8 diphthongs. Scottish English has only 10 monophthongs and 4 diphthongs.

Vowels are described using the CARDINAL VOWEL system as a framework. The twelve monophthongs are classified as

front   vowels (with the front part of the tongue higher than any other part): /iː/, /ɪ/, /e/, and /æ/ (as in seat, sit, set, sat)

central vowels (with the centre of the tongue raised towards the middle of the roof of the mouth): /ʌ/, /ɜː/, /ə/, and /ʊ/ (as in sun, hurt, ago, put)

back   vowels (with the tongue raised towards the back of the mouth): /ɑː/, /ɒ/, /ɔː/, and /uː/ (as in art, hot, saw, boot)

At the same time vowels are described in terms of tongue height.

High (or close) vowels have the tongue raised relatively close to the roof of the mouth. E.g. /iː/ as in *seat* is a high front vowel; and /uː/ (in *food*) is a high back vowel.

Low (or open) vowels have the whole tongue low in the mouth. English /æ/ as in the RP pronunciation of *hat* is a low front vowel, and /ɑː/ (e.g. in *heart, hard*) is a low back vowel.

Vowels that are neither high nor low are sometimes classified as *half close* or *half open*. With diphthongs the tongue glides from one position to another.

For the standard pronunciation of English vowels, see THE SOUNDS OF ENGLISH p. 265. For the various spellings of vowels, see also LENGTH (for pure vowels) and DIPHTHONG.

W

weak form

Many so-called form words (grammatical words) have two pronunciations—a *weak form*, containing a *weak vowel*, and a STRONG FORM.

As these grammatical words are usually unstressed and in a non-prominent position, the weak form is the pronunciation that is usually heard. Strong forms are used in sentence-final position, because this is prominent, even when the word is unstressed ('You may not think so, but'I do).

> Common words having weak forms are:
> (determiners) *a, an, the, some, his, your*
> (auxiliaries) *am, are, be, been, is, was, were, can, could, do, does, had, has, have, must, shall, should, will, would*
> (nouns) *Saint, Sir*
> (prepositions) *at, for, from, of, to*
> (pronouns) *he, her, him, me, she, them, us, we, who, you*
> (conjunctions and adverbs) *and, but, as, not, than, that, there*

Some words have more than one *weak form*. For example, the word *do* (strong form /duː/) —as in sentence final position above may be

> /du/ before a vowel sound, as in *What do I care?*
> /du/ or /də/ before a consonant sound, as in *Why do we bother?*
> /d/ in rapid speech, as in *D'you know what I think?*

weak vowel

The vowel /ə/ (*schwa*) and certain other vowels occurring in unstressed, unprominent syllables are *weak vowels*, in contrast to *strong vowels*.

The vowel /ə/ only occurs in unstressed syllables and is the prime weak vowel of English. Many strong vowels lose their distinct quality and are replaced by /ə/ when they lose stress or prominence. E.g. /'lænd/ *land*, but /'ɪŋglənd/ *England*; /'fɔː/ *for*, but /fə'get/ *forget*; /ˌʌn'taɪ/ *untie*, but /ən'les/ *unless*.

In other unstressed contexts two other weak vowels have been identified, roughly equivalent to the short vowels /ɪ/ and /ʊ/ and usually equated with them except in very precise analysis.

Weak vowels are sometimes so unimportant that the phonemic distinction between /ə/ and /ɪ/ is neutralized. Thus *believe* and *possible* may be pronounced as /brˈliːv/ or /bəˈliːv/, /ˈpɒsɪb(ə)l/ or /ˈpɒsəb(ə)l/.

A weak syllable does not mean an unstressed syllable, but a syllable containing a weak vowel.

wh-word

One of a small class of interrogative or relative words beginning with *wh-*. The main *wh-*words are: *what*, *which*, *who*, *whom*, *whose*; *when*, *where*, *why*, and (note) *how*. A question beginning with one of these words is a *wh*-QUESTION.

Wh-words are sometimes intensified by adding *ever*, often as a separate word (and always separate after *why*):

Who ever would have guessed?

Why ever didn't you say?

This usage is grammatically distinct from similar-looking compounds used as subordinators (e.g. *Whoever may have guessed, nobody said anything*).

wishing

Wishing is sometimes singled out in grammatical description because tense usage in subordinate clauses after expressions of wishing must be in the hypothetical past tense, e.g.

I wish I knew/had known what to say

I would that I knew/that I had known

If only I knew/had known

Such expressions when referring to present or past time denote what is contrary to fact; e.g. *I wish I knew/had known* implies *I don't/didn't know*. With reference to the future, wishing implies something that may be unlikely, but not necessarily what is impossible, e.g.

I wish you would come tomorrow

word

1 A meaningful unit of speech, which when written or printed has spaces on either side.

Native speakers intuitively recognize the *word* as a distinct and grammatical unit of language. Individual words and their meanings form the main contents of dictionaries. Words are also the basic units which are combined to form phrases, clauses, and sentences.

Grammarians recognize smaller meaningful units (e.g. *morphemes*), but the *word* has distinct characteristics. It cannot normally have other elements inserted into it, and its parts cannot be rearranged as words in a sentence can. Contrast *rearrangement* (where no change is possible), and *Its parts can be rearranged* (which can be reordered as *Rearranged its parts can be, Can its parts be rearranged?*).

The word has also been defined as the smallest unit that can reasonably constitute a complete utterance, as in

Do you accept? *Yes/Maybe/Naturally*

Some words fail this test (e.g. *a, an, the*), but the definition is largely accurate.

2 A word as found in a dictionary plus all its variants—sometimes distinguished from sense (1) as LEXEME.

Although this is a more abstract sense of *word*, this is a common meaning (e.g. *see, sees, seeing, saw, seen* are all parts of the same 'word' *see*).

word class

A *word class* groups together words that broadly share the same syntactic characteristics.

This is much the same as the more traditional classification of words into PARTS OF SPEECH, but prefers definitions based on syntax rather than on meaning. Word classes usually also include some precise extra categories such as ARTICLES, DETERMINERS, and NUMERALS.

See p. 165 PARTS OF SPEECH.

word ending

The same as SUFFIX.

word formation

1 The whole field investigated by MORPHOLOGY, including both INFLECTION and DERIVATION.

2 More narrowly, DERIVATION and the formation of entirely new words, but omitting inflection, which is seen as part of syntax.

See p. 145 NEW WORDS.

word order

The order in which words come in clauses and sentences is part of the grammar of a language. In inflected languages such as Latin, word order may be comparatively 'free', because a word's function is often indicated by its ending. English, having few inflections, has a much more 'fixed' word order. The basic unmarked word order is SVO (Subject Verb Object). See p. 42 CLAUSES.

....

Y

....

yes-no question

A question that could be answered with a straight 'yes' or 'no'. *Yes-no questions* contrast with *alternative questions* and *wh*-QUESTIONS as one of the three major QUESTION types.

Syntactically yes-no questions must begin with subject-operator INVERSION, e.g.

Are you ready?
Are you sitting comfortably?
Have you quite finished?
Can anybody explain this?

Z

zero

Zero is an abstraction, symbolized by Ø, representing a gap where there could theoretically be, or in comparable grammatical contexts there is, some sound, syllable, or word.

The concept of *zero* is used as a way of making rules more comprehensive and more 'regular' than they would otherwise be.

* **zero article**: a *zero article* is said to occur before an uncountable noun or a plural count noun when either is used with an indefinite meaning. Thus Ø alternates with *a/an* (used before a singular count noun) in a paradigmatic relationship, e.g. Ø *food*, Ø *vegetables*, *a cauliflower*.

* **zero genitive**: a genitive word lacking the genitive *-s* inflection because the word already ends in *-s*. This is the usual genitive with regular plural nouns, as in *the athletes' achievements*, where the form is identical in speech with the ordinary plural form (*athletes*), and only differs in the written form by the addition of an apostrophe. *Zero genitive* also occurs with some singular words, particularly foreign names ending with /z/, e.g. *Aristophanes' plays*.

By contrast, irregular plurals not ending in *-s* show a marked contrast of form between plural common case (e.g. *men*) and the genitive (e.g. *the men's achievement*), as do singular forms (e.g. common case—*woman*; genitive—*woman's*).

* **zero plural**: some count nouns have no distinct plural form, e.g. *sheep*, *cod*, *deer*. Other nouns for animals have both zero and regular plurals, e.g. *fish/fishes*, *pheasant/pheasants*. Zero plural is often the norm with nouns of measurement and quantity (*He's six foot three*, *We need six dozen*) and is obligatory with some foreign plurals (e.g. *a series/two series*).

* **zero that-clause**: a zero *that*-clause is a noun clause or a relative clause which could be introduced by *that*, but where *that* has been omitted:

He said *he was sorry* (= that he was sorry)

I am surprised *you don't know* (= that you don't know)

Here's the map *I promised to lend you* (= that I promised to lend you)

A *zero relative clause* is a relative clause lacking a relative pronoun (e.g. *I promised to lend you* above). It is more usually called a CONTACT CLAUSE.

Diag. 1. THE CONSONANTS OF ENGLISH

	Place of articulation							
Manner of articulation	Bilabial	Labiodental	Dental	Alveolar	Palato-alveolar	Palatal	Velar	Glottal
Plosive	p b			t d			k g	
Fricative		f v	θ ð	s z	ʃ ʒ			h
Affricate					tʃ dʒ			
Nasal	m			n			ŋ	
Lateral				l				
Semi-vowel	w					j	(w)	
Frictionless continuant					r			

Notes: The places of articulation are shown from left to right, going from *bilabial* at the front of the mouth to *glottal* at the back. The different manners of articulation are indicated at the side. For explanations of these place and manner terms, see individual entries (e.g. PLOSIVE, BILABIAL).

For the sounds represented, see PHONEMES.

Where phonemes are shown in pairs, the first in each pair is voiceless, and the second voiced. The frictionless continuant /r/ is strictly speaking described as post-alveolar (i.e. somewhere between alveolar and palato-alveolar).

Diag. 2. THE SOUNDS OF ENGLISH

Vowels

'Pure vowels'

1	iː	as in see
2	ɪ	as in sit
3	e	as in ten
4	æ	as in hat
5	ɑː	as in arm
6	ɒ	as in got
7	ɔː	as in saw
8	ʊ	as in put
9	uː	as in too
10	ʌ	as in cup
11	ɜː	as in fur
12	ə	as in ago

Diphthongs

13	eɪ	as in page
14	əʊ	as in home
15	aɪ	as in five
16	aʊ	as in now
17	ɔɪ	as in join
18	ɪə	as in near
19	eə	as in hair
20	ʊə	as in pure

Consonants

1	p	as in pen
2	b	as in bad
3	t	as in tea
4	d	as in did
5	k	as in cat
6	g	as in got
7	tʃ	as in chin
8	dʒ	as in June
9	f	as in fall
10	v	as in voice
11	θ	as in thin
12	ð	as in then

13	s	as in so
14	z	as in zoo
15	ʃ	as in she
16	ʒ	as in vision
17	h	as in how
18	m	as in man
19	n	as in no
20	ŋ	as in sing
21	l	as in leg
22	r	as in red

Semi-vowels

23	j	as in yes
24	w	as in wet

Notes: The table shows the phonemes of standard (RP) English. Many variants of these symbols have been used in the past, with consequent confusion. The symbols shown here have gained general acceptance. They are the symbols used in the *Concise Oxford Dictionary* (1990) and standard works from other publishers. A variant found in some modern books is the use of /ɛ/ for vowel no.3, instead of /e/. This use affects vowels 13 and 19, which may appear as /ɛɪ/ instead of /eɪ/ and /ɛə/ instead of /eə/.

The different ways in which these phonemes may be spelt will be found for the 'pure' vowels at LENGTH; and for the diphthongs at DIPHTHONG. Spellings for consonants are given at the entries for various manners of articulations (e.g. at PLOSIVE, AFFRICATE, etc.).

Diag. 3 THE SPEECH ORGANS

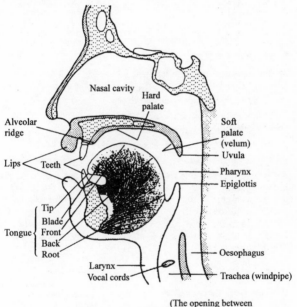

(The opening between
the cords is the glottis)

Some Common Usage Problems—and how to avoid them

1 We must agree!

A Subject-verb agreement (see p. 17)

1 * He is one of those people who enjoys every second of his life and is always having adventures.
2 * One lesson in four are inadequate.
3 * Each of the victims were offered counselling.
4 * All except one of them has wasted their money.
5 * The problem with jet skis are they can go at 50 mph.

Rule: A verb must agree with its subject in number and person. In 1, the subject of *enjoys* is *who* following plural *people*. So, correct to 'people who enjoy'. In 2 the subject is *one lesson* (in four), so we need '*is inadequate*'. In 3, although there were clearly several victims, the word *each* is singular and stresses the individual, so reword as 'each . . . *was* asked'. 4 should be '*all . . . have*' and 5, '*The problem . . . is*'.

Tip: If there is a phrase rather than a simple subject, decide which noun is the important one that really controls the verb.

B those sort, there's, neither . . . nor

6 * Do bring him. We love those sort of people.
7 * You board at Waterloo International, settle into your reserved seat, flash your passport and then there's no interruptions, no stops, no changes.
8 * Neither Andrew nor Tom appear to understand the problem.

Some people object strongly to *those/these* (plural) being followed by singular *sort/kind/type*, though this usage is very common. You can often reword: *that sort of person, those sorts of people, people of that sort, people like that.*

There's (or *There is*) is grammatically followed by a singular or an uncountable noun (*There is a buffet-car/There is air-conditioning*). But *There's* (not the full form) + a plural noun or more than one singular is sometimes used as here. Easily avoided by using *There are . . .*

Sentence 8 is an example of notional concord – a plural verb because two people appear not to understand. Acceptable to many people, but in strict grammar *Neither A nor T appears . . .*

C none . . .

9 * None of the bodies so far recovered [was/were] wearing a life jacket.

10 * The team [have/has] worked extremely hard and [deserves/deserve] our support.

None (9) may take a singular or plural verb according to sense. Here, where we have a singular 'life jacket', singular *was* is preferable. (But a plural verb is better in *None of their friends were present.*) *Team* (10) is a collective noun (see p. 45), so singular or plural verbs are acceptable, but don't mix them in the same sentence. Either say *have worked . . . and deserve* or *has worked . . . and deserves.*

D less

Strictly speaking *less* is used with uncountable nouns (*less bread*) and *fewer* with countables (*fewer loaves*). But *less* is increasingly used with countables (*less people, less worries*) and is acceptable to many people. *Less* (*than*) is correct with numbers seen as a single unit (*less than £20, less than five miles, 20 people or less*).

2 Adjective or adverb?

A Is it likely?

Many adjectives (pp. 6–8) have corresponding manner adverbs (p. 131) formed by adding *-ly* (e.g. *bad, badly; nice, nicely*). But there are many adverbs that do not end in *-ly*, and some adjectives that do. Can you sort the following words into two lists – adjectives and adverbs? Do any words belong in both lists?

better early elder elderly fast hardly lone lonely likely quicker soon straight

Answers: adjectives – *elder, elderly, lone, lonely*; adverbs – *hardly, soon*; both – *better, early, fast, quicker, straight* and to some extent *likely*.

Likely is an adjective (*a likely result; he is likely to forget*), but its use as an adverb (? *He will likely come*) is more problematic. In British English adverbial use is more acceptable when qualified: They've *most likely* forgotten; He'll *very likely* telephone). Tip: If in doubt, use *probably*!

B bad or badly?

We use adverbs when we say how an action is done (*The meeting went badly*) but after a linking verb (p. 128), which says what the subject is or becomes, we use an adjective (*The meat went bad*). Similarly we paint the town *red*, or something goes *wrong* or your blood runs *cold*.

Complete the following with clear/clearly, slow/slowly:

1a Stand . . . of the doors. b Please speak . . . .

2a Please drive . . . through the village. b The union have ordered everyone to go . . . (Answers: 1a clear, 1b clearly; 2a slowly, 2b slow.)

C elder? youngest?

Comparative forms (p. 48) are correct when comparing two things (It's *hotter* today than yesterday); superlative forms (p. 230) are used when more than two are involved. So how do you react to the following?

? I was the youngest of two children.

? Should she watch the BBC where her eldest son will be fronting the coverage . . . or should she tune into ITV where her younger son will . . . be taking the helm?

? Her youngest daughter is unmarried. Her elder died of cancer last year.

All these quotes are from quality newspapers – but all break the rules, and with a little care could have been avoided.

D only

A common position for the focusing adverb *only* (see p. 11) is just before the verb, and this is acceptable even when the word limits, not the verb, but some later part of the sentence. Thus *They only arrived yesterday* is understood to mean 'only yesterday', and *I was only thinking the other day that I hadn't seen you for ages* means 'only the other day'.

However, where ambiguity can arise, or an absurd interpretation is possible, it may be better to reword. *I can only say 'I love you' in Russian* does suggest 'I can't say "I love you" in any other language'. The probable meaning would be clearer as 'The only thing I can say in Russian is "I love you"'.

3 Don't be more negative than you need be

A More than one negative word

Sentences containing a single negative word are usually straightfor-ward. Problems may arise when there is more than one or when there are SEMI-NEGATIVE words (e.g. *hardly*) or words with a rather 'negative' meaning. (See pp. 72, 143, 210.)

   * The judge said: Anyone reading the case could not fail to miss the disgraceful piece of behaviour by the landlord . . . [news-paper report]

This does not make sense. Perhaps the judge said, or should have said, 'could not fail to notice' or 'could not miss'.

B Negatives and linked clauses

Care also needs to be taken with sentences containing a negative followed by a linked clause. Can you rewrite these?

1 * They all told me not to change anything, which is exactly what I intend to do.

2 * Doctors also advise osteoporosis patients not to smoke and drink alcohol in moderation only.

3 * Not enough young people apply for these courses or fail to get good enough A-level grades to qualify for entry.

In 1 'which is what I intend to do' grammatically refers to 'to change anything'. Rewrite . . . *and I don't intend to* or *which is advice I shall follow.* In 2, however, the *not* carries over (*not to smoke and drink . . . in moderation*). Rewrite 'not to smoke and *to* drink etc'. In 3 the negative subject carries over to the second clause, giving 'not enough young people fail . . .'.

So a new positive subject is needed – *and some of them fail to get* ...

C all/every .... not

? All of you will not agree.

? Every food doesn't have to be nutritious.

Opinion is divided about the acceptability of negative sentences beginning with *all* or *every*. They are better reworded, especially where the meaning is unclear. The first sentence here could mean 'Not all of you will agree' (but some will) or 'You will all disagree' (ie, none of you will agree).

D no question

There was no question that the standards required had been changed.

Theoretically this means that undoubtedly the standards had been changed. But a careful reading of the news item suggests that standards had NOT been changed. The phrase 'no question that' is now used with opposite meanings and is best avoided. *There's no question of* (something happening) means it certainly has not or will not. (*There's no question of lowering the standards* means the standards will NOT be lowered.)

4 Personally speaking: a look at pronouns

The personal pronouns (pp. 155, 172, 226) have subject and object forms:

Subject: I you he/she/it we you they
Object: me you him/her/it us you them

A Pronouns in phrases

As the second person forms are all *you*, problems only arise with 1st and 3rd person. As a general rule, a subject form is used for the subject of a verb (*He is here*); and an object pronoun is used for the object of a verb (*Help me*) and as the object of a preposition (*That's for her*).

These rules still apply when the pronoun is part of a phrase. Perhaps eventually faulty usage will be fully acceptable. Meanwhile try to get them right. Tip: What pronoun would you use if you were using one pronoun by itself?

Which of the following are incorrect?

1 Often the designer will hand the costumier the sketchiest of indications of textile and cut and expect he or she to supply the artistry as well as the stitching.

2 It is not for you nor I to question his motives.

3 The press has in general been honest and kind about Harry and I.

4 I shall attempt to give you some sense of the effect this had on we in the hospitals.

5 This was obvious to we the audience.

6 Treasury officials cannot sail serenely on, dismissing we little wealth-creating folk with a gentle patrician smile.

7 Me and Les were like brothers.

8 You don't think that us battle-hardened troops are just going to lie down now and say we are satisfied?

9 It was she who supported the family during those five difficult years.

10 It was I who discovered him.

In 1–6 subject pronouns have been wrongly used where object pronouns are needed (1 *expect him or her to supply*; 2 *not for you or me* (or *not for you nor for me*); 3 *about Harry and me*; 4 *for us*; 5 *obvious to us*; 6 *dismissing us*). In 7 and 8 subject pronouns are needed – *Les and I were . . . You don't think we . . . are going to lie down.*

9 and 10 are correct, because subject pronouns are usual in the structure BE (*It is/was*) + pronoun + *who*-clause (when *who* is the subject). However, in simple sentences containing BE + a pronoun, an object pronoun is normal (*It's me, That's them*) and a subject pronoun is formal, even pompous (*It is I*).

B who or whom?

1 Target audiences include Australian tourists whom the company hopes will be attracted by the prospect of tracing ancestors.

2 This would have happened, whomever was Chancellor.

3 Each time one receives a reply-paid envelope, it should be posted empty to whomever sent it.

The writers here are all trying too hard. *Whom* is the object case, and in each case subject *who* is needed (*who . . . will be attracted*; *whoever was . . .*). The third quotation is a bit tricky because 'to whom' looks right. But in fact we need *whoever sent it* (subject-verb-object). The object of the preposition is not the pronoun but the whole phrase *to* + *whoever sent it*.

Tip: As *whom* is falling into disuse, the simplest course is – if in doubt, use *who*. The only time when *whom* is really needed is when it follows a preposition: *To whom it may concern*. But this is formal usage. When the preposition comes later, *who* is possible, and indeed usual (e.g. *Who were you talking about?*).

C as I? than me?

Henry was a couple of years older than I, and I didn't know as much about the world as he.

The use of subject pronouns after *than* and *as* in comparisons when nothing further follows is formal. But the use of object pronouns, though common (e.g. *than me, as him*) is regarded as wrong by some people. A possible solution is to use subject pronouns but add the verbs (*. . . than I was; . . . as he did*).

D he and she?

1 ? Everyone sitting in a traffic jam on the M1 for example will agree that the Government ought to spend more of his money subsidising the railways (so that other drivers will be persuaded to travel by train).

2 ? As long as passengers have only hand-baggage, he or she can bypass the check-in desk and go directly to security.

3 ? Next day we visit a camp shaded by lush greenery. We recline on cushions and are waited on by an incredibly handsome boy. Someone is lying on his back trying to shoot birds out of the trees above us.

Traditionally, masculine pronouns and determiners (*he, him, his*) have been used even when both men and women are referred to, but many people now feel that this is 'sexist'. But using *he or she* (*him or her* etc), though sometimes possible, is self-conscious, and clumsy if repeated reference is needed.

The simplest avoidance strategy is to reword in the plural wherever possible, and this takes care of 1 and 2: *Drivers . . . will agree that the Government ought to spend more of their money*; *As long as passengers have . . . they can bypass. (Passengers . . . he or she . . . is* actually ungrammatical here, anyway!)

Sentence 3 presents more of a problem. The writer was presumably unwilling to write 'Someone is lying on their back', but *his back* at least momentarily suggests that someone (male or female) is lying on the boy's back. It would have been clearer to write something like 'There is a man lying on his back trying to . . .'.

Actually the indefinite pronouns (e.g. *everybody, someone, anyone*) are often followed by plural pronouns etc, and in some cases there is no realistic alternative (e.g. *Everyone knows that, don't they?*). In fact the use of *they, them, their* as 'singular and gender-free' is a common feature of English, though objected to by purists.

E   Don't be vague!

1 * Our 8 day journey is a rare chance to share in a summer celebration that is very much part of the Swedish soul. Join
   ᵗhem as they swim, fish, bicycle or just bask in the summer warmth . . .

2 * *Ollie the escaped parrot ends up behind bars*
   As the parrot's worried owner searched for him, Ollie got through the prison's ventilation system into E Wing. There he was looked after by a man serving a life sentence who keeps budgerigars. He grew so fond of the new cell-mate that he fed him his precious supply of chocolate biscuits . . .

3   It was certainly sporting of David Astor to allow the author to reprint the absurdly pompous letter of rebuke he sent to Cyril not long before he persuaded his father to sack him. . .

Pronouns should not be used instead of nouns unless it is clear what they refer to. In (1) *them* hangs ungrammatically in the air. The writer could have written 'Join the Swedes as they . . .'. In (2) we have two consecutive sentences beginning with a subject *he* ('he was looked after . . .' followed by 'He grew so fond . . .'). Both *he*'s therefore refer to the parrot. It is only when we read on that we realize this is not the intended meaning. (Rewrite as 'The man/ The prisoner grew so fond . . .'.)

Sentence 3, from a book review, is not ungrammatical and might be clear to readers who knew the background of the various people involved. But repeating some of the names would make it easier to work out who persuaded whose father to sack whom!

5 A look at prepositions

A Which preposition?

Many adjectives, nouns and verbs are particularly linked with particular prepositions – e.g. *adjacent to, bored by* (not *of*), *fond of, compatible with; pride in; believe in, hope for,* and care should be taken over them.

After *different, from* is regarded as the most correct form, and therefore the safest, but there is nothing actually wrong with *different to* (*It will mean enduring public scrutiny on an entirely different scale to anything they have experienced before*). *Different than* is useful when a clause follows (*We live a very different life than we used to*).

B How many prepositions?

* The Singapore government yesterday published its own version of these events and has talked to far more of the participants than Mr L now has access.

This sentence needs another *to* (*. . . than Mr L now has access to*). Perhaps the writer was afraid of ending the sentence with a preposition.

The reverse problem is shown in: *He will visit Cornwall, from where his forebears emigrated from in 1841.* Cut out a surplus *from*.

Using the same word twice in succession can be awkward, as in the newspaper heading *James Stewart lives on on the Web,* but it would be wrong to use only one. (The first *on* is actually an adverb, and only the second a preposition.)

A different problem is shown in: *Patients should not be afraid and embarrassed of having it sorted out.* Although it is acceptable when two words need the same preposition for the first one to be elided (e.g. *We hoped and prayed for a miracle*) this is not the case here. Rewrite as *. . . should not be afraid of, or embarrassed at, having . . .*

C like

When using a prepositional phrase beginning with *like,* be sure to compare like with like! Do not say * *Like so many other animals,* *the numbers of rhino have dwindled.* Say *Like so many other animals, the rhinos have dwindled in number.*

6 Knowing when to stop: a look at punctuation

A Run-on sentences and sentence fragments

A common mistake is to run two sentences together with a comma:

* I like pop art, however my sister doesn't.

This should be *I like pop art. However, my sister doesn't.*

The reason is that *however* is a conjunct or connector (p. 53). Other common ones are *accordingly, anyhow, anyway, besides, consequently, furthermore, indeed, meanwhile, moreover, nevertheless, on the other hand, otherwise.* These words refer back to something previously said, but are grammatically more detached than conjunctions (p. 54), and usually need their own sentences.

The reverse mistake is to turn what should be a single sentence into two

   * I like pop art. While my sister doesn't.

The mistake here is to treat a subordinate clause (p. 228), introduced by a conjunction, as a separate sentence. Subordinating conjunctions (subordinators) are very numerous. They include *after, although, because, before, if, unless, until, when, while* and many others.

Subordinating conjunctions may be distinguished from connectors in various ways. Unlike connectors, these conjunctions can often introduce a non-finite or verbless clause (e.g. *when buying a ticket*; *if in doubt*). Another characteristic of many subordinate clauses is that they can come before their main clause: *While my sister doesn't like pop art, I do.*

This sort of reversal is not possible with connectors, which refer back to a previous sentence.

   * However, my sister doesn't. I like pop art.

B and, but, or

Coordinating conjunctions (p. 58) share some characteristics of both connectors and subordinating conjunctions. They resemble connectors in that they must come between the words or phrases they are joining, and cannot come at the beginning. They resemble subordinating conjunctions in usually joining two (or more) elements in the same sentence. Thus, normally when *and, but* or *or* is joining one clause to another, there is no punctuation mark or just a comma:

> Ask the school for your daughter's standardised scores and keep a close eye on her homework.
> Our 10-year-old's teacher says he's bright, but they continually complain about his poor handwriting.

This has led to considerable prejudice against using these words to begin a sentence. However, such usage is perfectly grammatical, as a stylistic device, if the connector refers back to the preceding sentence.

> I had been informed darkly that he was now in hospital. I expected to find him seriously ill. And perhaps, in his mind, he was.

In fact it is even possible to begin a new paragraph with *And, But* or *Or*. But this should not be overdone!

C Help your readers

Punctuation is intended as an aid to comprehension. Do not throw marks around like confetti, but think about your readers. Where would a comma or commas be useful here?

> On the other hand, a Dartmoor farmer told me that because of the damp barley and oats grown on the moor were very susceptible to diseases such as rusts and smuts.

This would be clearer as . . . *told me that, because of the damp, barley and oats* . . .

7 Don't let it all hang out

Hanging and misrelated participles are explained on p. 103. Often the meaning is clear, and the sentence could easily be recast. Thus the examples given could be rephrased as:

> *When I spoke to her on the phone the other day* . . .
> *When you are buying statuary,* . . . .
> *Every afternoon, instead of dozing listlessly in their beds,* . . . *they are offered organized entertainment.*

However, sometimes a misrelated participle makes the sentence ambiguous or absurd.

1 * Having upset almost all sections of the community, his opponents are growing in number.
2 * Walking the dogs in the field the next morning, the donkey came up to me.
3 * After travelling by road all day, the 123-room Sahara Palace is an air-conditioned all-mod-con watering hole.
4 * The Garden Centre is here to stay. Set up with a loan on a site rented from the borough council, the goal is to be self-financing.

Rewrite: 1 *Having upset . . . he has a growing number of opponents.* 2 *When I was walking the dogs . . .* 3 *After an all-day road journey . . .* 4 *Set up with a loan . . . , the Centre aims to be . . .*

8 More mismatches

A Prepositional phrases

Prepositional phrases (p. 185) can also appear in the wrong place with confusing or absurd results. A journalist described by another journalist as a 'bald man with a beard called Bill' protested that his beard had no name! Here are some more unfortunate errors of word order:

* A move to build boarding kennels has been turned down by planners because of fears about noise from neighbours and health officials.
* As a true hermaphrodite whose story was documented on television last July, I must compliment [E . . . H . . .] on her excellent article on the Androgen Insensitivity Syndrome . . . [letter to a newspaper]

The first quote is easily understood, and could easily have been rephrased (*fears from neighbours . . . about noise*). The second is actually confusing. Grammatically (*As a true hermaphrodite . . . . I*), the letter writer is referring to herself. But as the letter later shows that she is a doctor interested in unusual sexual pathology, it seems probable that by 'a true hermaphrodite' she meant E . . . H . . . If that was the intended meaning she should have written *As a true hermaphrodite, E . . . H . . . is to be complimented . . .*

B Other verbless phrases

Various other verbless phrases can be wrongly attached or left hanging.

1 * I first met him in Jerusalem. *Short, dark, with large prominent teeth*, wherever he goes there is laughter.

2 * *Now noticeably slimmer*, her talents as an actress seem doomed to be obscured by her notoriety.

3 * *Back again in Delhi last November*, more of the streets were tree-lined.

Rewrite: 1 *Short, dark, . . . he arouses laughter . . .* 2 *Now noticeably slimmer, she seems doomed to have her acting talents obscured . . .* 3 *Back again in Delhi, we noticed that more and more streets. . . .*

9 Pairs

Correlative pairs are explained on p. 59.

A Balance

1 * The dietician's instructions seem to me to be not only a little daft, but I am just not bothering to take any notice of them at all.

2 * He neither managed to get himself nor one of his candidates chosen.

3 * He thought that the poet must have been either colour blind or had never been there.

The two words in a pair should join words or phrases that are grammatically balanced. All the above break this rule. The first is particularly awkward, and even if it is rewritten with grammatically balanced clauses (*Not only do the dietician's instructions seem to me to be odd, but I am just not bothering . . .*) the result is unsatisfactory. Perhaps the sense would be better conveyed as 'The dietician's instructions seem to me to be not only odd, but actually not worth taking any notice of at all'.

The second could be easily rewritten: *. . . he managed to get neither himself nor one of his candidates . . .*

The third is rather trickier, and obviously ungrammatical, linking as it does an adjective (*colour blind*) with a verb phrase. One possibility is *. . . he thought either the poet must have been colour blind or he had never been there.* Alternatively – *he thought the poet either must have been colour blind or could never have been there.*

B What is a pair?

1 * This writer is concerned not so much with impact than with a need to communicate something.

2 * The marketing of this documentary raises more questions and doubts about the hype and self-promotion of the television industry, as about the conduct of the troops and their colonel in the battle.

3 * No sooner had the applause died down when we heard the distinct sound of gunfire.

4 * We hardly had time to run for cover than we realized it was a hoax.

Comparative pairs (p. 49) basically express equivalence – *as/so . . . as* (and its negative *not so . . . as*), or they express greater or lesser degree (*better, nicer, etc more/less . . . than*). The first sentence should therefore be '*not so much* with . . . *as* with . . .' Sentence 2 should read . . . '*more* questions and doubts about the hype . . . . *than* about . . .' [Notice that the joined items are equivalent, since we mentally supply the ellipted words – *more questions and answers about the hype than [questions and answers] about . . .*

Sentences 3 and 4 show similar confusions between different pairs. *No sooner* (note the *-er* ending) is followed by *than. Hardly*, and also *scarcely*, when part of a correlative pair, is followed by *when* or *before.* (*We hardly had time to run for cover before we realized it was a hoax.*) Notice also in 3 the inversion of subject and auxiliary verb after a negative opening (*No sooner had the applause . . .*). See p. 120.

C A note on *prefer*

* The parents, who lived in extreme poverty, preferred their children to live as rich beggars abroad than in poverty at home.

Though the verb *prefer* is concerned in a way with comparison, *prefer X to Y* is the normal pattern. 'Prefer . . . than' is considered unacceptable. The problem here is the presence of 'to live': to avoid this, *rather than* may be used. (*They preferred their children to live as rich beggars abroad rather than in poverty at home.*)

More drastically, the sentence could be reworded with a different verb – 'They *would rather* their children lived as rich beggars abroad *than* in poverty at home'.

10 Some verb problems

A Subjunctive (see p. 227)

In general there is little need to use subjunctives, as other tenses are usually possible (see suasive verb, p. 225). The only subjunctive that is desirable, particularly in formal styles, is the *were*-subjunctive, the use of *I/he/she/it were* (rather than *was*) when talking about hypothetical situations:

> If she were younger she might marry again.
> Would you accept the job if it were offered to you?
> He talked to me as if I were a child.

What about these?

> We all wondered if it were true.
> We had no idea if he were at home or not.

Answer: *were* is wrong in both sentences here, and *was* is needed. Tip: do not use *were* after *I/he/she/it* when you are talking about the past and when *if* could be replaced by *whether*.

B may or might?

> * The Queen had several suitors whom she may have married before Prince Philip.

May have is increasingly being used where *might have* is preferable. *May* and *might* are sometimes interchangeable, though *might* implies a remoter possibility (e.g. *Take an umbrella. It may/might rain*). When we are discussing the past, *may have* implies that we do not know – we are guessing. So our quotation suggests that perhaps the Queen married more than once before finally marrying Prince Philip! This absurd implication would not arise with *might have*, which implies that there was some possibility or opportunity in the past that was not acted upon.

The use of *may have* instead of correct *might have* is noticeable in some conditional sentences:

> * There were fears yesterday that squatters on the floor above may have died in the flames, but they later reported to the police that they had escaped without injury.

The second half of the sentence makes it clear that there were fears the squatters *might have* died, but that we know that they did not.